'Computer Know-how fo

CW00742975

The Computer Jargon Book

Clement K. Djidonu

B.Sc., Ph.D., MICS, MIIE, Euro. IE, C.Stat., FIAP

UNIVERSITY PUBLISHING INC.
AMERICAN NATIONAL BANK BUILDING
1912 CAPITOL AVENUE
CHEYENNE, WY 82001 USA

British Library Cataloguing in Publication Data

Djidonu Clement Kwaku
   The Computer Jargon Book: An Illustrated Guide to Over
   10,000 Three-Letter Acronyms, Abbreviations and Terminologies
   Relating to Hardware, Software, Networks, Data
   Communications and Telecommunications.-
   (*'Computer Know-how for All'* Series)
   I. Title II. Series
   004

ISBN 1- 874443- 03-3

Dedicated to Thomas Xodzise and Kofi Kove

This book is part of the *'Computer Know-how for All'* **Series** published by University Publishing Inc.

Other books in the series by the same Author.

Demystifying the Computer: A Quick and Easy Guide for All Newcomers to Computers. (ISBN **1-874443-06-8**)

All You Need To Know About Computers: From Hardware through Software to Computer Networks, Data Communications and Telecommunications. (ISBN **1-874443-04-1**)

Simplified Illustrated Guide to Computer Hardware Jargon: A Practical Guide to Over 5000 Standard Abbreviations, Acronyms and Terminologies. (ISBN **1-874443-00-9**)

Desktop Guide to Computer Software, Processing and Applications Jargon: Simplified and Easy Guide to Over 5000 Basic Terminologies, Abbreviations and Acronyms. (ISBN **1-874443-02-5**)

Beginner's and Expert's Guide to Computer Networks, Data Communications and Telecommunications Jargon: A Quick Guide to Over 5000 Commonly-used Acronyms, Terminologies and Abbreviations (ISBN **1-874443-01-7**)

Any of these books can be obtained from your local bookshop or by ordering direct from your local distributor:

PEC Publications International
Suite 146, 2 Old Brompton Road
London SW7 3DQ
Fax: 071-5814445

Preface

Computers touch all aspects of our lives: work, home and leisure. Rarely will someone not at some time come into contact with computers in one form or another. More and more people are using computers on a daily basis. Most organizations and businesses are computerized. Schools, colleges and universities are rapidly introducing computer training into their standard course syllabuses; employers are stating computer literacy as a basic requirement for most job openings. Despite this rapid spread in the use of computers and their unparalleled importance to all aspects of modern life, the computer field and industry is a jargon jungle.

It is true that every specialized field has its own jargon in which the experts in that field communicate: medicine is one such field, law is another. However the computer field has been described as one of the most jargon-riddled; even the experts find it extremely difficult to get by without a helping hand in the form of a jargon handbook like this one. Every now and then a new term pops up unannounced. It is difficult to read a single page of a newspaper or magazine article on computers without being swamped by unexplained acronyms, abbreviations and terminologies. Computer books, magazines, journals and sales literature are littered with unintelligible-looking jargon. It is difficult to follow a simple conversation relating to computers without being overwhelmed by computer jargon of all shapes, shades and sizes. Most people, including computer professionals, find it difficult to figure out what even the most commonly used acronyms and abbreviations stand for and what they mean. The vast majority of these are three-lettered.

Here we offer a unique reference handbook to guide you through the computer jargon maze of three-letter acronyms, abbreviations and terminologies. This guide, which is part of the 'computer know-how for all' series, is aimed at all computer users in every field. It is for both the newcomer and the computer professional. We have put together in this easy-to-use invaluable reference guide over 10,000 commonly used three-letter acronyms, abbreviations and terminologies relating to hardware, software, networks, data communications and telecommunications. Illustrations are also used throughout the book to enrich the reader's understanding of key computer terminologies and concepts.

We hope this unique, well-researched guide will assist you in understanding and using computers and enable you to get the most value from your investments in computer products, training and education.

AAC: Automatic Aperture Control
AAD: Authorized Apple Dealer
AAP: Associative Array Processor
AAP: Attached Applications Processor
AAR: Associative Array Register
ABC: Automatic Brightness Control Circuit
ABE: Arithmetic Building Element
ABI: Applications Binary Interface
ABM: Alternate Bus Master
ABP: Actual Block Processor
ABT: Advanced Backplan Technology
ABT: Advanced BiCMos Technology
ABT: Air Blast Transformer
ACB: Air Circuit Breaker
ACC: ACCumulator
ACC: Automatic Color Control
ACD: ConDuctivity, Analyzer
ACD: Authorized Computer Distributors
ACD: Destination ACcumulator
ACE: Acceptance Checkout Equipment
ACE: Adaptive Computer Experiment
ACE: Advanced Computing Environment
ACE: Advanced Control Experiment
ACE: Automated Computing Engine
ACE: Automatic Checkout Equipment
ACE: Automatic Computer Evaluation
ACE: Automatic Cross-connection
      Equipment
ACH: Attempts per Circuit per Hour
ACI: Advanced Chip Interconnection
ACI: Automatic Card Identification
ACL: Advanced Complementary
      MOS Logic
ACM: Access Control Mechanism
ACM: Address Calculation Machine
ACM: Alterable Control Memory
ACM: Association of Computing Machinery
ACP: Advanced Computational Processor
ACP: Advanced CoProcessor
ACP: Ancillary Control Processor
ACP: Arithmetic and Control Processor
ACR: Access Control Register
ACR: Address Control Register
ACR: Audio Cassette Recorder
ACR: Automatic Compression Regulator

ACS: ACcumulator Switch
ACS: Advance Computer System
ACS: Advanced Control System
ACS: Alternating Current Synchronous
ACS: Attitude Control System
ACS: Automatic Checkout System
ACS: Auxiliary Cooling System
ACS: Auxiliary Core Storage
ACT: Advanced CMos with TTL Inputs.
ACT: Analogical Circuit Technique
ACU: ACknowledgement Signal Unit
ACU: Address Control Unit
ACU: Arithmetic Control Unit
ACU: Association of Computer Users
ACV: Alarm Check Valve
ADA: Analog Differential Analyzer
ADB: Apple Desktop Bus
ADB: Audio Digitizer Board
ADC: Airborne Digital Computer
ADC: Air Data Computer
ADC: Analog-to-Digital Converter

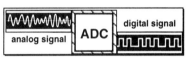

A/DC: Analog to Digital Converter
ADD: Advanced Diagnostic Diskette
ADD: Alphanumeric Display Device
ADE: Automated Design Engineering
ADE: Automated Design Equipment
ADE: Automatic Drafting Equipment
ADF: Automatic Document Feeder
ADH: Automatic Document Handler
ADI: Alternating Direction Implicit
ADI: Alternating Direction Iterative
ADI: Altitude Director Indicator
ADI: Automatic Direction Indicator
ADP: Acoustic Data Processor
ADP: Airborne Data Processor
ADR: Analog-Digital Recorder
ADS: Accurately Defined System
ADS: Advanced Digital Systems
ADS: Analog Digital Subsystem
ADS: Auto Data Switches
ADT: Application Dedicated Terminal
ADT: Automatic Data Transfer
ADT: Automatic Design Tools
ADU: Automatic Data Unit
ADU: Automatic Dialing Unit
AEA: American Electronics Association
AEB: Auxiliary Equipment Building

AED:	Association of Equipment Distributors	ALF:	Automatic Line Feed
AEE:	Airborne Evaluation Equipment	ALP:	Arithmetic and Logic Processor
AEI:	Accept Sequence Error Indicator	ALP:	Automated Language Processing
AEI:	Automatic Equipment Identification	ALS:	Allocated Logical Storage
AEM:	Association of Electronic Manufacturers (USA)	ALS:	Approach-Light System
		ALT:	ALTernator
AEO:	Acoustic-Electric Oscillator	ALU:	Advanced Logical Unit
AEP:	American Electric Power	ALU:	Arithmetic and Logic Unit
AES:	Aerospace and Electronic Systems	AMA:	Associative Memory Array
AES:	Auto-Electronic Selector	AMC:	Automatic Mixture Control
AFF:	Automatic Fast Feed	AMD:	Advanced Micro Devices (Computer Company)
AFI:	Automatic Fault Isolation		
AFK:	Alternate Function Key	AME:	Angle Measuring Equipment
AFM:	Automated Fader Mixing Equipment	AME:	Automatic Monitoring Equipment
		AMM:	Additional Memory Module
AFR:	Advanced Fault Recognition	AMP:	Access Module Processor
AFR:	Advanced Fault Resolution	AMP:	AMPlifier
AFT:	Analog Facility Terminal	AMP:	Associative Memory Processor
AFU:	Autonomous Functional Unit	AMR:	Arithmetic Mask Register
AGE:	Aerospace Ground Support Equipment	AMS:	Acoustic Monitor System
		AMS:	Advanced Memory System
AGS:	Alternating Gradient Synchrotron	AMS:	Atmospheric Monitor System
AGV:	Automatically Guided Vehicle	AMT:	Advanced Manufacturing Techniques
AHM:	Amperes Hour Meter		
AIB:	Add-In Boards	AMT:	Advanced Manufacturing Technology
AIC:	Add-In Cards		
AIC:	Analog Input Channel	AMT:	Automated Microfiche Terminal
AIC:	Automatic Initiation Circuit	ANC:	ANCillary Logic Unit
AID:	Alternate Installation Disk	ANE:	Aeronautical and Navigational Electronics
AID:	Analog Interface Device		
AIG:	Address Indicating Group	ANI:	Automatic Number Identification
AIL:	Array Interconnection Logic	ANL:	Automatic Noise Limiter Circuit
AIM:	Access Isolation Mechanism	ANO:	ANOde
AIM:	American Interactive Multi-media	AOC:	Automatic Output Control
AIM:	Avalanche Induced Migration	AOC:	Automatic Overload Control
AIO:	Analog Input/Output Board	AOM:	Acoustic-Optic Modulator
AIP:	Alphanumeric Impact Printer	AOU:	Arithmetic Output Unit
AIS:	Analog Input System	AOU:	Associative Output Unit
AIS:	Automatic Interface Switching	APC:	Auto Plot Controller
AIT:	Advanced Information Technology	APD:	Addressed Packet Diode
AIT:	American Institute of Technology	APD:	Avalanche PhotoDiode
AIU:	Abstract Information Unit	APM:	Air Particulate Monitor
AKR:	Address Key Register	APM:	Analog Panel Meter
ALB:	Arithmetic and Logic Box	APM:	Automatic Predictive Maintenance
ALC:	Adaptive Logic Circuit		
ALC:	Analog Leased Circuit	APO:	Automatic Power-Off
ALC:	Automatic Level Control	APP:	Associative Parallel Processor
ALC:	Automatic Load Control	APP:	Auxiliary Power Plant
ALD:	Advanced Logic Design	APR:	Active Page Register
ALD:	Analog Line Driver	APR:	Airborne Profile Recorder
ALD:	Automated Logic Diagram	APS:	Allocated Physical Storage
ALE:	Address Latch Enable		

APS: Alphanumeric Photocomposer System
APS: Automatic Patching System
APS: Auxiliary Power System
APT: Automation Planning & Technology
APU: Analog Processing Unit
APU: Arithmetic Processing Unit
APU: Auxiliary Power Unit
APU: Auxiliary Processing Unit
AQL: Acceptable Quality Level
AQT: Acceptable Quality Test
ARC: Attached Resource Computer
ARC: Automatic Relay Calculator
ARC: Average Response Computer
ARL: Acceptable Reliability Level
ARM: Acorn Risc Machine
ARM: Atmosphere Radiation Monitoring
ARR: Address Recall Register
ARR: Address Record Register
ARS: Adjunct Register Set
ART: Actual Retention Time
ARU: Address Recognition Unit
ARU: Application Resource Unit
ARU: Auxiliary Read-Out Unit
ASA: Advanced System Architecture
ASA: American Standards Association
AS/B: Auto Sharer/Buffer
ASC: Advanced Scientific Computer
ASC: Alternate Sector Cylinder
ASC: Alternative System Console
ASC: Associative Structure Computer
ASC: Automatic System Controller
ASD: Anti-Static Devices
ASE: Airborne Search Equipment
ASE: Automatic Support Equipment
ASF: Auxiliary Supporting Feature
ASI: American Standards Institute
ASI: Axial Shape Index
ASM: Asynchronous State Machine
ASO: Auxiliary Switch Open
ASP: Association Storing Processor
ASP: Attached Support Processor
ASR: Active Status Register
ASR: Address Shift Register
ASR: Airborne Surveillance Radar
ASR: Airport Surveillance Radar
ASS: Alternate Screen Size
ASU: Add/Subtract Unit
ASU: Apparatus Sliding Unit

ASV: Angle Stop Valve
ASV: Automatic Self Verification
ASW: Auxiliary SWitch
ATC: Advanced Technology Components
ATC: Applied Technology Council
ATE: Artificial Traffic Equipment
ATE: Automatic Test Equipment
ATG: Automatic Test Generator
ATL: Analog-Threshold Logic
ATL: Automatic Tape Library
ATM: Advanced Technology Maintenance
ATM: Automatic Teller Machine

Automatic Teller Machine

ATP: Attended Trail Printer
ATR: Audio Tape Recorder
ATR: Automatic Traffic Recorder
AT&T: American Telephone & Telegraph Company
ATU: Analysis and Transformation Unit
AUI: Attachment Unit Interface
AUT: Advanced User Terminals
AUT: Assembly Under Test
AUT: Automated Unit Test
AUX: AUXiliary
AVC: Automatic Valve Control
AVC: Automatic Vent Control
AVL: Automatic Vehicle Location
AVM: Automatic Vehicular Monitoring
AVM: Automatic Voltage Margin
AVP: Addressable Vertical Position
AVP: Attached Virtual Processor
AVR: Automatic Voice Regulator
AVR: Automatic Voltage Regulator
AWC: Active Wiring Concentrator
AWF: Acceptable Work-Load Factor
AWN: Automated Weather Network
AWS: Active Work Space
AXD: AuXiliary Drum
AXP: Associative Crosspoint Processor

B

BAC: Bus Adapter Control
BAF: Bonded Acetate Fiber
BAR: Base Address Register
BAR: Buffer Address Register
BAS: Bothways Auto-Switch
BAT: BATtery
BAT: Best Available Technology
BBD: Bucket Brigade Device
BBU: Battery Back-Up
BBU: BIT Buffer Unit
BCH: Bits per Circuit per Hour
BCL: Base Coupled Logic
BCM: Basic Control Memory
BCO: Bridge Cut-Off
BCR: Bar Code Reader
BCR: Byte Count Register
BCS: Bar Code Scanner

bar code scanner

BCS: Basic Combined Subset
BCT: BiCMos Technology
BCT: Bushing Current Transformer
BCU: Basic Counting Unit
BCU: Binary Counting Unit
BDC: Binary Differential Computer
BDD: Binary to Decimal Decoder
BDF: Base Detonating Fuse
BDU: Basic Device Unit
BDU: Basic Display Unit
BDV: BreakDown Voltage
BED: Bridge-Element Delay
BEM: Basic Editor Monitor
BEP: Back-End Processor
BEU: Basic Encoding Unit
beV: billion electron-Volts
BFO: Bit Frequency Oscillator
BIC: Bipolar Integrated Circuits
BIC: Buffer Interface Controller
BIL: Basic Impulse Insulation Level
BIL: Basic Impulse Isolation Level

BIL: Basic Insulation Level
BIM: BIT Image Memory
BIM: Bus Interface Module
BIP: Binary Image Processor
BIR: Bus Interface Register
bit: binary digit
BIT: Built-In Test
BIT: Burn-In Test
BIU: Basic Information Unit
BIU: Buffer Image Unit
BIU: Bus Interface Unit
BJT: Base Junction Transistor
BJT: Bipolar Junction Transistor
BLC: Board Level Computer
BLD: Beam-Lead Device
BLL: Below Lower Limit
BLM: Basic Language Machine
BLU: Basic Link Unit
BLU: Basic Logic Unit
BLU: Bipolar Line Unit
BMC: Bubble Memory Controller
BMC: Bulk Media Conversion
BMD: Benchmark Monitor Display
BMD: BioMetric Device
BMT: Block Mode Terminal Interface
BNC: Bayonet Nut Coupler
BOB: Back Office Box
BOC: Block-Oriented Computer
BOD: Break Over Diode
BOM: Basic Operating Monitor
BOR: Bus Out Register
BPD: Bushing Potential Device
BPH: Ballistic Print Head
BPI: Bits Per Inch
BPN: Breakdown Pulse Noise
BRS: Big Red Switch
BRT: Binary Run Tape
BRU: Basic Resolution Unit
BSC: Back-of-Store Computer
BSD: Bulk Storage Device
BSM: Batch Spool Monitor
BSM: Bit Slice Microprocessor
BSR: Board of Standards Review
BTB: Branch Target Buffer
BTD: Bomb Testing Device
BTE: Battery Terminal Equipment
BTF: Bomb Tail Fuse
BTT: Bank Teller Terminal
BUC: BUs Control
BUF: BUFfer
BUR: Back-Up Register
BWC: Buffer Word Counter

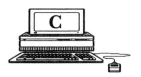

CAC: Computer Acceleration Control
CAD: Cartridge-Activated Device
CAD: Computer Access Device
CAD: Computer Activated Device
CAD: Computer-Aided Design
CAD: Computer-Aided Drafting
CAE: Common Application Environment
CAF: Content Addressable Filestore
CAK: Command Access Keys
CAM: Central Address Memory
CAM: Computer Addressed Memory
CAM: Computer-Aided Manufacturing
CAM: Content-Addressable Memory
CAM: Cybernetic Anthropomorphous
Machine
CAP: CAPacitor

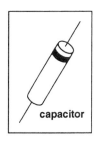

capacitor

CAP: Computer-Aided Production
CAP: Computer-Assisted Production
CAP: Content Addressable Processor
CAP: Crytron Associative Processor
CAR: Channel Address Register
CAR: Current Address Register
CAT: Channel-Attached Terminal
CAS: China Association for
Standardization
CAS: Circuits And Systems
CAS: Column Address Strobe
CAT: Capacity Activated Transducer
CAT: Computer-Assisted Testing
CAT: Controlled Attenuator Timer
CAT: Credit Authorization Terminal
CAU: Controller Adapter Unit
CAU: CPU Access Unit
CAU: Crypto Auxiliary Unit
CBA: Centralized Bus Architecture
CBA: Computer-Based Automation

CBC: Chain Block Controller
CBC: Collector Base Capacitance
CBT: Computer-Based Terminal
CCA: Channel to Channel Adapter
CCA: Computer Communications
Architecture
CCB: Circuit Concentration Bay
CCB: Configuration Control Board
CCC: Canadian Computer Conference
CCD: Charged-Coupled Device
C⁴D: Conductivity-Connected Charged-
Coupled Device
CCD: Core Current Driver
CCF: Central Computing Facility
CCF: Controller Configuration Facility
CCH: Channel Check Handler
CCI: Combined form of CCIR and CCIT
C³L: Complementary Constant
Current Logic
CCM: Call Count Meter
CCM: Computer Coupled Machines
CCO: Current-Control Oscillator
CCP: Conditional Command Processor
CCP: Console Command Processor
C&CP: Corrosion & Cathodic Protection
CCR: Channel Command Register
CCR: Channel Control Reconfiguration
CCR: Condition Code Register
CCR: Control ContractoR
CCS: Central Computer System

Central Computer System

CCS: Custom Computer System
CCT: Card Coding Technique
CCT: Carriage Control Tape
CCT: CirCuiT

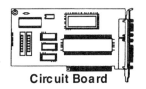

Circuit Board

CCT: Computer Compatible Tape

CCT:	Constant Current Transformer
CCU:	Central Control Unit
CCU:	Cluster Control Unit
CCU:	Command Chain Unit
CCU:	Common Control Unit
CCU:	Communication Control Unit
CCU:	Computer Control Unit
CCU:	Concurrency Control Unit
CCV:	Control Configured Vehicle
CDB:	Common Data Bus
CDC:	Computer Display Channel
CDD:	Character Display Device
CD+G:	Compact Disc + Graphics
CDI:	Cluster Disk Interface
CDI:	Collector, Diffused Isolation
CD-I:	Compact Disk-Interactive
CDP:	Central Data Processor
CDP:	Checkout Data Processor
CDR:	Command Destruct Receiver
CDR:	Recordable Compact Disk
CDS:	Component Disassembly Station
CDS:	Comprehensive Display System
CDS:	Computer Duplex System
CDS:	Control Display System
C/DS:	Cache/Disk System
CDT:	Control Data Terminal
CDU:	Cartridge Disk Unit
CDU:	Central Display Unit
CDU:	Control and Display Unit
CDX:	Control-Differential Transmitter
CEA:	Common Element Assembly
CEC:	Central Electronic Complex
CED:	Capacitance Electronic Disk
CED:	Computer Entry Device
CEE:	International Commission on Rules for the Approval for Electrical Equipment
CEI:	Chip Enable Input
CEO:	Chip Enable Output
CER:	Complete Engineering Release
CEU:	Channel Extension Unit
CEU:	Communications Expansion Unit
CFA:	Cascade-Failure Analysis
CFA:	Computer Family Architecture
CFA:	Cross-Field Amplifier
CFD:	Compact Floppy Disk
CFF:	Critical Flicker Frequency
CFM:	Cathode Follower Mixer
CFP:	Continuous-Form Paper
CGA:	Color Graphics Adapter
CGC:	Color Graphic Card
CGM:	Color Graphics Metafile

CGP:	Color Graphics Printer
CHD:	Cartridge Hard Disk
CHE:	CHip Enable
CHR:	CHannel Reconfiguration Hardware
CIA:	Computer Industry Association
CIB:	Channel Interface Bus
CIB:	Command Input Buffer
CIC:	Custom Integrated Circuit
CID:	Charge-Injection Imaging Device
CID:	Component IDentification Number
CIE:	Computer Interrupt Equipment
CIM:	Computer Input Microfilm
CIM:	Computer Interface Monitor
CIM:	Computer Integrated Manufacturing
CIM:	Console Interface Module
CIM:	Continuous Image Microfilm
CIP:	Compatible Independent Peripherals
CIP:	Current Injection Probe
CIR:	Color Infra-Red
CIR:	Current Instruction Register
CIS:	Containment Isolation System
CIU:	Central Interface Unit
CIU:	Channel Interface Unit
CIU:	Computer Interface Unit
CJB:	Cold Junction Box
CJP:	Communication Jamming Processor
CKD:	Count-Key-Data Device
ckt:	circuit
CKV:	ChecK ,Valve
CLA:	Computer Lessors Association
CLB:	Central Logic Bus
CLC:	Course Line Computer
CLD:	Current-Limiting Device
CLF:	Capacitive Loss Factor
CLK:	CLocK
CLR:	Computer Language Recorder
CLR:	Current Limiting Resistor
CLS:	Closed Loop System
CLU:	Central Logic Unit
CLU:	Circuit Line Up
CMA:	Computer Monitor Adapter
CMA:	Contact-Making Ammeter
CMC:	Circuit-Mode Control
CME:	Central Memory Extension
CMF:	Coherent Memory Filter
CMF:	Common Mode Failure
CMK:	Cursor Movement Keys
CMM:	Core Mechanical Mockup
CMP:	Configuration Management Plan
CMS:	Circuit Maintenance System
CMS:	Current Mode Switching

CMT:	Cassette Magnetic Tape	CRU:	Combined Rotating Unit
CMT:	Conversational Mode Terminal	CRU:	Communication Register Unit
CMU:	Control Maintenance Unit	CRU:	Customer Replaceable Unit
CMU:	Control Memory Unit	CSA:	Canadian Standards Association
CMV:	Common Mode Voltage	CSD:	Constant Speed Drive
CNC:	Computerized Numerical Control	CSE:	Control System Engineering
COB:	Card On Board	CSE:	Core Storage Element
COM:	Certificate Of Maintainability	CSF:	Containment Support Fixture
COM:	Computer Output Microfiche	CSF:	Cut Sheet Feeders
COM:	Computer Output Microfilm	CSM:	Continuous Sheet Memory
COM:	Computer Output Microfilmer	CSP:	Control Storage Processor
COM:	Computer Output Microfilming	C/SP:	Communications/Symbiont
COM:	Computer Output Micrographics		Processor
COM:	Computer Output on Microfilm	CSR:	Channel Select Register
CON:	CONtroller	CSR:	Control Status Register
COP:	COmmunication Processor	CSU:	Central Switching Unit
COS:	Connection-Oriented Service	CSW:	Control Power SWitch
COS:	Corporation for Open Systems	CTA:	Compatibility Test Area
COT:	Control Operator's Terminal	CTB:	Concentrator Terminal Buffer
COT:	Customer Oriented Terminal	CTC:	Chargeable Time Clock
CPC:	Card Programmed Calculator	CTC:	Counter Timer Chip
CPC:	Clock Pulse Control	CTC:	Counter Timer Circuit
CPC:	Common Peripheral Channel	CTD:	Charge-Transfer Device
CPC:	Computer Power Center	CTE:	Customer Terminal Equipment
CPC:	Core Protection Calculator	CTL:	Cassette Tape Loader
CPC:	Core Protection Computer	CTL:	Complementary Transistor Logic
CPC:	Cycle Program Counter	CTL:	Core Transistor Logic
CPE:	Central Processing Element	CTO:	Charge Transforming Operator
CPE:	Customer Premises Equipment	CTP:	Construction Test Procedure
CPI:	Common Physical Interface	CTR:	Certified Test Results
CPP:	Card Punching Printer	CTR:	Common Technical Regulation
CPS:	Circuit Package for Schematic	CTS:	Coaxial Terminal Switch
CPS:	Compact Printer Sharer	CTS:	Computer Telewriter System
CPT:	Control Power Transformer	CTS:	Computer Tomography Scanners
CPU:	Central Processing Unit	CTS:	Conformance Testing Service
CPU:	Collective Protection Unit	CTU:	Central Terminal Unit
CPU:	Computer Peripheral Unit	CUA:	Circuit Unit Assembly
CPX:	Charged Pigment Xerography	CUE:	Computer Updating Equipment
CPX:	Control Panel EXtensions	CUM:	Central-Unit Memory
CRA:	Computer Retailers Association	CUT:	Circuit Under Test
CRM:	Core Resistance Mechanism	CUT:	Control Unit Tester
CRM:	Core Restraint Mechanism	CVI:	Certified Vendor Information
CRM:	Count Rate Meter	CVR:	Cockpit Voice Recorder
CRN:	Computer Room Network	CVR:	Constant Voltage Regulator
CRO:	Cathode-Ray Oscilloscope		
CRQ:	Console Reply Queuing		
CRS:	Computer Recognition Systems		
CRS:	Containment Rupture Signal		
CRT:	Cathode Ray Tube		
CRT:	Circuit Requirement Table		
CRU:	Card Reader Unit		

DAC: Design Augmented by Computer
DAC: Digital to Analog Converter

DAC: Digital Analysis Converter
DAC: Display Analysis Console
DAD: Direct Access Device
DAM: Data Addressed Memory
DAM: Direct Access Memory
DAP: Distributed Array Processor
DAR: Data Access Register
DAR: Destination Access Register
DAS: Data Acquisition System
DAT: Data Abstract Tape
DAT: Digital Audio Tape
DAT: Director of Advanced Technology
DAU: Data Access Unit
DAU: Data Acquisition Unit
DAU: Data Adapter Unit
DAV: Direct Above Voice
DBC: Data Base Computer
DBE: Data Bus Enable
DBM: Data Buffer Module
DBR: Data Buffer Register
DCB: Data Control Bus
DCC: Data Channel Converter
DCC: Data Circuit Concentrator
DCC: Data Communication Controller
DCC: Device Cluster Controller
DCC: Device Control Character
DCC: Direct Control Channel
DCC: Disk Control Cards
DCE: Data Circuit Terminating Equipment
DCE: Data Conversion Equipment
DCE: Digital Control Element
DCE: Distributed Computing Environment
DCF: Disk Controller/Formatter
DCG: Display Character Generator
DCP: Digital Computer Processor
DCP: Document Conversion Processor
DCR: Data Coordinator and Retriever
DCS: Design Control Specifications
DCU: Data Capture Unit

DCU: Data Command Unit
DCU: Data Control Unit
DCU: Device Control Unit
DCU: Digital Control Unit
DDC: Digital Display Converter
DDC: Direct Digital Computer
DDC: Direct Digital Control
DDD: Dual Disk Drives

DDE: Director Design Engineering
DDI: Device Driver Interface
DDM: Device Descriptor Module
DDP: Digital Data Processor
DDR: Data Direction Register
DDR: Dynamic Device Reconfiguration
DDS: Data Display System
DDS: Digital Dynamics Simulator
DDT: Digital Debugging Tape
DDT: Direct Device Transfer
DEA: Display Electronics Assemblies
DEC: Digital Electronic Corporation
DEE: Data Encryption Equipment
DEE: Digital Evaluation Equipment
DEF: Data Entry Facility
DES: Digital Expansion System
DES: Disk Encoding Scheme
DEU: Data Encryption Unit
DEU: Data Entry Unit
DEU: Data Exchange Unit
DFB: Distributed Feed-Back
DFB: Distribution Fuse Board
DFD: Dual Floppy Drive
DFI: Digital Facility Interface
DFK: Data Function Keyboard
DFL: Design For ManufacturabiLity
DFR: Decreasing Failure Rate
DFS: Dynamic Flight Simulator
DFT: Digital Facility Terminal
DFT: Diskette-Formatted Tape
DGB: Disk Gap Bond
DGS: Data Ground Station
DGX: Direct Graphics Technology

DHE: Data Handling Equipment
DIA: Digital Input Adapter
DIA: Direct Interface Adapter
DIA: Dual Interface Adapter
DIC: Data Insertion Converter
DIC: Digital Incremental Computer
DIC: Digital Integrating Computer
DID: Daily Initialization Diskette
DID: Data Input Device
DIG: Digital Image Generator
DIG: Digital Input Gate
DIL: Dual In Line Chip
DIP: Display Information Processor
DIP: Dual In-Line Package

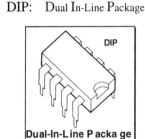

Dual-In-Line Packa ge

DIS: Device Interface System
DIU: Digital Input Unit
DKI: Device Kernel Interface
DLA: Daisy Chain Out Left
DLA: Data Link Adapter
DLB: Daisy Chain In Left
DLC: Digital Leased Circuit
DLS: Digital Line System
DLS: Digital Local Switch
DLT: Depletion-Layer Transistor
DLU: Data Line Unit
DMA: Direct Memory Access
DMA: Drum Memory Assembly
DMC: Digital Micro-Circuit
DMD: Diskette Magazine Drive
DME: Distance Measuring Equipment
DMM: Data Multi-Meter
DMM: Digital Multi-Meter
DMP: Dot Matrix Printer

dot matrix printer

DMR: Dynamic Modular Replacement

DMU: Digital Message Unit
DMU: Dual Maneuvering Unit
DNC: Direct Numerical Control
DNL: Dynamic Noise Limiter
DOB: Data Output Bus
DOC: Data Optimizing Computer
DOD: Digital Optical Disk
DOL: Dynamic Octal Load
DOM: Digital Ohm-Meter
DOP: Digital Optical Processor (AT&T)
DOT: Digital Optical Tape
DOT: Digital Optical Technology
DPA: Display Printer Adapter
DPE: Data Processing Equipment
DPG: Digital Pattern Generator
DPM: Data Processing Machine
DPM: Digital Panel Meter
DPM: Dual-Ported Memory
DPS: Dedicated Printer Sharer
DPU: Data Processing Unit
DPU: Disk Pack Unit
DRA: Daisy Chain In Right
DRB: Daisy Chain Out Right
DRC: Design Rule Checking
DRD: Data Recording Device
DRE: Dead Reckoning Equipment
D/RE: Disassembly/Reassembly
        Equipment
DRM: Digital RadioMeter
DRO: Doubly Resonant Oscillator
DRP: Dead Reckoning Plotter
DRS: Disassembly/Reassembly Station
DRS: Disk Real-Time System
DRT: Device Rise Time
DRU: Data Reference Unit
DSA: Data Set Adapter
DSA: Distributed Systems Architecture
DSB: Data Switch Boxes
DSD: Digital System Design
DSD: Digital System Diagram
DSD: Diskette Storage Device
DSD: Diskette Storage Drive
DSD: Disk Storage Device
DSD: Disk Storage Drive
DSD: Double-Sided Disk
DSE: Data Storage Equipment
DS/E: Digital Scrambler/Encoder
DSF: Disk Storage Facility

DSI:	Display Station Indicator
dsk:	disk
dsk:	diskette

diskette

DSL:	Drawing and Specification Listing
DSR:	Device Status Register
DSS:	Device Support Station
DSU:	Data Service Unit
DSU:	Data Storage Unit
DSU:	Disk Storage Unit
DTC:	Desk Top Computer
DTE:	Data Transmission Equipment
DTI:	Data Terminal Installation
DTL:	Diode-Transistor Logic
DTO:	Digital Testing Oscilloscope
DTP:	Directory Tape Processor
DTR:	Data Transfer Register
DTR:	Disposable Tape Reel
DTR:	Distribution Tape Reel
DTS:	Digital Termination System
DTT:	Dark Trace Tube
DTU:	Data Transfer Unit
DTU:	Digital Tape Unit
DTU:	Digital Transmission Unit
DUT:	Device Under Test
DVC:	CapacitiVe Diode
DVM:	Demand-Paged Virtual Memory
DVM:	Digital Volt Meter
DVM:	Displaced Virtual Machine
DWP:	Daisy Wheel Printer
DXA:	Document EXchange Architecture

EAD:	Equipment Allowance Document
EAE:	Extended Arithmetic Element
EAL:	Equipment Air Lock
EAM:	Electrical Accounting Machines
EAM:	Electronic Automatic Machine
EAN:	European Article Number
EAR:	Extended Address Register
EBL:	Electron Beam Lithography
EBS:	Electron-Beam Semiconductor
EBS:	Electron Bombarded Semiconductor
ECA:	Electronics Control Assembly
ECC:	Electronic Components Conference
ECG:	ElectroCardioGram
ECK:	Enhanced Contoured Keyboard
ECL:	Emitter Coupled Logic
ECL:	Equipment Component List
ECM:	Electric Coding Machine
ECM:	ElectroChemical Machining
ECM:	Electronic Counter Measures
ECM:	Extended Core Memory
ECO:	Electron Coupled Oscillator
ECR:	Electronic Cash Register
ECR:	Embossed Character Reader
ECS:	Electronic Control Switch
ECS:	Embedded Computer System
ECS:	Extended Control Storage
ECU:	Electronic Conversion Unit
EDC:	Electronic Desk Calculator
EDC:	Electronic Digital Computer
EDC:	Extended Device Control
EDC:	External Disk Channel
EDC:	External Drum Channel
EDD:	Expert Database Designer
EDD:	External Disk Drive
EDE:	Emitter Dip Effect
EDM:	Electrical Discharge Machining
EDT:	Electric Discharge Tube
EDT:	Engineering Design Text
EDT:	Expedited Data Transfer
EDU:	Electronic Display Unit
EDU:	Error Detection Unit
EEA:	Electronic Engineering Association
EEC:	Electronic Engine Control
EED:	Electro-Explosive Device
EEM:	Electronic Equipment Monitoring
EEP:	Electronic Evaluation and Procurement
EET:	Edge Enhancement Technology
EFA:	Extended Finite Automation
EFD:	External Floppy Disk
EFI:	Electronic Flight Instruments
EFI:	Electronic Fuel Injection
EFP:	Electronic Field Production
EGA:	Enhanced Graphics Adapter

EGM: Electronic Governor Module
EHD: External Hard Disk
EHP: Electric Horse Power
EHV: Extra High Voltage
EIA: Electronic Industries
     Association (USA)
EIB: Electronics Installation Bulletin
EIC: Equipment Identification Code
EIL: Electron Injection Laser
EKG: ElectroCardioGram
ELD: Edge Lit Display
ELD: ElectroLuminiscent Display
ELE: Equivalent Logic Element
ELP: Electronic Line Printer
ELR: Error Logging Register
ELS: Emulsion Laser Storage
ELV: ELectrically Operated Valve
EMA: Extended Memory Area
EMA: Extended Mercury Autocoder
EMB: EMulator Board
EMB: Extended Memory Block
EMC: Electro-Magnetic Compatibility
EMC: Electro-Magnetic Conformance
EMC: Engineered Military Circuits
EMC: Expanded Memory Card
EMF: Electro-Magnetic InterFerence
EMF: Electro-Motive Force
EMI: Electro-Magnetic Induction
EMI: Electro-Magnetic Interference
EMI: Electro-Magnetic Isolation
EMI: Electron Magnetic Interference
EMM: Electro-Magnetic Measurement
EMP: Electro-Magnetic Pulse
EMP: Electro-Mechanical Power
EMP: Electronic Market Place
EMP: External Monitor Port
EMS: Electro-Magnetic Susceptibility
EMS: Embedded Microprocessor System
EMS: Expanded Memory Specification
EMS: Extended Main Store
EMS: Extended Memory Specification
EMS: Extended Memory Susceptibility
EM&S: Equipment Maintenance
     & Support
EMU: Electro-Magnetic Unit
EMU: Emulator Microprocessing Unit
EMU: Extended Memory Unit
EOD: Erasable Optical Disks

EOS: End-Of-Screen
EPA: Enhance Performance
     Architecture
EPF: Electronic Power Feed Unit
EPO: Emergency Power-Off
EPR: Error Pattern Register
EPS: Switch-mode Power Supply
EPT: Electro-Static Printing Tube
EPT: Exciter Power Logic
EPT: Execution Processing UniT
EPU: Electrical Power Unit
ERA: Electronic Reading Automation
ERP: Effective Radiated Power
ERU: External Run Unit
ERW: Electronic Resistance Welding
ESA: Enterprise System
     Architecture (IBM)
ESC: Electro-Static Compatibility
ESD: Electro-Static Deflection
ESD: Electro-Static Discharge
ESE: Electrical Support Equipment
ESF: Extended Spooling Facility
ESG: Electrically Suspended Gyroscope
ESG: Electronically Suspended
     Gyroscope
ESG: Electro-Static Gyroscope
ESN: Electronic Serial Number
ESP: Electro-Static Precipitator
ESP: Electro-Static Printer
ESR: Electron Spin Resonance
ESR: Equivalent Series Resistance
ESS: European Silicon Structures
EST: Electro-Static Storage Tube
ESU: Electro-Static Unit
ETP: Electrical Tough Pitch
EUV: Extreme Ultra-Violet
EVA: Electronic Velocity Analyzer
EVC: EISA Video Controller
EVM: Electronic Volt-Meter
EVM: Extended Virtual Machine
EXD: EXternal Device

FAC: Field ACcelerator
FAE: Field Application Engineer
FAM: Fast Access Memory
FAM: Fast Auxiliary Memory
FAP: Field Application Panel
FAR: File Address Register
FBM: Foreground and Background Monitor
FBP: Flat-Bed Plotters
FBR: Feed-Back Resistance
FBS: Flat-Bed Scanner

flat-bed scanner

FCA: Functional Configuration Audit
FCC: Flight Control Computer
FCI: Flux Change Per Inch
FCL: Feed-Back Control Loop
FCL: Functional Capabilities List
FCM: Firmware Control Memory
FCP: File Control Processor
FCU: File Control Unit
FDC: Floppy Disk Controller
FDD: Fixed Disk Drive
FDD: Flexible Disk Drive
FDD: Floppy Disk Drive
FDF: Fixed Disk Formatting
FDP: Future Data Processors
FDR: Flight Data Recorder
FDS: Fixed Disk Storage
FDS: Flexible Disk System
FDS: Floppy Disk System
FDU: Floppy Disk Unit
FEB: Functional Electronic Block
FEC: Front-End Computer
FED: Field Effect Diode
FEL: Free Electron Laser

FEM: Field Effect Modified
FEP: Fuse Enclosure Processor
FET: Field-Effect Transistor
FFC: Flip Flop Circuit
FFC: Flip-Flop Complementary
fff: flicker fusion frequency
FFN: Full Function Node
FGC: First Generation Computer
FHD: Fixed Head Disk
FIP: Finance Image Processor
FIR: File Indirect Register
FLB: Full-Length Board
FLF: Follow-The-Leader Feed-Back
FLM: First Logic Machine
FLS: FLow Switch
FLS: Full-Length Slot
FLT: Fault Location Technology
FMS: Flexible Manufacturing System
FMS: Flux Monitoring System
FMV: Full Motion Video
FOD: Functional Operational Design
FOR: Fiber Optics Recording
FOS: Ferrous Oxide Spots
FPB: Floating Point Board
FPC: Functional Processor Cluster
FPM: File Protect Memory
FPM: Floppy-Disk Processor Module
FPP: Floating Point Processor
FPR: File Protect Ring
FPU: File Processing Unit
FPU: Floating Point Unit
FRD: Functional Reference Device
FRU: Field Replaceable Unit
FSA: Finite State Automation
FSM: Finite State Machine
FSR: Feed-back Shift Register
FSS: Fail Safe System
FSS: Fail Soft System
FST: Flat-Screen Technology
FSU: Final Signal Unit
FTC: Fault-Tolerant Computers
FTR: Functional Test Requirement
FTT: Financial Transaction Terminal
FVU: File Verification Unit
FWA: Forward Wave Amplifier

GAB: Graphic Adapter Board
GAL: Genesis Array Logic
GAT: Graphics Art Terminal
GDU: Graphic Display Unit
GFI: Guided Fault Isolation
GIC: General Input/Output Channel
GIC: Generalized Impedance Converter
GJP: Graphic Job Processor
GMS: General Maintenance System
GOE: Ground Operation Equipment
GOM: Group Occupancy Meter
GOR: General Operations Requirement
GOS: Grade Of Service
GPA: General-Purpose Array
GPC: General Peripheral Controller
GPC: General-Purpose Computer
GPF: General Protection Fault
GPP: General-Purpose Processor
GPR: General-Purpose Register
GPT: General-Purpose Terminal
GPU: General Processing Unit
GRS: General Register Stack
GSE: Ground Support Equipment
GSI: Grand Scale Integration
GSM: Gray Scale Monitor
GSP: General Synthetic Processor
GSP: Guidance Signal Processor
GTD: Graphic Tablet Display
GTO: Gate Turn-Off
GVA: Graphic Volt-Ampere
GVS: Guided-Vehicle System

HAC: Hierarchical Abstract Computer
HAL: Hard Array Logic
HAR: Home Address Register
HAU: Horizontal Arithmetic Unit
HAU: Hybrid Arithmetic Unit
HCC: Hardware Capability Code
HCC: Hercules Compatible Card
HCG: Hardware Character Generator

HCI: Host Computer Interface
HCI: Human-Computer Interface
HCI: Hybrid Computer Interface
HCL: Header Control Label
HCM: Hayes Compatible Modem
HCP: Hard Copy Printer
HCP: High-Speed Channel Processor
HCR: Hardware Check Routine
HCS: Hard Copy System
HCT: High-Speed CMOS with TTL
HDA: Head/Disk Assembly
HDB: High Density Bipolar
HDC: Hardware Disk Cache
HDD: Head Down Display
HDD: Hard Disk Drive

Hard Disk Drive

HDD: High Density Disk
HDF: High Density Flexible
HDL: Hardware Description Languages
HDM: Hard Disk Manager
HDT: High Density Tape
HDV: Hard Dollar Value
hdw: hardware
HFE: Human Factors Engineering
HGA: Hercules Graphic Adapter
HGC: Hercules Graphic Card
HHC: Hand-Held Calculator

Hand -Held Calculator

HHC: Hand-Held Computer
HHS: Hand-Held Scanner
HIC: Hybrid Integrated Circuit
HIM: Hardware Interface Module

15

HIP:	Host Interface Processor		IAR:	Instruction Address Register
HIT:	High Isolation Transformer		IAR:	Interrupt Address Register
HIT:	Homing Interceptor Technology		IAS:	Immediate Access Store
HLA:	High-Speed Line Adapter		IAT:	Institute for Advanced Technology
HLD:	Hardware Logic Diagram		IAT:	Institute of Automatics and Telemechanics (Russia)
HLU:	Host Logical Unit			
HMA:	High Memory Area		IAU:	Information Access Unit
HMI:	Hardware Monitor Interface		IAU:	Interface Adapter Unit
HMI:	Human Machine Interface		IBC:	Integrated Block Controller
HMM:	Hardware Multiply Module		IBM:	International Business Machines (Computer Company)
HMO:	Hardware Micro-Code Optimizer			
HPA:	High Power Amplifier		IBT:	Integrated Business Terminal
HPD:	High Power Density		ICA:	Integrated Communication Adapter
HPF:	High Pass Filter		ICA:	Inter-Computer Adapter
HPT:	Heads Per Track		ICB:	Inter-Computer Bus
HRC:	High Rupturing Capacity		ICB:	Interface Control Board
HRC:	Hypothetical Reference Circuit		ICB:	Internal Common Bus
HRG:	High Resolution Graphics		ICC:	Integrated Circuit Chips

HIP: Host Interface Processor
HIT: High Isolation Transformer
HIT: Homing Interceptor Technology
HLA: High-Speed Line Adapter
HLD: Hardware Logic Diagram
HLU: Host Logical Unit
HMA: High Memory Area
HMI: Hardware Monitor Interface
HMI: Human Machine Interface
HMM: Hardware Multiply Module
HMO: Hardware Micro-Code Optimizer
HPA: High Power Amplifier
HPD: High Power Density
HPF: High Pass Filter
HPT: Heads Per Track
HRC: High Rupturing Capacity
HRC: Hypothetical Reference Circuit
HRG: High Resolution Graphics
HRI: High Resolution Imagesetter
HRM: Hardware Read-In Mode
HRP: High Resolution Printer
HSB: High-Speed Buffer
HSD: Hard-Sectored Disk
HSI: High-Speed Interface
HSI: Horizontal Situation Indicator
HSM: High-Speed Memory
HSP: High-Speed Printer
HSR: High-Speed Reader
HTE: Hypergroup Translating Equipment
HTS: Head, Track and Sector
HTS: Head Track Selector
HTU: Heat Transfer Unit
HVR: Hardware Vector to Raster
HVR: High Voltage Regulator
HWI: HardWare Interpreter
HWL: Hard-Wired Logic
HWP: Hot Wire Printer
HYB: HYBrid System

IAR: Instruction Address Register
IAR: Interrupt Address Register
IAS: Immediate Access Store
IAT: Institute for Advanced Technology
IAT: Institute of Automatics and Telemechanics (Russia)
IAU: Information Access Unit
IAU: Interface Adapter Unit
IBC: Integrated Block Controller
IBM: International Business Machines (Computer Company)
IBT: Integrated Business Terminal
ICA: Integrated Communication Adapter
ICA: Inter-Computer Adapter
ICB: Inter-Computer Bus
ICB: Interface Control Board
ICB: Internal Common Bus
ICC: Integrated Circuit Chips

IC Chip

ICC: Interrupt Controller Chips
ICE: Immediate Cable Equalizers
ICE: In-Circuit Emulator
ICE: Input Checking Equipment
ICE: Integrated Cooling for Electronics
ICL: International Computers Limited
ICM: Instruction Control Memory
IC/P: Intelligent Copier/Printer
ICR: Independent Component Release
ICR: Indirect Control Register
ICR: Input Control Register
ICR: Interrupt Control Register
ICS: Integrated Control System
ICT: Image Creation Terminal
ICU: Instruction Control Unit
ICU: Integrated Control Unit
ICU: Interface Control Unit
ICU: Interrupt Control Unit
IDA: Integrated Digital Avionics
IDA: Intelligent Drive Array
IDB: Input Data Buffer
IDC: Insulation Displacement Connector
IDC: Internal Data Channel
IDE: Integrated Drive Electronics
IDE: Intelligent Drive Electronics
idl: idle
IDS: IDle Signal
IDS: Information Display System

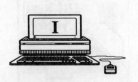

IAB: Interrupt Address to Bus
IAC: Integration, Assembly, Checkout
IAD: Initiation Area Discriminator CRT
IAM: Initial Address Memory
IAO: Internal Automation Operation
IAP: Image Array Processor

IDS:	Intelligent Display System	IMT:	Intelligent Micro-Image Terminal
IDS:	Interactive Display System	IMU:	Increment Memory Unit
IDT:	Intelligent Data Terminal	IMU:	Instruction Memory Unit
IDT:	Inter-Digital Transducer	IOA:	Input/Output Adapter
IEC:	Integrated Equipment Components	IOB:	Input/Output Buffer
IEC:	International Electrotechnical Commission	IOC:	Initial Operational Capacity
		IOC:	Input/Output Connector
IEE:	Institution of Electrical Engineers (UK)	IOC:	Input/Output Controller
		IOC:	Integrated Optical Circuit
IES:	Illuminating Engineering Society	IOD:	Input-Output Device
IES:	Intelligent Emulation Switching	IOP:	Input-Output Port
IES:	International Electrotechnical Vocabulary	IOP:	Input Output Processor
		IOR:	Input Output Register
IFD:	Internal Floppy Drive	IOS:	Input-Output Selector
IFE:	Intelligent Front-End Processor	IOS:	Input/Output System
IFL:	Integrated Fuse Logic	IOU:	Input/Output Unit
IFP:	Integrated File Processor	IOW:	Input/Output Wire
IFP:	InterFace Processor	IPA:	Integrated Peripheral Adapter
IFR:	InterFace Register	IPA:	Integrated Photodetection Assemblies
IFS:	Intelligent File Store		
IFU:	Instruction Fetch Unit	IPA:	Integrated Printer Adapter
IGS:	Integrated Graphics System	IPA:	Intermediate Power Amplifier
IGT:	Interactive Graphics Terminal	IPB:	Integrated Processor Board
IHF:	Inhibit Halt Flip-Flop	IPB:	Inter-Processor Buffer
IIL:	Integrated Injection Logic	IPB:	Inter-Processor Bus
I2L:	Integrated Injection Logic	IPC:	Illustrated Parts Catalog
IIU:	Instruction Input Unit	IPC:	Institute of Printed Circuits
IJP:	Ink-Jet Printer	IPC:	Integrated Packet Channel
IKB:	Intelligent KeyBoard	IPC:	Integrated Peripheral Channel
ILA:	Intelligent Line Adapter	IPC:	Integrative Protective Circuits
ILA:	Intermediate Level Amplifier	IPC:	International Private Circuits
ILD:	Injection Laser Diode	IPC:	Inter-Process Controller
ILE:	Interfacing Latching Element	IPC:	Inter-Process Coupler
ILM:	Information Logic Machine	IPE:	Information Processing Equipment
ILM:	Inter-Laced Monitor	IPI:	Intelligent Printer Interface
ILM:	Intermediate Language Machine	IPM:	Intelligent Peripheral Monitor
ILO:	Injection-Locked Oscillator	IPP:	Imaging PhotoPolarimeter
ILP:	Intermediate Language Processor	IPU:	Instruction Processing Unit
ILS:	Integrated Logistic Support	IPU:	Integrated Processor Unit
ILT:	Inquiry Logical Terminal	IPU:	Inter-Processor Unit
IMA:	Institute for Manufacturing Automation	IQL:	Incoming Quality Level
		IRA:	Instruction Register Address
IMB:	Inter-Mode Bus	IRH:	Induction Recording Head
IMD:	Integrated Microcomputer Division	IRM:	Inspection, Repair and Maintenance
IME:	International Microcomputer Exposition	IRR:	Interrupt Return Register
		IRW:	Inverted Rib Waveguide
IML:	Initial Microprogram Load	ISA:	Industry Standard Architecture (IBM)
IMP:	Injection into Microwave Plasma	ISD:	Intermediate Storage Device
IMP:	Integrated Microwave Products	ISE:	In-System Emulator
IMP:	Intelligent Message Processor	ISE:	Interrupt System Enable
IMP:	Interface Message Processor	ISL:	Integrated Schottky Logic
IMR:	Interrupt Mask Register		

ISO: International Standards Organization
ISP: Indexed Sequential Processor
ISP: Instruction Set Processor
ISP: Integrated System Peripheral
ISU: Initial Signal Unit
ISU: Instruction Storage Unit
ISU: Interface Sharing Unit
ISU: Interface Switching Unit
ITA: Interface Test Adapter
ITA: International Tape Association
ITB: Internal Transfer Bus
ITF: Integrated Test Facility
ITI: Industrial Technology Institute
ITI: Interactive Terminal Interface
ITI: International Technology Institute
ITL: Integrated Transfer Launch
ITM: Indirect Tag Memory
ITP: Integrated Transaction Processor
ITS: Interactive Terminal Support
ITU: Incremental Tape Unit
ITV: Instructional TeleVision
IUL: In-Use Light
IUS: Interchange Unit Selector
IUS: Interchange Unit Separator
IVM: Initial Virtual Memory
IVM: Interface Virtual Machine
IVP: Installation Verification Procedure
IVR: Intermediate Voltage Regulator
IVS: Interactive Videodisk System
IVT: Integrated Video Terminal
IWB: Instruction Word Buffer
IWS: Independent Work Station
IWS: Intelligent Work Station
IWU: Internet Working Unit
IXU: Index Translation Unit

JOT: Job-Oriented Terminal
JPU: Job Processing Unit
JQE: Journal of Quantum Electronics
JRR: Journal Roll Reader
JRS: Junction Relay Set
JSA: Japanese Standards Association
JSP: Job Stream Processor
JTE: Junction Tandem Exchange

KBL: KeyBoard Layout
KBL: KeyBoard Listener
KCC: Keyboard Common Contact
KCU: Keyboard Control Unit
KDP: Keyboard, Display, and Printer
KDR: Keyboard Data Recorder
KDS: Key Display System
KDS: Key-to-Disk System
KDT: Key Data Terminal
keV: kilo-electron-Volt
Khm: Kilohm
KIR: Kyocera Image Refinement
Technology
KPH: Keystrokes Per Hour
KPM: Key Punch Machine
KPO: Key Punch Operator
KPR: Key Punch Replacement
KSU: Key Service Unit
KTR: Keyboard Typing Reperforator
kVA: kiloVolt-Ampere
KWH: KiloWatt Hour
KXU: Keyword Transformation Unit

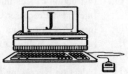

JAR: Jump Address Register
JAW: Just Another Workstation
JCC: Job Control Card
JCC: Joint Computer Conference
JID: Job Input Device
JIS: Japanese Industrial Standard
JIT: Just-In-Time
JMD: Jointly Managed Device
JOD: Job Output Device

LAD: Location Aid Device
LAD: Logical Amplitude Devices
LAR: Limit Address Register
LAU: Lobe Attaching Unit
LBA: Linear Bounded Automation
LBA: Local Bus Adapter
LBC: Local Bus Controller

LBP: Laser Beam Printer
LBR: Laser Beam Recorder
LBS: Laser Beam Sweep
LCA: Line Control Adapter
LCA: Local Communication Adapter
LCA: Low Cost Automation
LCC: Leadless Chip Carrier

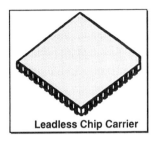

Leadless Chip Carrier

LCC: Ledger Card Computer
LCC: Liquid Crystal Cell
LCD: Liquid Crystal Diode
LCD: Liquid Crystal Display
LCE: Launch Complex Equipment
LCF: Language Central Facility
LCJ: Low Cost Junction
LCL: Lower Control Limit
LCM: Large Core Memory
LCR: Inductance-Capacitance-Resistance
LCS: Liquid Crystal Shutter
LCT: Low Cost Technology
LCU: Level Converter Unit
LCU: Local Control Unit
LDA: Latitude DAta Computer
LDA: LoaD in Accumulator
LDC: Local Device Controller
LDD: Lightly Doped Drains
LDF: LoaD Factor
LDO: Logical Device Order
LDR: Light Dependent Resistor
LDS: Large Disk Storage
LEA: Longitudinally Excited
     Atmosphere
LED: Light-Emitting Diode

Light-Emitting Diode

LEF: Light-Emitting Film

LEM: Logical End of Medium
LEM: Logical Enhanced Memory
LEO: Lyons Electronic Office
LEP: Lower End Plug
LFE: Laboratory For Electronics
LFO: Low Frequency Oscillator
LFU: Least Frequently Used
LGI: Linear Gate and Integrator
LHF: List Handling Facility
LHM: Loop Handling Machine
LIA: Laser Industry Association
LIA: Laser Institute of America
LIA: Low-Speed Input Adapter
LIC: Linear Integrated Circuit
LID: Leadless Inverted Device
LID: Locked-In Device
LIM: LIMulator
LIS: Line Isolation Switch
LIT: Liquid Injection Technique
LKM: Low Key Maintenance
LLA: Leased Line Adapter
LLD: Low Level Detector
LLI: Low Level Interface
LLS: Liquid Level Switch
LNA: Low Noise Amplifier
LNB: Local Name Bus
LNC: Low Noise Converter
LND: Limited Number of Devices
LOA: Low-Speed Output Adapter
LOF: Look Ahead On Fault
LOT: Light Operated Typewriter
LPC: LooP Control Relay
LPE: Liquid Phase Epitaxy
LPO: Low Power Output
LPR: LooP Control Relay
LPS: Long Persistence Screen
LPU: Language Processor Unit
LPU: Line Printer Unit
LPU: Line Processor Unit
LQP: Letter-Quality Printer
LRM: Limited Register Machine
LRU: Least Recently Used
LSA: Limited Space-Charge
     Accumulation Diode
LSI: Large Scale Integration
LSI: Large System Integration
LSM: Letter Sorting Machine
LSP: Laser Scanning Power
LSP: Low-Speed Printer
LSR: Local Storage Register
LSR: Low Shifting Resistor
LSR: Low-Speed Reader

LSU:	Least Significant Unit
LSU:	Library Storage Unit
LSU:	Line Selection Unit
LSU:	Load Storage Unit
LSU:	Local Storage Unit
LSX:	LSI-UNIX System
LTC:	Lap-Top Computer

Laptop Computer

LTC:	Local Terminal Controller
LTD:	Line Transfer Device
LTM:	Long-Term Memory
LVD:	Liquid Crystal Visual Display
LVP:	Low Voltage Protection

M

MAB:	MacroAddress Bus
MAC:	Machine-Aided Cognition
MAC:	Module Auxiliary Connector
MAC:	Multi-Access Computer
MAC:	Multiple Access Computer
MAD:	Magnetic Airborne Detector
MAD:	Magnetic Anomaly Detector
MAD:	Maintenance Assembly-Disassembly
MAD:	Michigan Algorithm Decoder
MAD:	Multi-Aperture Device
MAD:	Multiple Access Device
MAE:	Memory Address Extension
mag:	magnetic
MAM:	Multi-Access to Memory
MAM:	Multi-Application Monitor
MAP:	Macro-Arithmetic Processor
MAP:	Manufacturing Automation Protocol
MAP:	Memory Allocation Protection
MAP:	Micro-Programmed Array Processor
MAP:	Multi-Programmed Array Processor
MAR:	Macro-Address Register
MAR:	Member Address Register
MAR:	Memory Address Register

MAR:	Micro-Program Address Register
MAT:	Micro-Alloy Transistor
MAU:	Memory Access Unit
MBC:	Memory Bus Control
MBC:	Memory Bus Controller
MBD:	Magnetic Bubble Device
MBD:	Manual BoarD
MBE:	Molecular Beam Epitaxy
MBI:	Memory Bank Interface
MBM:	Magnetic Bubble Memory
MBR:	Memory Base Register
MBR:	Memory Buffer Register
MBT:	Metal Base Transistor
MBU:	Memory Buffer Unit
MCA:	Micro-Channel Architecture (IBM)
MCB:	Memory Controller Board
MCB:	Micro-Computer Board
MCB:	Module Circuit Board
MCC:	Main Control Circuit
MCC:	Maintenance Control Center
MCC:	Maintenance Control Circuit
MCC:	Micro-CPU Chip
MCC:	Multiple Chip Carrier
MCF:	Military Computer Family
MCH:	Machine Check Handler
MCI:	Machine Check Interrupt
MCM:	Magnetic Core Memory
MCM:	Mainframe-Centric Model
MCM:	Multiplexed Circuit Modem
MCM:	Multi-Scan Color Monitors
MCP:	Math CoProcessors
MCP:	Memory Centered Processor
MCR:	Magnetic Card Readers
MCR:	Magnetic Character Readers
MCR:	Master Control Register
MCR:	Memory Control Register
MCS:	Magnetic Card Storage
MCS:	Magnetic Core Storage
MCS:	Master Control System
MCS:	Micro-Computer System
MCS:	Modular Computer Systems
MCS:	Motor Circuit Switch
MCS:	Multi-Console System
MCS:	Multiple Console Support
MCU:	Main Control Unit
MCU:	Maintenance Control Unit
MCU:	Management Control Unit
MCU:	Master Control Unit
MCU:	Memory Control Unit
MCU:	Microprocessor Control Unit
MCU:	Microprogram Control Unit
MCU:	Multi-Chip Unit

MCV: Movable Closure Valve
MDA: Manufacturing Defects Analyzer
MDA: Monochrome Display Adapter
MDA: Multi-Dimensional Array
MDA: Multi-Docking Adapter
MDC: Memory Disk Controller
MDC: Micro-Computer Development Center
MDD: Magnetic Disk Drive
MDF: Multiple Device File
MDI: Medium Dependent Interface Unit
MDL: Maintenance Diagnostic Logic
MDL: Microprocessor Development Lab
MDP: Micro-Display Processor
MDR: Memory Data Register
MDS: Magnetic Disk Storage
MDS: Magnetic Disk Store
MDS: Magnetic Drum Storage
MDS: Main Distribution Socket
MDS: Malfunction Detection System
MDS: Memory Disk System
MDS: Microprocessor Development System
MDT: Manufacturers Delegated Test
MDU: Magnetic Disk Unit
MDU: Magnetic Drum Unit
MDU: Maintenance Diagnostic Unit
MDU: Monitor and Display Unit
MEB: Modem Evaluation Board
MED: Micro-Electronic Device
MEG: MEGa-Ohm
MEL: Many-Element Laser
mem: memory
MEM: Minimum Essential Medium
MEO: Memory Expansion Option
MEP: Microfiche Enlarger Printer
MES: Manual Entry Subsystem
MES: MEtal Semiconductor
MEU: Memory Expansion and Protection Unit
MEU: Memory Expansion Unit
MeV: Million electron Volts
MFB: Mixed Functional Block
MFC: Micro-Functional Circuit
mfd: microfarad
MFF: Match Flip Flop
MFP: Multi-Form Printer
MGA: Multi-Sense Graphic Adapter
MGC: Missile Guidance Computer
MGC: Mono Graphic Card
MGE: Modem Gateway Equipment
MGH: Mono Graphic Hercules
MGP: Monochrome Graphic Printer

MHD: Movable Head Disk
MHD: Moving Head Disk
MHE: Materials Handling Equipment
MHS: Magnetic Hand Scanner
MIA: Metal Interface Amplifier
MIA: Multiplex Interface Adapter
MIB: Manual Input Buffer
MIB: Micro-Instruction Bus
MIB: Multi-Layer Interconnection Board
MIC: Medium Interface Connector
MIC: Michigan Instructional Computer
MIC: MICrometer
MIC: Microwave Integrated Circuit
MIC: Minimum Ignition Current
MIC: Monolithic Integrated Circuit
MIC: Multi-Chip Integrated Circuit
MIR: Manual Input Register
MIR: Memory Information Register
MIR: Memory Input Register
MIS: Metal Insulator Semiconductor
MIT: Master Instruction Tape
MIT: Massachusetts Institute of Technology
MIX: Micro-Program IndeX Register
MIX: Modular Interface EXtension
MLA: Matching Logic and Adder
MLA: Memory Location Address
MLB: Multi-Layer Board
MLC: Multi-Layer Ceramic Capacitor
MLS: Microprocessor Line Set
MLU: Memory Logic Unit
MLU: Multiple Logic Unit
MMA: Major Maintenance Availability
MMB: Multi-Port Memory Bank
MMC: Multi-Port Memory Controller
MMF: MagnetoMotive Force
MMI: Main Memory Interface
MMI: Man-Machine Interface
MMM: Main Memory Module
MMP: Main Micro-Processor
MMP: Multiple Micro-Processors
MMR: Main Memory Register
MMS: Maintenance Mode Switch
MMS: Man-Machine Systems Group
MMU: Main Memory Unit
MMU: Memory Management Unit
MNA: Multi-Share Network Architecture
MNF: Multi-System Network Facility
MNS: Metal Nitride Semiconductor
MOA: Matrix Output Amplifier
MOC: Memory Operating Characteristic
MOC: Mission Operation Computer

MOD: Magneto-Optical Disks	MSD: Mass Storage Device
MOR: Memory Output Register	MSF: Monitor Screen Filters
MOS: Memory Oriented System	MSI: Machine Sensible Information
MOS: Metal Oxide Semiconductor	MSI: Medium Scale Integration
MOS: Metal Oxide Silicon	MSM: Memory Storage Module
MOV:Metal-Oxide Varistors	MSM: Metal-Semiconductor-Metal
MPA: Multiple Peripheral Adapter	MSP: Machine Space Point
MPC: Margin-Punched Card	MSP: Machine Storage Pool
MPC: Micro-Program Counter	MSP: Main Storage Partition
MPC: Modular Peripheral	MSP: Main Storage Processor
Interface Converter	MSR: Magnetic Slot Reader
MPC: Multi-Media Personal Computer	MSR: Magnetic Stripe Reader
MPC: Multi-Point Connection	MSR: Main Storage Region
MPD: Multi-Lingual Product Description	MSR: Mark Sense Reader
MPE: Memory Parity Error	MSR: Memory Select Register
MPF: MicroProcessor Family	MSR: Missile Site Radar
MPI: Magnetic Particle Inspection	MSS: Mass Storage System
MPI: MicroProcessor Interface	MSS: Master Slave System
MPI: Multi-Bus Peripheral Interface	MSS: Multi-Spectral Scanner
MPM: Micro-Program Memory	MST: Master STation
MPP: Multi-Programmable Processor	MST: Mean Service Time
MPP: Multiprogrammable Processor Port	MST: Monolithic System Technology
MPR: Micro-Program Register	MSU: Mass Storage Unit
MPS: Mapped Physical Storage	MSU: Memory Storage Unit
MPS: MicroProcessing System	MSV: Mean Square Voltage
MPS: MicroProcessor System	MSV: Multi-Service Vendor
MPU: Memory Protection Unit	MTA: Magnetic Tape Adapter
MPU: MicroProcessing Unit	MTA: Multi-Terminal Adapter
MPU: MicroProcessor Unit	MTC: Machine Tool Conference
MQW: Multi-Quantum Well	MTC: Magnetic Tape Cartridge
MRB: Magnetic Recording Borescope	MTC: Magnetic Tape Cassette
MRC: Machine Readable Code	MTC: Magnetic Tape Channel
MRC: Microform Reader Copier	MTC: Magnetic Tape Code
mrc: mid-range Computers	MTC: Magnetic Tape Controller
MRH: Magneto-resistive Recording Head	MTC: Maintenance Time Constraint
MRK: Margin Release Key	MTC: Manual Toning Control
MRM:Machine Readable Medium	MTC: Memory Test Computer
MRM:Margin Release Mechanism	MTD: Magnetic Tape Deck
MRO: Maintenance, Repair and Operating	MTD: Magnetic Tape Drive
MRP: Microform Reader Printer	MTE: Multiple Terminal Emulator
MRS: Multifunction Rotary Switches	MTF: Mean Time to Failure
MRT: Maximum-Repair-Time	MTH: Magnetic Tape Handler
MRT: Mean-Repair-Time	MTI: Machine Tools Industry
MRT: Multiple Requester Terminal	MTL: Magnetic Tape Label
MRU: Machine Records Unit	MTL: Magnetic Tape Leader
MRU: Minimum Resolvable Unit	MTL: Merged-Transistor Logic
MSA: Mass Storage Adapter	MTR: Magnetic Tape Reader
MSC: Mark Sensing Card	MTR: Magnetic Tape Recorder
MSC: Mass Storage Controller	MTR: Mean Time Repair
MSC: Module Segment Connector	mtr: monitor
MSC: Multiple Systems Coupling	MTS: Magnetic Tape Station
MSC: Multi-System Coupling	

MTS: Magnetic Tape Storage
MTS: Magnetic Tape System
MTS: Multiple Terminal System
MTT: Magnetic Tape Terminal
MTT: Magnetic Tape Trailer
MTT: Magnetic Tape Transport
MTU: Magnetic Tape Unit

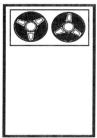

Magnetic Tape Unit

MTU: Master Terminal Unit
MTU: Memory Transfer Unit
MTU: Multiplexer and Terminal Unit
MUM:Multi-User Monitor
MUP: Multiple Utility Peripheral
MUR: Multi-User Register
MUS: Multi-User System
MVA:MegaVolt-Ampere
MVM:Manager Virtual Machine
MVP: Most Valuable Peripheral
MWL:MilliWatt Logic
MWS:Multi-Work Station
MWV: Maximum Working Voltage
MXM: MatriX Memory

NAD: No Apparent Defect
NAF: National Association OF
Independent Computer Companies
NBC: Non-Blocking Configuration
NBC: Note Book Computer
NBS: National Bureau of Standards (USA)
NBT: Null-Balance Transmissometer
NCC: National Computer Center (UK)
NCC: National Computer Conference
NCI: National Computer Institute
NCI: National Computing Industries

NCI: Northeast Computer Institute (USA)
NCO: Number Controlled Oscillator
NCP: Numeric CoProcessor
NCR: National Cash Register
NCS: National Computer Systems
NCS: Netherlands Computer Society
NDC: Normalized Device Coordinates
NDF: No Defect Found
NEA: National Electronics Association
NEC: National Electrical Code
NEC: National Electronics Conference
NEC: Nippon Electric Corporation (Japan)
NED: No Expiration Date
NEG: NEGative
NEL: Naval Electronics Laboratory
NEV: Non- EquiValent Gate
NFF: No Fault Found
NIB: Negative Impedance Booster
NIC: Negative Impedance Converter
NIH: Not Invented Here
NIM: Non-Interlaced Monitor
NIP: Non-Impact Printer
NIS: Neutron Instrumentation System
NIT: Non-Intelligent Terminal
NKP: Numeric Key Pad

Numeric Key Pad

NMA: National Microfilm Association
NMA: National Micrographics Association
NMR: Nuclear Magnetic Resonance
NMS: Neutron Monitoring System
NMV: Normal Mode Voltage
NOI: Node Operator Interface
NPD: Network Protector Device
NPH: Needle-Print Head
N-P-N: Negative-Positive-Negative
NPP: Non-Postscript Printer
NPS: Numerical Plotting System
NRL: Normal Rated Load
NSA: National Standards Association (USA)
NSA: Netherlands Society for Automation
NSI: Non-Standard Item
NSK: Not Specified by Kind

NSL: Non-Standard Label
NSN: National Stock Number
NSO: National Standards Organization (USA)
NTA: National Technology Agreement
NTC: National Transformers Committee (USA)
NTC: Nonstore Through Cache
NTD: Neutron Transmutation Doping
NTE: Network Terminating Equipment
NTR: Next Task Register
NTS: Navigation Technology System
NVM: Non-Volatile Memory
NVR: No Voltage Release
NXM: Non-EXistent Memory

OAC: One Address Computer
OAP: Orthogonal Array Processor
OAR: Overhaul And Repair
OAR: Operand Address Register
OBC: On-Board Computer
OBC: Optical Bar Code
OBP: On-Board Processor
OBR: Optical Bar Code Reader
OBS: Optical Beam Scanner
OCC: Operational Computer Complex
OCC: Optical Circuit and Component
OCI: Optically Coupled Isolator
OCI: Oxide Control and Indication
OCM: Optical Counter Measures
OCM: Oscillator and Clock Module
OCP: Operational Control Panel
OCP: Operator Control Panel
OCP: Order Code Processor
OCR: Optical Character Reader
OCR: Optical Character Recognition

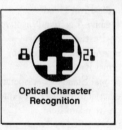

Optical Character Recognition

OCR: Output Control Register
OCR: Over-Current Relay
OCS: Open/Cabling Strategy
OCS: Optical Character Scanner
OCT: Operational Cycle Time
OCU: Operational Control Unit
ODB: Output Data Buffer
ODB: Output to Display Buffer
ODC: Optical Disk Controller
ODD: Optical Data Digitizer
ODD: Optical Data Disk
ODD: Optical Digital Disk
ODR: Output Definition Register
ODS: Output Data Strobe
ODU: Output Display Unit
OEM: Obscure Equipment Methodology
OEM: Original Equipment Manufacturer
OER: Original Equipment Replacement
OES: Output Enable Serial
OFT: Optical Fiber Tube
OGE: Operational Ground Equipment
OIC: Optical Integrated Circuit
OIL: Operation Inspection Log
OIP: Optical Image Processor
OIS: Operational Instrumentation System
OIS: Optical Image Sensor
OLC: OnLine Computer
OLD: Optical Laser Disk
OLM: OnLine Monitor
OLR: Office Loop Repeater
OLV: Open-Frame Low Voltage
OMA: Operations Monitor Alarm
OMC: Operation and Maintenance Center
OMC: Operations Monitoring Computer
OMM: Operation and Maintenance Manual
OMP: Optical Mark Printer
OMR: Optical Mark Reader
OMT: OrthoMode Transducer
OMU: Optical Measuring Unit
OOF: Office Of the Future
OPD: One Per Desk
OPO: Optical Parametric Oscillator
OPP: Octal Print Punch
OPR: Optical Page Reader
OPS: OnLine Process Synthesis
OPU: Operations Priority Unit
ORA: Output Register Address
ORC: OnLine Reactivity Computer
ORC: Orthogonal Row Computer
ORE: Output Register Empty
ORU: OnLine Replacement Unit
OSA: Open Systems Architecture

OSB:	Option SpaceBar		PAT:	Peripheral Allocation Table
osc:	oscillator		PAT:	Personalized Array Translator
OSD:	Optical Scanning Device		PAT:	Priority Access Timer
OSE:	Operational Support Equipment		PAT:	Production Acceptance Testing
OSG:	Operand Select Gate		PAT:	Program for Advance
OSR:	Operand Storage Register			Technology (EEC)
OSR:	Output Shift Register		PAU:	Pattern Articulation Unit
OST:	Office of Science and Technology		PAX:	Parallel Architecture EXchange
OSW:	Operational SWitching Unit		PBC:	Peripheral Bus Computer
OTA:	Office of Technology		PBC:	Personal Business Computer
	Assessment (USA)		PBE:	Panasonic Business Equipment
OTA:	Open Test Assembly		PBJ:	Pater-Braided Jute
OTA:	Operational Transconductance		PBP:	Push Button Panel
	Amplifier		PBS:	Push Button Switch
OTC:	Operational Test Center		PBU:	Push Button Unit
OTP:	One-Time-Programmable		PCA:	Physical Configuration Audit
OTS:	OnLine Terminal System		PCA:	Printed Circuit Assembly
OTT:	One-Time Tape		PCA:	Protective Connecting Arrangement
OTU:	Office of Technology Utilization		PCA:	Pulse Code Adapter
OTU:	Operational Test Unit		PCA:	Pulse Counter Adapter
OVD:	Optical Video Disk		PCB:	Power Circuit Breaker
OVP:	Over-Voltage Protection		PCB:	Printed Circuit Board
OWF:	Optimum Working Facility		PCD:	Power Control Device
OWL:	OnLine Without Limits		PCD:	Production Common Digitizer
			PCE:	Process Control Equipment
			PCE:	Punched Card Equipment
			PCF:	Printed Card Form

			PCF:	Programmed Cryptographic Facility
			PCI:	Panel Call Indication Switches
			PCI:	Peripheral Controller Interface
			PCK:	Phase Control Keyboard
			PCK:	Processor Controlled Key
PAC:	Package Assembly Circuit		PCM:	Parallel Conversion Method
PAC:	Pedagogic Automatic Computer		PCM:	Plug Compatible Mainframe
PAC:	Personal Analog Computer		PCM:	Plug Compatible Manufacturer
PAC:	Pneumatic Analog Computer		PCM:	Plug Compatible Memory
PAC:	Pneumatic Auxiliary Console		PCM:	Punched Card Machine
PAC:	Programmable Analog Controller		PCP:	Parallel Cascade Processor
PAD:	Positioning Arm Disk		PCP:	Plug Compatible Peripherals
PAF:	Production Assembly Facility		PCP:	Process Control Processor
PAI:	Parts Application Information		PCP:	Punched Card Punch
PAI:	Pre-Arrival Inspection		PCR:	Print Command Register
PAI:	Precise Angle Indicator		PCR:	Program Control Register
PAK:	Product Authorization Key		PCR:	Punched Card Reader
PAL:	Programmable Array Logic		PCR:	Punched Card Requisition
PAL:	Prototype Application Loop		PCS:	Personal Computing System
PAM:	PAnel Monitor		PCS:	Plastic-Clad Silicon Optical Fiber
PAM:	Peripheral Adapter Module		PCS:	Plato Computer System
PAO:	Pulsed Avalanche Diode Oscillator		PCS:	Pointing Control System
PAR:	Page Address Register		PCS:	Process Computer System
PAR:	Performance And Reliability		PCS:	Process Control System
PAR:	Program Address Register		PCS:	Punched Card System

PCT:	Peripheral Control Terminal	PFR:	Paper Feed Rollers
PCT:	Photon-Coupled Transistor	PFR:	Power Fail Recovery
PCU:	Peripheral Control Unit	PFR:	Power Fail Restart
PCU:	Port Contention Unit	PFR:	Power Full Recovery
PCU:	Power Control Unit	PF/R:	Power Full/Restart
PCU:	Processor Control Unit	PFT:	Paper Feed Tray
PCU:	Programmable Control Unit	PGA:	Pin Grid Array Chip
PCU:	Punch Card Unit		

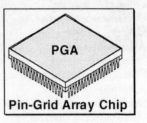

Pin-Grid Array Chip

PDA:	Parallel Data Adapter		
PDA:	PushDown Automation		
PDC:	Parallel Data Controller	PGA:	Programmable Gate Array
PDC:	Performance Data Computer	PGC:	ProGram Counter
PDC:	Photo-Data Card	PGD:	Planar Gas Discharge
PDC:	Programmable Desk Calculator	PGP:	Programmable Graphics Processor
PDM:	Physical Distribution Management	PGR:	Precision Graphic Recorder
PDM:	Push Down Memory	PHD:	Parallel Head Disk
PDP:	Plasma Display Panel	PIA:	Parallel Interface Adapter
PDP:	Procedure Definition Processor	PIA:	Peripheral Interface Adapter
PDP:	Program Digital Processor	PIB:	Programmable Input Buffer
PDP:	Programmed Data Processor	PIC:	Peripheral Interface Channel
PDP:	Public Dial Port	PIC:	Plastic Insulated Cable
PDQ:	Programmed Data Quantizer	PIC:	Polyethylene-Insulated Conductor
PDR:	Page Data Register	PIC:	Priority Interrupt Control Chip
PDR:	Peripheral Data Register	PIC:	Priority Interrupt Controller
PDR:	Processed Data Recorder	PIC:	Programmable Interrupt Controller
PDS:	Power Distribution System	PID:	Peripheral Interface Device
PDS:	Processor Direct Slot	PID:	Personal Identification Device
PDT:	Programmable Data Terminal	PID:	Pictorial Information Digitizer
PDT:	Push Down Transducer	PID:	Pseudo Interrupt Device
PDU:	Plasma Display Unit	PIE:	Parallel Interface Element
PDU:	Power Distribution Unit	PII:	Peripheral Interconnect Interface
PDU:	Programmable Delay Unit	PII:	Positive Immittance Inverter
PEB:	Pulse Electron Beam	PIL:	Precision In-Line
PEC:	Photo-Electric Cell	PIM:	Processor Interface Module
PEE:	Photo-FerroElectric Effect	PIN:	Personal Identification Number
PEF:	Physical Electronics Facility	PIN:	Position INdicator
PEL:	Production Error Log	pin:	positive-intrinsic-negative transistor
PEM:	Photo-Electro-Magnetic	PIO:	Peripheral Input Output
PEM:	Processing Element Memory	PIP:	Primary Indicating Position
PEO:	Peripheral Equipment Operators	PIP:	Programmable Integrated Processor
PEP:	Peripheral Event Processor	PIS:	Process Interface System
PEP:	Planar Epiaxial Passivated Transistor	PIT:	Peripheral Input Tape
PES:	Photo-Electric Scanner	PIT:	Program Instruction Tape
PET:	Peripheral Equipment Tester	PIU:	Path Information Unit
PEU:	Port Expander Unit	PIU:	Plug-In Unit
PFB:	Pre-Fetch Buffer	PIU:	Process Interface Unit
PFI:	Physical Fault Insertion		
PFK:	Program Function Keyboard		
PFM:	Paper Feed Mechanism		
PFP:	Pre-Fetch Processor		
PFP:	Program File Processor		

PIV:	Peak Inverse Voltage	POD:	Physical Output Device
PKC:	Position Keeping Computer	POD:	Point of Origin Device
PKD:	Portable Keying Devices	POF:	Point Of Failure
PKD:	Programmable Keyboard/Display	POK:	Power-On Key
PKE:	Public-Key Encryption	POM:	Print-Out Microfilm
PLA:	Programmable Line Adapter	PON:	Power ON
PLA:	Programmable Logic Array	POP:	Power On/Off Protection
PLA:	Programmed Logic Array	pos:	positive
PLC:	Power-Line Carrier	POS:	Printer Operating Speed
PLC:	Programmable Line Controller	POT:	POtenTiometer
PLC:	Programmable Logic Controller	PPA:	Parallel Processor Architecture
PLD:	Phase-Lock Demodulator	PPB:	PROM Programmer Board
PLD:	Programmable Logic Device	PPC:	Personal Programmable Calculator
PLD:	Pulse Length Discriminator	PPC:	Platform Position Computer
PLE:	Pipe-Line Element	PPC:	Portable Personal Computer
PLM:	Passive Line Monitor	PPC:	Print Position Counter
PLM:	Pulse Length Manual	PPC:	Pulsed Power Circuit
PL/M:	Programming Language for Microprocessor	PPD:	Primary Paging Device
		PPE:	Pre-Modulation Processor Equipment
PLO:	Phase Locked Oscillator	PP/E:	Parallel Print/Extract
PLP:	Procedural Language Processor	PPF:	Production Possibility Frontier
PLS:	Programmable Logic Sequencer	ppi:	pixels per inch
PLT:	Program Library Tape	PPI:	Programmable Parallel Interface
PLU:	Peripheral Logical Unit	PPM:	Parts Per Million
PMA:	Pre-Amplifier Module Assembly	PPM:	Planned Preventive Maintenance
PMA:	Preferred Machine Assist	PPM:	Previous Processor Mode
PMA:	Prime Micro-Assembler	PPP:	Parallel Pattern Processor
PMB:	Procedure Memory Bus	PPP:	Parallel Printer Port
PMB:	PROM Memory Board	PPS:	Preferred Power Supply
PMB:	Proprietary Memory Bus	PPS:	Primary Power System
PMC:	Performance Management Computer	PPT:	Punched Paper Tape
PMC:	Programmable Machine Controller	PPU:	Peripheral Processing Unit
PME:	PhotoMagnetoelectric Effect	PPU:	Primary Processing Unit
PME:	Process and Manufacturing Engineering	PRA:	Program Reader Assembly
		PRC:	Procession Register Clock
PME:	Processor Memory Enhancement	PRE:	Picture Response Equipment
PMI:	Parallel Machine Interface	PrE:	Printer Emulator
PML:	Physical Memory Loss	PRI:	PRinter Interface
PMM:	Programmable Micro-Computer Module	prl:	parallel
		PRL:	PRocessor Level
PMP:	Parallel Micro-Programmed Processor	PRN:	PRiNt
PMP:	Parts-Material-Packaging	pro:	processor
PMP:	Pre-Modulation Processor	PRR:	Pseudo Resident Reader
PMR:	Power Master Reset	PRS:	Pattern Recognition System
PMS:	Physical Main Storage	PRS:	Primary Register Set
PMS:	Processor Memories and Switches	PRT:	Pattern Recognition Technology
PMT:	PhotoMultiplier Tube	PRT:	Portable Remote Terminal
PMT:	Program Master Tape	PRU:	Physical Record Unit
PNP:	Positive-Negative-Positive-Type Transistor	PRU:	PRinter Unit
		PRV:	Peak Inverse/Reverse Voltage
P-N-P:	Positive-Negative-Positive	PSA:	Parametric Semiconductor Amplifier
POC:	Power On Clear	PSC:	PhotoSensitive Cell

PSC:	Processable Scored Card	PUP:	Peripheral Unit Processor
PSD:	Phase Shifting Device	PUP:	Peripheral Universal Processor
PSF:	Pattern Sensitive Fault	PUT:	Program Update Tape
PSF:	Point Spread Function	PUT:	Programmable Unijunction Transistors
PSM:	Peak Selector Memory	PVC:	Position and Velocity Computer
PSM:	Power Supply Module	PVC:	Program and Velocity Computer
PSM:	Programming Support Monitor	PVD:	Physical Vapor Deposition Technology
PSM:	Proportional Spacing Machine		
PSP:	Portable Service Processor	PVI:	Programmable Video Interface
PSP:	PostScript Printer	PVM:	Preferred Virtual Machine
PSR:	Performance Summary Report	PVP:	Pipe-Lined Vector Processor
PSR:	Processor State Register	PVR:	Prefix Value Register
PSR:	Program Status Register	PVS:	Performance Verification System
PSS:	Printer Storage System	PVS:	Power Visualization System
PS/2:	Personal System/2 Computer (IBM)	PVT:	Page View Terminal
		PWA:	Printed Wire Assembly
PST:	Periodic Self-Test	PWB:	Printed Wiring Board
PST:	Pressure-Sensitive Tablet	PWR:	Processor WRite
PST:	Program Selected Terminal		

PSU:	Peripheral Switching Unit		
PSU:	Power Supply Unit		
PSU:	Problem Statement Unit		
PSU:	Processor Service Unit		
PSU:	Processor Speed Up	QAR:	Quality Assurance Requirements
PSU:	Processor Storage Unit	QAS:	Questions & Answers System
PSU:	Program Storage Unit	QBT:	Quad Bus Transceiver
PSV:	Pain Shield Video	QCE:	Quality Control Engineering
PSW:	Processor Status Word	QCR:	Quality Control Reliability
PTA:	Paper Tape Accessory	QDC:	Quarantine Delivery Control
PTA:	Planar Turbulence Amplifier	QDI:	Quasi-Differential Inputs
PTA:	Programmable Translation Array	QDP:	QuickDraw Printer
PTA:	Pulse Torquing Assembly	QEA:	Quantum Electronics & Applications
PTC:	Palm Top Computer	QFP:	Quad Flat Pack
PTC:	Paper Tape Code	QIC:	Quarter Inch Cartridge
PTC:	Perforated Tape Code	QIC:	Quarter Inch Committee
PTD:	Parallel Transfer Disk Drive	QIL:	Quad In-Line
PTE:	Pressure-Tolerant Electronics	QLR:	Quadruple Length Register
PTM:	Programmable Timer Module	QOD:	Quick-Opening Device
PTP:	Paper Tape Perforator	QPM:	Quality Program Manager
PTP:	Paper Tape Punch	QRP:	Query Reporting Processor
PTP:	Processor To Processor	QTM:	Thermistor
PTR:	Paper Tape Reader	QVT:	Quality Verification Testing
PTR:	Perforated Tape Reader	QXI:	Queue EXecutive Interface
ptr:	printer		
PTR:	Punched Tape Reader		
PTS:	Paper Tape System		
PTS:	Programmable Terminal System		
PTS:	Pure Time Sharing		
PTT:	Program Test Tape		
PTU:	Package Transfer Unit		
PTV:	Punched Tape Verifier		
PUC:	Processing Unit Cabinet		

RAA: Random Access Array
RAD: Random Access Device
RAD: Random Access Disk
RAD: Rapid Access Device
RAD: Rapid Access Disk
RAG: ROM Address Gate
RAM: Random Access Memory
RAM: Remote Access Monitor
RAP: Relational Associative Processor
RAR: Return Address Register
RAR: ROM Address Register
RAS: Rapid Access Storage
RAS: Reliability, Availability,
 Serviceability
RAS: Row Address Strobe
RAT: Remote Area Terminal
RAT: Reserve Auxiliary Transformer
RAU: Remote Acquisition Unit
RBM: Rod Block Monitor
RBR: Read-Back Registers
RBS: Remote Batch System
RBT: Remote Batch Terminal
RCA: Remote Control Adapter
RCC: Real-Time Computer Complex
RCD: Registered Connective Device
RCD: Removable Cartridge Drive
RCE: Reliability Control Engineering
RCE: Remote Control Equipment
RCL: Reloadable ControL Storage
RCL: Resistance Capacitance
 and Inductance
RCP: Receive Clock Pulse
RCP: Recognition and Control Processor
RCP: Remote Computer Pool
RCR: Return Code Register
RCS: Reloadable Control Storage
RCS: Remote Computer System
RCS: Remote Computing Service
RCS: Remote Control Switch
RCT: Resolves Control Transformer
RCT: Reversible CounTer
RCU: Remote Concentrator Unit
RCU: Remote Control Unit
RCV: Remote Controlled Vehicle
RDD: Raster Display Device
RDD: Replaceable Database Drivers
RDL: Resistor Diode Logic

RDM: Recording Demand Meter
RDP: Relational Database Processor
RDP: Remote Data Processor
RDQ: Reusable Disk Queuing
rdr: reader
RDR: Receive Data Ready
RDR: Receive Data Register
RDT: Remote DigiTal Readout
REC: REmote Console
reg: register
REM: REcognition Memory
REN: Remote ENable
REP: Re-Entrant Processor
REQ: REquest for Quotation
RET: Remote Enquiry Terminal
RET: Resolution Enhancement
 Technology
REU: Ready Extension Unit
RFS: Remote File Server (AT&T)
RGB: Red, Green, Blue Monitor
RGP: Rate Gyro Package
RGP: Remote Graphics Processor
RGS: Rocket Guidance System
RGT: Resonant Gate Transistor
RHR: Receiver Holding Register
RIA: Removable Instrument Assembly
RIA: Robot Institute of America
RIF: Reliability Improvement Factor
RIM: Register Indirect Mode
RIP: Raster Image Processor
RIR: Relative Index Register
RIR: ROM Instruction Register
RIS: Raster Input Scanner
RIS: Rotating Image Scanner
RIT: Resolution Improvement
 Technology
RJE: Remote Job Entry Processor
RJP: Remote Job Processor
RKR: RacK Register
RLA: Remote Line Adapter
RLA: Remote Loop Adapter
RLC: Resistance-Inductance-Capacitance
RLC: ROM Location Counter
RLE: Receiver Latch Enable
RLR: Record Length Register
RMA: Reactive Modulation Amplifier
RMA: Reliability, Maintainability,
 Availability
RMA: Return Material Authorization
 Number
RMA: Return Mechandise Authorization
 Number

RMC: Rack-Mounted Computer
RMC: Rod Memory Computer
RME: Rack-Mount Extender
RMM:Read Mostly Memory
RMM:Remote Maintenance Monitor
RMU: Remote Maneuvering Unit
RMU: Resource Management Unit
RNG: Random Number Generator
ROC: Remote Operator's Console
ROC: Required Operations Capability
ROM: Read Only Memory
ROP: Receive Only Printer
ROP: Register-Oriented Processor
ROT: Remaining Operating Time
RPC: Remote Position Control
RPD: Radar Planning Device
RPE: Remote Peripheral Equipment
RPM: Read Program Memory
RPM: Revolutions Per Minute
RPM: Rotations Per Minute
RPQ: Request Price Quotation
RPS: Remote Printing System
rps: revolutions per Second
RPS: Rotational Position Sensing
RPU: Radio Phone Unit
RPU: Radio Propagation Unit
RPU: Regional Processing Unit
RPU: Remote Processing Unit
RQL: Rejectable Quality Level
RRO: RAM Refresh Operation
RRV: Remote Reconnaissance Vehicle
RSB: Remote System Base
RSD: Responsible System Designer
RSP: Reader/Sorter Processor
RSP: Rotating Shield Plug
RSS: ReSet Switch
RST: Re-Set Trigger
RSU: Register Storage Unit
RSU: Relay Storage Unit
RTA: Real-Time Accumulator
RTA: Reliability Test Assembly
RTA: Remote Technical Assistance
RTC: Reader Tape Contact
RTC: Real-Time Clock
RTC: Real-Time Computer
RTC: Relative Time Clock
RTD: Resistance Temperature Detector
RTD: Resistance Temperature Device
RTF: Raceway-Type Floor
RTL: Register Transfer Level
RTL: Resistor-Transistor Logic
RTM: Real-Time Monitor

RTP: Real-Time Peripheral
RTP: Remote Terminal Processor
RTP: Remote Test Processor
RTP: Requirement and Test Procedures
RTS: Remote Terminal System
RTT: Resistive Thermal Transducers
RTU: Remote Terminal Unit
RUF: Resource Utilization Factor
RUG: Resource Utilization Graph
RUP: Remote Unit Processor
RUT: Resource Utilization Time
RVC: Relative Velocity Computer
RWC: Reduced Write Current
RWH: Read-Write Head
RWM:Read/Write Memory
RWO: Read-Write Optical
RWP: Read/Write Protection
RWR: Read/Write Register
RWS: Read/Write Slot
RWT: Read/Write Tested
RWT: Right When Tested
RXM: Read/Write EXpandable Memory

SAA: Systems Application Architecture (IBM)
SAB: Solid Assembly Block
SAB: Speech Adapter Box (Philips)
SAC: Servo Adapter Coupler
SAC: Stand Alone Computer
SAC: Storage Access Channel
SAC: Store Access Controller
SAE: Shaft Angle Encoder
SAI: Sub-Architectural Interface
SAM: Semantic Analyzing Machine
SAM: Sequential Access Memory
SAM: Serial Access Memory
SAM: Systems Adapter Module
SAM: Systems Analysis Machine
SAR: Segment Address Register
SAR: Source Address Register
SAR: Storage Address Register
SAR: Successive Approximation Register
SAS: Serial Associative Storage

SBA:	Static Buffer Allocation	SDP:	Software Development Process
SBC:	Sensor-Based Computer	SDR:	Storage Data Recorder
SBC:	Single Board Computer	SDR:	Storage Data Register
SBC:	Small Business Computer	SDS:	System Data Synthesizer
SBD:	Schottky-Barrier Diode	SDU:	Station Display Unit
SBI:	Screen Burn-In	SDV:	Soft Dollar Value
SBM:	StandBy Monitor	SEC:	Secondary Electron Conduction
SBP:	Semiconductor Bipolar Processor	SEC:	Secondary Emission Conductivity
SBR:	Storage Buffer Register	SEC:	Simple Electronic Computer
SBS:	Sensor-Based System	SEE:	Systems Effectiveness Engineering
SBT:	Surface Barrier Transistor	SEF:	Storage Extension Frame
SBU:	Security BackUp	sel:	selector
SBU:	Station Buffer Unit	SEL:	Stanford Electronics Laboratory
SBU:	System Back Up	SEM:	Scanning Electron Microscope
SBV:	Spill Backup Volume	SEM:	Standard Electronic Module
SCA:	Simulated Core Assembly	SEM:	Systems Engineering Management
SCC:	Single-Conductor Cable	SEP:	Space Electronic Package
SCC:	Single-Cotton Covered Wire	SEP:	Standard Electronic Package
SCC:	Standards Coordinating	SER:	Sequential Events Recorder
	Committee (IEEE)	SES:	Systems Engineering Services
SCD:	Serial Cryptographic Device	SET:	Space Electronics and Telemetry
SCE:	Signal Conversion Equipment	SET:	Stepped Electrode Transistor
SCE:	Signal Conversion Equivalent	SFA:	Single Failure Analysis
SCF:	Single Cluster Feature	SFB:	Semiconductor Functional Block
SCM:	Small Core Memory	SFD:	System Function Description
SCM:	Super Conducting Magnet	SFL:	Substrate Fed Logic
scn:	scanner	SFP:	Security Filter Processor
SCP:	Secondary Command Processor	SFR:	Special Function Registers
SCR:	Scan Control Register	SFT:	System Fault Tolerance
SCR:	Semiconductor-Controlled Rectifier	SFU:	Special Front End Unit
SCR:	Sequence Control Register	SFU:	Special Function Unit
SCR:	Silicon Control Rectifier	SGC:	Second Generation Computers
SCR:	System Change Request	SHA:	Solid Homogenous Assembly
SCS:	Silicon-Controlled Switch	SHA:	Special Handling Area
SCS:	Small Computer System	SHE:	Subject Headings for Engineering
SCT:	SCanning Telescope	SHF:	Storage Handling Facility
SCT:	Service Counter Terminal	SHM:	Society for Hybrid Micro-Electronics
SCU:	Sequence Control Unit	SHP:	Standard Hardware Program
SCU:	Station Control Unit	shr:	share
SCU:	Storage Control Unit	SIA:	Semiconductor Industry Association
SCU:	System Control Unit	SIA:	Standard Interface Adapter
SDB:	Storage Data Bus	SIA:	System Integration Area
SDC:	Scratch Data Cartridge	SIB:	Screen Image Buffer
SDC:	Source Data Card	SIB:	Serial Input Output Board
SDC:	Stabilization Data Computer	SIB:	Serial Interface Board
SDF:	Single Device File	SIB:	Spool Intercept Buffer
SDM:	Selective Dissemination	SIB:	System Image Buffer
	of Microfiche	SIB:	System Interface Bus
SDM:	Semiconductor Disk Memory	SIC:	Semiconductor Integrated Circuit
SDM:	Shut Down Mode	SIC:	Standard Industrial Classification
SDP:	Site Data Processor	SID:	Silicon Imaging Device

SID:	Standard Input Device	SMF:	Storage Mapping Function
SID:	Syntax Improving Device	SMF:	Systems Management Facilities
SIL:	Single In-Line	SMI:	Simulated Machine Indexing
SIM:	Sequential Inference Machine	SMI:	Static Memory Interface
SIP:	Single-In-Line Package	SMI:	System Memory Interface

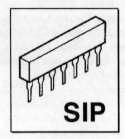

SIP

		SMM:	Semiconductor Memory Module
		SMM:	Shared Main Memory
		SMM:	Shared Multiport Memory
		SMP:	Simple Mail Protocol
		SMS:	Shared Mass Storage
		SMS:	Standard Modular System
		SMT:	Surface Mount Technology
		SMT:	System Master Tape
		SMU:	Store Monitor Unit
		SMU:	System Monitoring Unit
SIR:	Segment Identification Register	SOD:	Standard Output Device
SIT:	Stand-Alone Intelligent Terminal	SOD:	System Output Device
SIT:	Static Induction Transistor	SOI:	Silicon On Insulator
SIU:	System Interface Unit	SOJ:	Small Outline J-Lead
SJP:	Serialized Job Processor	SOR:	Specific Operating Requirement
SKB:	SKew Buffer	SOR:	Specific Operational Requirement
SLA:	Service Level Agreement	SOS:	Silicon On Sapphire
SLA:	Shared Line Adapter	SPA:	Shared Peripheral Area
SLA:	Stored Logic Array	SPB:	Stored Program Buffer
SLC:	SeLeCtor	SPC:	Serial Parallel Cards
SLC:	Simulator Linguistic Computer	SPC:	Small Peripheral Controller
SLD:	System List Device	SPC:	Special Purpose Computer
SLD:	System Log Device	SPC:	Static Power Converters
SLI:	Suppress Length Indicator	SPC:	Stored Program Computer
SLI:	Synchronous Line Interface	SPD:	Secondary Paging Device
SLO:	Swept Local Oscillator	SPD:	Stored-Program Device
SLP:	Source Language Processor	SPD:	Surged Protective Devices
SLR:	Storage Limits Register	SPE:	Single-Photo-Electric Cell
SLS:	Shared Logic System	SPE:	Special Purpose Equipment
SLT:	Solid Logic Technique	SPE:	System Performance Effectiveness
SLT:	Solid Logic Technology	SPI:	Shared Peripheral Interface
SLU:	Secondary Logic Unit	SPI:	Single Processor Interface
SLU:	Serial Line Unit	SPK:	Soft Programmable Keys
SLU:	Special Line Unit	SPM:	Scratch Pad Memory
SMA:	Surface Mounting Applicator	SPM:	Session Protocol Machine
SMA:	System Management Automation	SPM:	Sequential Processing Machine
SMB:	System Monitor Board	SPM:	Special-Purpose Memories
SMC:	Secondary Memory Cache	SPM:	Symbol Processing Machine
SMC:	Storage Module Controller	SPO:	Synchronized Power-On
SMC:	System Monitor Controller	SPP:	Simultaneous Print/Plot
SMD:	Storage Module Device	SPP:	Special Purpose Processors
SMD:	Storage Module Drive	SPP:	Surge Protection Package
SMD:	Surface Mountable Devices	SPP:	Surge Protector Plug
SMD:	Systems Measuring Device	SPR:	Stack Pointer Register
SME:	Society of Manufacturing Engineers	SPR:	Storage Protection Register
		SPS:	Serial Parallel Serial
		SPS:	SPeed Switch

SPT:	Sectors Per Track	STR:	STatus Register
SPT:	Symbolic Program Tape	STS:	Standard Technical Specifications
SPU:	Slave Processing Unit	STT:	Seven Track Tape
SPU:	System Processing Unit	STT:	Sublimation Thermal Transfer
spx:	simplex circuit	STU:	Segment Time Unit
SRA:	Shop Replaceable Assembly	STU:	Subscriber Terminal Unit
SRD:	Step-Recovery Diode	SUD:	System Utility Device
SRL:	Shift Register Latch	SUE:	System User Engineered
SRM:	Source Range Monitors	SUI:	Standard Universal
SRO:	Singly Resonance Oscillator		Identifying Number
SRR:	Shift Register Recognizer	SUS:	Silicon Unilateral Switch
SRS:	Secondary Register Set	SUT:	System Under Test
SRS:	Simulated Remote Sites	SVA:	Shared Virtual Area
SRS:	Slave Register Set	SVP:	SerVice Processor
SSA:	Static Storage Allocation	SVR:	Super Video Recorder
SSC:	Solid State Component	SVS:	Single Virtual Storage
SSC:	Solid State Computer	SVS:	Single Virtual System
SSC:	Subsystem Store Controller	SVT:	System Validation Testing
SSD:	Single-Sided Disk	SXE:	Data Switching Equipment
SSD:	Soft-Sectored Diskette	SXS:	Step By Step Switch
SSD:	Solid State Disk	sys:	system
SSD:	Start-Stop Devices		
SSE:	Special Support Equipment		
SSI:	Sector Scan Indicator		
SSI:	Small Scale Integration		
SSI:	Small System Integration		

SSM:	Semiconductor Storage Module		
SSM:	Small Semiconductor Memory		
SSN:	Segment Stack Number	TAB:	Tape Automated Bonding
SSP:	System Status Panel	TAC:	Terminal Access Controller
SSP:	System Support Processor	TAC:	Time-to-Amplitude Converter
SSR:	Serially Shared Resource	TAC:	Transformer Analog Computer
SSS:	Start-Stop System	TAC:	Transistorized Automatic Computer
SST:	Scanned Storage Tube	TAC:	Transistorized Automatic Control
SSU:	System Services Unit	TAG:	Technical Advisory Group
SSW:	Synchro SWitch	TAG:	Time Automated Grid
STB:	Subsystems Test Bed	TAP:	Terminal Access Processor
STC:	Seven-Track Compatibility	TAR:	Terminal Address Register
STC:	Store Through Cache	TAR:	Track Address Register
STC:	System Test Complex	TAR:	Transfer Address Register
STE:	Special Test Equipment	TAS:	Terminal Automation System
STE:	Standard Test Equipment	TAU:	Test Access Unit
STE:	Subscriber Terminal Equipment	TBC:	Toss Bomb Computer
STE:	Supergroup Translating Equipment	TBP:	Type-Bar Printer
STH:	Spherical Type Head	TBR:	Table Base Register
STL:	Schottky Transistor Logic	TCA:	Technical Computer Adapter
STL:	System Test Loop	TCA:	Thermal Critical Assembly
STM:	Short Term Memory	TCC:	Technical Computer Center
STM:	System Master Tape	TCC:	Test Controller Console
STN:	Symbolic Terminal Name	TCE:	Telemetry Checkout Equipment
STP:	Selective Tape Print	TCF:	Technical Control Facility
STP:	Shielded Twisted Pair		

TCF:	Terminal Configuration Facility	TOC:	Time Out Circuit
TCK:	Testability ClocK	TPB:	Teletype Printer Buffer
TCL:	Transfer Chemical Laser	TPD:	Thermoplastic-Photoconductor Device
TCM:	Terminal to Computer Multiplexer		
TCO:	Thermal Cut-Off Devices	TPI:	Tracks Per Inch
TCP:	Transport Control Protocol	TPM:	Technical Performance Measures
TCR:	Tape Cassette Recorder	TPM:	TeleProcessing Monitor
TCS:	Terminal Control System	TPS:	Tape to Print System
TCS:	Terminal Countdown Sequencer	TPU:	Task Processing Unit
TCT:	Teletype Compatible Terminal	TPU:	Terminal Processing Unit
TCU:	Tape Control Unit	TPW:	Twisted-Pair Wire
TCU:	Teletypewriter Control Unit	TQC:	Total Quality Control
TCU:	Terminal Control Unit	TQE:	Time Queue Element
TCU:	Timing Control Unit	TRK:	TRacK
TCV:	Terminal Configured Vehicle	TRL:	Transistor-Resistor Logic
TDA:	Tunnel Diode Amplifier	TRM:	Terminal Response Monitor
TDC:	Tandem Data Circuit	TRR:	Tape Read Register
TDK:	Test Drive Kit	TRS:	Tandy Radio Shack
TDM:	Template Descriptor Memory	TRS:	Terminal Receive Side
TDR:	Tape Data Register	TSA:	Time Slot Access
TDR:	Time Domain Reflectometry	TSC:	Three State Control
TDS:	Transaction Driven System	TSC:	Time Share Control
TDU:	Tape Deck Unit	TSF:	Time to System Failure
TEA:	The Electronic Aveary	TSM:	Time Sharing Monitor
TET:	Thermo-Electric Transducer	TSP:	Time Series Processor
TFD:	Thin-Film Disk	TSR:	Technical Summary Report
TFM:	Thin Film Memory	TSR:	Temporary Storage Register
TFT:	Thin-Film Transistor	TSR:	Translation State Register
TGC:	Telegraph Grade Circuit	TSS:	Touch-Sensitive Screen
TGC:	Terminator Group Controller	TST:	Touch Screen Technology
THP:	Terminal Handling Processor		
THP:	Terminal Holding Power		
THR:	Transmitter Holding Register		
TIB:	Terminal Input Buffer		
TIE:	Terminal Interface Equipment		
TIP:	Terminal Interface Processor		
TIP:	Transaction Interface Processor		
TIR:	Target Instruction Register		
TIR:	Total Internal Reflection		

TIS:	Terminal In Service	TSV:	Turnkey Systems Vendor
TIU:	Terminal Interface Unit	T²L:	Transactor-Transistor Logic
TIU:	Trusted Interface Unit	TTL:	Transistor-Transistor Logic
TKS:	Turn Key System	TTM:	Tape Transport Mechanism
TLA:	Three-Letter Acronym	TTP:	Test Transfer Port
TLB:	Table Lookaside Buffer	TTP:	Thermal Transfer Printer
TLB:	Translation Lookaside Buffer	TTU:	Terminal Time Unit
TLI:	Transport Level Interface	TVS:	Task Virtual Storage
TLR:	Triple-Length Register	TVM:	Transistor Volt-Meter
TLT:	Typewriter-Like Terminals	TVS:	Transient Voltage Suppressor
TMC:	Tape Management Catalog	TWA:	TypeWriter Adapter
tml:	terminal	TWC:	Two Wire Circuit
TNC:	Total Numerical Control	TWD:	Thin Window Display
		TWR:	Tape Writer Register

UAR: Unit Address Register
UBC: Universal Buffer Controller
UBD: Utility Binary Dump
UBT: Unit Buffer Terminal
UCB: Unit Control Block
UCB: Universal Character Buffer
UCP: Uninterruptible Computer Power
UDB: Up Data Buffer
UDH: Unthinkable Domestic
Hexadecimal Cable
UDR: Universal Document Reader
UDS: Unprotected Dynamic Storage
UET: Universal Emulating Terminal
UFC: Universal Frequency Counter
UFF: Universal Flip-Flop
UFI: Usage Frequency Indicator
UGA: Unity Gain Amplifier
UHM: Universal Host Machine
UHR: Ultra-High Reduction
UIM: Ultra-Intelligent Machine
UIO: Units In Operation
UIR: User Instruction Register
UIS: Unit Identification System
UKB: Universal KeyBoard
ULA: Uncommitted Logic Array
ULC: Uniform Loop Clock
ULC: Universal Logic Circuit
ULE: Unit Location Equipment
ULM: Universal Logic Module
ULS: Unallocated Logical Storage
UMB: Upper Memory Block
UMF: Ultra-MicroFiche
UMI: Ultra-MIcrofiche
UOC: Ultimate Operating Capability
UOL: User Operated Language
UPC: Universal Peripheral Controller
UPC: Universal Product Code
UPI: Universal Peripheral Interface
UPP: Universal PROM Programmer
UPS: Unallocated Physical Storage
UPS: Uninterrupted Power Supply
UPS: Uninterruptible Power Supply
UPS: Uninterruptible Power System
UPS: Unmapped Physical Storage
URE: Unit Record Equipment
URP: Unit Record Processor
UTD: Universal Transfer Device

UTP: Unattended Trail Printer
UTR: Unprogrammed Transfer Register
UTS: Universal Timing-Sharing System
UUT: Unit Under Test
UVD: Under Voltage Device
UVE: Ultra-Violet Erasers
UVP: Under-Voltage Protection

VAC: Vector Analog Computer
VAC: Voltage Alternating Current
VAD: Voltmeter Analog-to-Digital
Converter
VAM: Virtual Access Method
VAR: Value-Added Remarketer
VAT: Voice Activation Technology
VAU: Vertical Arithmetic Unit
VAX: Virtual Address EXtension
VBP: Virtual Block Processor
VBR: Valid BIT Register
VCA: Valve Control Amplifier
VCA: Voltage Control Amplifier
VCB: Video Capture Board
VCC: Video Compact Cassette
VCD: Variable Capacitance Diode
VCF: Voltage Controlled Filter
VCG: Verification Condition Generator
VCG: Voltage Controlled Generator
VCO: Voltage Controlled Oscillator
VCR: Video Cassette Recorder
VCR: Virtual Card Reader
VCS: Video Computer System
VCS: Virtual Computing System
VCS: Virtual Console Spooling
VCT: Voltage Control Transfer
VDB: Vector Data Buffer
VDB: Video Display Board
VDC: Video Data Controller
VDC: Video Display Controller
VDC: Voltage Direct Current
VDC: Voltage Doubler Circuit
VDD: Version Description Document
VDD: Virtual Disk Drive
VDE: Variable Display Equipment
VDE: Verband Deutsche
Electrotechniker (Germany)

VDG: Video Display Generator	VMC: Virtual Memory Computer
VDI: Video Display Interface	VMD: Vector Memory Display
VDM: Video Display Module	VME: Versa Module Europe
VDP: Video Data Processor	VME: Virtual Machine
VDP: Video Display Processor	Environment (ICL)
VDR: Vendor Data Request	VMF: Virtual Machine Facility
VDR: Voltage Dependent Resistor	VML: Virtual Memory Level
VDT: Video Data Terminal	VMM: Virtual Machine Monitor
VDT: Video Display Terminal	VMO: Virtual Machine Operator
VDT: Visual Display Terminal	VMS: Virtual Memory System
VDU: Video Display Unit	VMS: Voice Messaging System
VDU: Visual Display Unit	VMT: Video Matrix Terminal
VEC: VEctor Analog Computer	VMT: Virtual Memory Technique
VET: Visual Editing Terminal	VNC: Voice Numerical Control
VFB: Vertical Format Buffer	VOC: Variable Output Circuit
VFC: Voltage Frequency Channel	VOC: Video Overlay Card
VFC: Voltage-to-Frequency Converter	VOD: Voice Operated Device
VFO: Voice Frequency Oscillator	VOF: Variable Operating Frequency
VFS: Virtual File System	vom: voltOhmmeter
VFU: Vertical Format Unit	VOM: Volt-Ohm Millimeter
VGA: Versatile Graphics Array	VPC: Verge-Punched Card

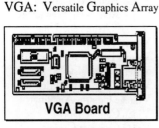

VGA Board

	VPM: Vendor Part Modification
	VPM: Virtual Processor Monitor
	VRC: Visible Record Computer
	VRD: Voice Recognition Device
	VRP: Visual Record Printer
	VRU: Voice Response Unit
VGA: Video Graphic Adapter	VSA: Voltage Sensitive Amplifier
VGA: Video Graphic Array	VSC: Virtual Subscriber Computer
VGD: Video Graphic Display	VSD: Virtual Spooling Device
VGU: Video Generation Unit	VSI: Visual Simulator Interface
VHD: Very High Density	VSM: Video Switching Matrix
VHM: Virtual Hardware Monitor	VSP: Video Signal Processor
VHR: Very High Resolution	VSP: Virtual Storage Partition
VHS: Video Home System	VSR: Virtual Storage Region
VIA: Versatile Interface Adapter	VSS: Video Storage System
VIC: Variable Instruction Computer	VSS: Virtual Storage System
VIE: Virtual Interactive Environment	VSS: Virtual Supervisor State
Workstation	VSS: Voice Synthesis System
VIN: Vehicle Identification Number	VSX: Verification Suite X /Open
VIP: Vector Instruction Processor	VSX: Videotex Storage and EXchange
VIP: Versatile Information Processor	VTA: Virtual Terminal Agent
VIR: Vendor Information Request	VTB: Video Terminal Board
VIR: Vendor Item Release	VTC: Virtual Terminal Control
VIU: Video Interface Unit	VTD: Vertical Tape Display
VLE: Vapor Levitation Epitaxy	VTI: Video Terminal Interface
VLR: Visitor Location Register	VTR: Video Tape Recorder
VLT: Video Layout Terminal	VTS: Virtual Terminal System
VMA: Valid Memory Address	VUA: Virtual Unit Address
VMA: Virtual Machine Assist (IBM)	VV&C: Verification, Validation and
	Certification

WCM: Wire-Core Matrix
WCM: Wired-Core Memory
WCM: Writable Control Memory
WCR: Word Control Register
WCR: Word Count Register
WCT: Wireless Computer Terminal
WDD: Winchester Disk Drives
WER: Write-Enable Ring
WIP: Work In Process
WIP: Work In Progress
WIR: Write Inhibit Ring
WOM: Write-Only Memory
WOM: Write-Optical Memory
WOR: Write-Only Registers
WPC: Wired Program Computer
WPM: Write Program Memory
WPM: Write Protect Memory
WPN: Write-Protect Notch
WPR: Write-Permit Ring
WPR: Write-Protect Ring
WPS: Work Place Share
WPT: Write-Protect Tab

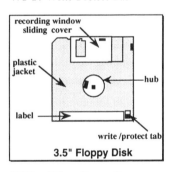

3.5" Floppy Disk

WSI: Wafer Silicon Integration
WTC: Write Through Cache

XBC: EXternal Block Controller
XBM: EXtended Basic Mode
XCO: Crystal-Controlled Oscillator

XDR: EXternal Data Representation
xdr: transducer
XES: Xerox Engineering System
XFM: X-Band Ferrite Modulator
XGA: EXchange Graphics Array
XGA: EXtended Graphics Array
XIM: EXtended I/O Monitor
XI/O: EXecute Input/Output
XLP: EXtra Large Scale Packaging
XMS: EXtended Memory Specification
XOT: EXtra Output Terminal
XPG: X/Open Portability Guide
XPI: Cross Polarization Interference
XRM: EXtended Relational Memory
XSP: EXtended Set Processor
XUV: EXtreme Ultra-Violet

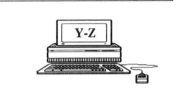

YYY

YDC: Yaw Damper Computer

ZZZ

ZAS: Zero Access Storage
ZIF: Zero Insertion Force
ZIL: Zigzag-In-Line
ZIP: Zigzag-In-Line Package
ZLB: Zero Length Buffer
ZWC: Zero Wind Computer

COMPUTER SOFTWARE,
PROCESSING
AND APPLICATIONS

AAA: American Accounting Association
AAC: Audio Active Compare
AAD: Authorized Apple Dealer
AAL: Absolute Assembly Language
AAP: Analyst Assistance Program
AAP: Apollo Applications Program
AAR: Automatic Alternative Routing
AAS: Advanced Administrative System
AAS: Arithmetic Assignment Statement
AAS: Automated Accounting System
AAS: Automatic Addressing System
AAT: Arbitrated Access Time
AAT: Average Access Time
ABC: Approach By Concept
ABI: Association des Bibliotheques
         Internationales
ABL: Accepted Batch Listing
ABL: Architectural Block
         Diagram Language
ABL: Atlas Basic Language
ABL: Automatic Bootstrap Loader
ABP: Advanced Business Processor
ABR: Automatic Band Rate
ABR: Automatic Band Recognition
ABT: Alpha Beta Technique
ABV: ABsolute Value
ACB: Access Control Byte
ACB: Application Control Block
ACC: Access Control Character
ACC: Application Control Code
ACC: Automatic Carrier Control
ACD: Accounting Check Digit
ACE: Animated Computer Education
ACE: Automatic Control Engineering
ACF: Access Control Field
ACF: Area Computing Facilities
ACG: Automatic Code Generator
ACH: Attempts per Circuit Hour
ACH: Automatic Clearing House
ACK: Affirmative ACKnowledge
ACL: Access Control List
ACL: Application Control Language
ACL: Association for Computational
         Linguistics (USA)
ACL: Atlas Commercial Language
ACL: Audit Command Language

ACM: Additive Color Mixing
ACM: Analog Command Module
ACP: Aerospace Computer Program
ACP: Airline Control Program
ACR: Aircraft Control Room
ACR: Alternative CPU Recovery
ACR: American Computer Referral (USA)
ACR: Automatic Carriage Return
ACS: Advanced Computer Services
ACS: Alphabetic Character Set
ACS: Alphabetic Character Subset
ACS: Alphanumeric Character Set
ACS: Alphanumeric Character Subset
ACS: Alternate Collating Sequence
ACS: Alternative Collating Sequence
ACS: ANSI Character Set
ACS: Assembly Control System (IBM)
ACS: Attitude Command System
ACS: Automated Commercial System
ACS: Automatic Catalog Search
ACS: Auxiliary Code Storage
ACT: Algebraic Compiler & Translator
ACT: Applied Computer Techniques
ACT: Automatic Code Translation
ACV: Address Control Vector
ACW: Access Control Word
ADA: Airborne Data Automation
ADA: Automatic Data Acquisition
ADA: Automatic Decimal Alignment
ADA: Lady ADA Lovelace
         (Programming Language)
ADB: Archival Data Base
ADB: Automatic Device Backup
ADC: Automatic Data Collection
ADD: ADDress
ADE: ADdress Error
ADE: Advanced Data Entry
ADE: Attribute Data Element
ADE: Automated Debugging Environment
ADE: Automatic Data Entry
ADF: Alphanumeric Data Fields
ADG: Applications Development Group
ADH: A -Digit Hunter
ADI: Alternate Digit Inversion
ADI: ADapter Support Interface
ADM: Activity Data Method
ADM: Adaptable Data Manager
ADM: Adaptive Database Manager
ADM: Adaptive Delta Modulation
ADO: Automatic Dial-Out
ADP: Administrative Data Processing
ADP: Advanced Data Path

ADP:	Advanced Data Processing	AIC:	Alternate Index Cluster
ADP:	Airport Development Program	AID:	Algebraic Interpretive Dialog
ADP:	Ammonia Duplicating Process	AID:	Attention IDentification
ADP:	Association of Database Producers (UK)	AID:	Automatic Information Distribution
ADP:	Assumed Decimal Pool	AID:	Automatic Interaction Detection
ADP:	Automatic Data Processing	AIL:	Arithmetic Input Left
ADQ:	Almost Differential Quasi-Tenery	AIM:	Administrative & InforMation Program (NASA)
ADR:	Alternate Data Retry	AIM:	Advanced Information in Medicine
ADR:	Application Definition Record	AIM:	American Interactive Multi-Media
ADR:	Audit Discrepancy Report	AIM:	Associative Index Method
ADS:	Accurately Defined System	AIM:	Automated Inventory Management
ADS:	Activity Data Sheet	AIM:	Avalanche Induced Migration
ADS:	Advanced Debugging System	AIR:	Aerospace Information Report
ADS:	Application Development System	AIR:	Automatic Interrogation Routine
ADT:	Active Disk Table	AIR:	Recorder, Indicating, Analyzer
ADT:	Application Dedicated Terminal	AIS:	Advanced Information Systems
ADT:	Automated Design Tools	AIS:	Application Information Services
ADT:	Automatic Design Tools	AIU:	Alternate Index Upgrade
ADT:	Automatic Data Translator	AIX:	Advanced Interactive EXecutive (IBM)
ADT:	Automatic Decimal Tab	AJE:	Autostart Job Entry
ADT:	Autonomous Data Transfer	AKG:	Automatic Key Generation
AED:	ALGOL Extended Design	ALB:	Application Load Balancing
AED:	Automated Engineering Design	ALB:	Assembly Line Balancing
AEG:	Active Element Group	ALC:	Assembly Language Coding
AEI:	Assicizio Electrotecnica Italiana	ALC:	Automatic Library Call
AEI:	Average Efficiency Index	ALF:	Application Library File
AEL:	Audit Entry Language	ALI:	Automatic Logic Implementation
AEP:	Automated Entry Processing	ALL:	Application Language Liberator
AFD:	Automatic Field Duplication	ALL:	Application Load List
AFE:	Apple File Exchange (Apple Computer, Inc.)	ALL:	Assembly Level Language
AFG:	Analog Function Generator	ALM:	Absolute Load Module
AFM:	Application Function Module	ALN:	Attribute Level Number
AFM:	Automatic Flight Management	ALP:	Assembly Language Pre-Processor
AFN:	All-Figure Numbering	ALP:	Assembly Language Program
AFO:	Advanced File Organization	ALP:	Automated Language Processing
AFP:	Apple Filing Protocol (Apple Computer, Inc.)	ALP:	Automated Learning Processing
		ALS:	Advanced Logistics System
AFP:	Apple Talk File Protocol (Apple Computer, Inc.)	ALS:	Arithmetic Logic Section
		ALS:	Automatic Line Spacing
AFR:	Advanced Fault Recognition	Alt:	Alter
AFR:	Advanced Fault Resolution	ALW:	Automatic Letter Writing
AFR:	Automatic Field Recognition	AMA:	Associative Memory Address
AFR:	Automatic Format Recognition	AMA:	Automatic Margin Adjust
AFS:	Automatic File Select	AMA:	Automatic Memory Allocation
AFS:	Automatic File Sort	AMC:	Automatic Message Counting
AFS:	Available File Space	AMD:	Associative Memory Data
AFT:	Automated Funds Transfer	AMD:	Active Matrix Display
AFT:	Automatic Funds Transfer	AME:	Application Management Environment
AGN:	Application Group Name		
AHP:	Addressable Horizontal Points	AME:	Automatic Microfiche Editor

AMH: Application Message Handler
AMI: Access Method Interface
AMI: Association Of Multi-Image
AMI: Average Mutual Information
AML: Advanced Math Library
AML: A Manufacturing Language
AML: Application Module Library
AML: Array Machine Language
AMR: Access Method Routine
AMR: Automated Management Reports
AMS: Access Method Services
AMT: Advanced Manufacturing
Techniques
AMT: Advanced Manufacturing
Technology
ANA: Article Number Association
ANA: Automatic Number Analysis
AND: Alpha Numeric Display
ANI: Automatic Number
Identification
ANL: American National Standards
Label
ANL: Automatic New Line
ANO: AlphaNumeric Output
ANS: American National Standard
AOD: Arithmetic Output Data
AOE: Auditing Order Error
AOF: Address Output File
AOF: Advanced Operating Facilities
AOG: AND/OR Graph
AOH: Add-On-Header
AOI: Acoustic-Optical Imaging
AOI: ADD-OR-Inverter
AOI: Advance Ordering Information
AOI: Automated Operator Interface
AOL: Application Oriented Language
AOQ: Average Outgoing Quality
AOS: Advance Operating System
AOS: Advanced Office System
AOS: Alternating Operating Systems
AOS: Apple Online Services (Apple
Computer, Inc.)
APA: All Points Addressable
APC: Adaptive Predictive Coding
APC: Additive Primary Colors
APC: Allocated Page Count
APC: Associative Processor Control
APC: Automatic Peripheral Control
APC: Automatic Program Control
APD: Approach Progress Display
APE: Application Program Evaluation

APE: Automatic Program Execution
APF: Application Processing Function
APF: Authorized Program Facility
APG: Application Program Generator
APG: Automated Priority Group
API: Application Program Image
API: Application Program Interface
API: Application Programming Interface
APL: A Programming Language
APL: Array Processing Language
APL: Association of Programmed
Learning
APL: Associative Programming Language
APL: Automatic Program Loading
APN: Automatic Page Numbering
APQ: Active Page Queue
APQ: Available Page Queue
APR: Active Page Register
APR: Automatic Programming
and Recording
APS: Array Processor Software
APS: Assembly Programming System
APS: Auxiliary Program Storage
APT: Augmented Programming Training
APT: Automatic Programmed Tool
APT: Automatically Programmed Tools
APT: Automatic Program Transfer
APX: Application Processor EXecutive
ARA: Attitude Reference Assembly
arb: arbitrary
ARE: Automated Responsive Environment
ARF: Automatic Report Feature
ARI: Applications Reference Index
ARK: Auto-Repeat Key
ARL: Average Run Length
ARP: Analogous Random Process
ARP: Automatic Recovery Program
ARS: Advanced Record System
ARS: Airline Reservation System

ARS: Audio Response System
ART: Authorization and Resource Table

42

ART: Automated Reasoning Tool
ASA: Addressed Sequential Access
ASA: American Standards Association
ASA: Automatic Storage Allocation
ASC: Adaptive Speed Control
ASC: Automatic Search Catalog
ASD: Application Structure Definition
ASE: Application Service Element
ASE: Application Service Entity
ASE: Application Support Environment
ASE: Application Swapping Extension
ASF: Active Segment Field
ASF: Advanced Sprocket Feed
ASI: American Standards Institute
ASL: Automated System Initialization
ASL: Association for Symbolic
Logic (USA)
asm: assembler
ASM: Association for Systems
Management
ASM: Auxiliary Storage Manager
ASO: Automatic Sequential Operation
ASP: Application Structure Preserving
ASP: Application Support Protocol
ASP: Association of Shareware
Professionals
ASP: Associative Storage Pool
ASP: Automated Spooling Priority
ASP: Automatic Schedule Procedures
ASR: Accumulators Shift Right
ASR: Application Structure Review
ASS: Application Structure Specification
AST: Advanced Simulation Technology
ASV: Automatic Self Verification
ASW: Application SoftWare
ATB: Access Type Bits
ATC: Automatic Toning Control
ATC: Automatic Train Control
ATC: Automation Training Center
ATD: Actual To Date
ATF: Automatic Text Formatter
ATG: Automatic Test Generation
ATI: Audio Tutorial Instruction
ATI: Automatic Track Initiation
ATL: Application Terminal Language
ATM: Adjust Test Mode
ATM: Adobe Type Manager
ATM: Automatic Tab Memory
ATP: Application Transaction Program
ATP: Attended Trail Printer
ATS: Absolute Task Set
ATT: Address Translation Table

AUQ: Available Unit Queue
AVA: Absolute Virtual Address
AVP: Addressable Vertical Positions
AVR: Automatic Volume Recognition
AVS: Automated Verification System
AVS: Automatic Volume Storage
AVS: Automatic Volume Switching
AVT: Automatic Vision Testing
AWA: Automatic Widow Adjust
AWC: Association for Women
in Computing
AWW: Automatic Word Wraparound
AZS: Automatic Zero Set

BAC: Beginning Attribute Character
BAK: BAcK-Up
BAL: Basic Access Level
BAL: Basic Assembly Language
BAL: Business Application Language
BAM: Basic Access Method
BAP: Basic Assembly Program
BAP: Bus Available Pulse
BAS: Basic Access Service
bat: batch
BBL: Basic Business Language
BBL: Branch Back and Load
BBP: Black Box Process
BBS: Bulletin Board System
BBS: Business Batch System
BBT: Bit Block Transfer
BCA: Bit Count Appendage
BCB: Bit Control Block
BCB: Block Control Byte
BCC: Block Cancel Character
BCC: Block Control Character
BCD: Binary Coded Decimal
BCE: Basic Comparison Element
BCH: Block Control Header
BCI: Basic Command Interpreter
BCL: Bar Coded Label
BCL: Basic Contour Line
BCL: Burroughs Common Language
BCM: Bound Control Module
BCO: Binary Coded Octal System
BCP: Bit Control Panel

BCP:	Byte Control Protocol	BIM:	Beginning of Information Marker
BCS:	Basic Combined Subset	BIM:	Business Information Managers
BCS:	Basic Control System	BIN:	Basic Identification Number
BCS:	Biomedical Computing Society	BIN:	BINary
BCS:	Block Check Sequence	BIO:	Buffered Input Output
BCS:	Boston Computer Society	BIP:	Basic Interpreter Package
BCS:	British Computer Society	BIS:	Bureau of Information Science
BCS:	Business Computer System	BIS:	Business Information System
BCT:	Between Commands Testing	bit:	binary Digit
BCW:	Buffer Control Word	BIU:	Basic Information Unit
BDB:	Bibliographic Data Base	BIX:	Byte Information EXchange
BDC:	Binary Decimal Counter	BJF:	Batch Job Foreground
BDE:	Batch Data Exchange	BLS:	Block Level Sharing
BDI:	Batch Data Interchange	BLT:	Basic Language Translator
BDL:	Build Definition Language	BMF:	Bit-Mapped Font
BDM:	Basic Data Management	BMG:	Bit-Mapped Graphics
BDO:	Bit Drop Out	BML:	Basic Machine Language
BDP:	Bi-Directional Printing	BMP:	Batch Message Processing
BDP:	Business Data Processing	BMP:	Bench Mark Program
BDS:	Business Definition System	BMS:	Balanced Merge Sort
BDT:	Binary Deck-to-Tape	BMS:	Basic Management System
BDX:	Bar Double-X	BMS:	Basic Mapping Support
BEC:	Backward Error Correction	BMW:	BeaM Width
BEC:	Beginning of the Equilibrium Cycle	BNF:	Backus Naur Form
BEI:	British Education Index	BNF:	Backus Normal Form
BEL:	BELl Character	BNS:	Binary Numbering System
BEP:	Back-End Processing	BOA:	Buffered Output Area
BES:	Basic Executive System	BOC:	Basic Operator Control
BFD:	Back Focal Distance	BOC:	Beginning Of Cycle
BFG:	Binary Frequency Generator	BOC:	Bell Operating Company
BFI:	Batch Freeform Input	BOC:	Byte Output Control
BFL:	Back Focal Length	BOI:	Beginning Of Information
BFR:	Backward File Recovery	BOI:	Branch Output Interrupt
BFS:	Balanced File Organization Scheme	BOP:	Binary Output Program
BFT:	Binary File Transfer	BOS:	Background Operating System
BFT:	Brute Force Technique	BOS:	Basic Operating System
BFT:	Bulk Function Transfer	BOS:	Batch Operating System
BGC:	BackGround Color	bos:	bit-Oriented Schemes
BGC:	BackGround Compatibility	BOS:	Business Operating System
BGP:	BackGround Process	BOT:	Beginning Of Tape
BGS:	BackGround Study	BPC:	Bi-Phase Code
BGS:	Basic Graphic System	BPC:	Buffer Pad Characters
BGU:	Business Graphics Utility	BPF:	Blue Print Files
BHA:	Base Helix Angle	BPI:	Bits Per Inch
BHR:	Block Handling Routine	BPI:	Bytes Per Inch
BIB:	Balanced Incomplete Block	BPL:	Basic Pascal Language
BIC:	Byte Input Control	BPL:	Binary Program Loader
BID:	Binary Image Data	BPM:	Batch Processing Monitor
BIF:	Basic In Flow	BPM:	Bi-Phase Mark
BIF:	Built-In Function	BPP:	Batch Processing Program
BIL:	Bit Inter-Leaving	BPS:	Basic Programming Support
BIL:	Block Input Length		

BPS: Basic Programming System
BPS: Binary Program Space
bps: bits per second
BPS: Bytes Per Second
BQL: Basic Query Language
BRA: Basic Rate Access
BRM: Binary Rate Multiplier
BRM: Bit Rate Multiplier
BRS: Bibliographic Retrieval
         Services Inc. (USA)
BRZ: Bipolar Return to Zero
BSA: Business Software Alliance
BSA: Business Systems Analyst
BSF: Blessed System Folder
BSI: British Standards Institute
BSK: BackSpace Key
BSL: Bit Serial Link
BSL: BootStrap Loader
BSM: Basic Storage Module
BSP: Business System Planning
BSR: Back Space Record
BSR: Blip-Scan Ratio
BSR: Board of Standards Review
BSS: Bulk Storage System
BTC: Batch Terminal Controller
BTC: Batch Transfer Controller
BTD: Binary To Decimal
BTL: Beginning Of Tape Label
BTL: Business Translation Language
BTP: Batch Transfer Program
BTP: Branch Technical Position
BTS: Batch Terminal Simulation
BTS: Bound Task Set
BTW: By The Way
BUD: Bottom-Up Design
BUF: Back-Up File
BUM: Bottom Up Method
BUS: Basic Utility System
BUT: Bottom Up Testing
BWD: Basic Word Data
BWD: Basic Working Display
BYP: BYPass

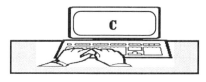

CAA: Computer-Assisted Accounting
CAC: Computer-Aided Classification
CAC: Containment Atmosphere Control
CAD: Character Assembler/Disassembler
CAD: Click-And-Drag
CAD: Computer-Aided Design
CAD: Computer-Aided Detection
CAD: Computer-Aided Dispatching
CAD: Computer-Aided Drafting
CAD: Computer Applications Digest
CAE: Computer-Aided Education

Computer-Aided Education

CAE: Computer-Aided Engineering
CAE: Computer-Assisted Enrolment
CAE: Computer-Assisted Estimation
CAF: Computer-Aided Fraud
CAG: Computer-Assisted Guidance
CAG: Cooperative Automation Group
CAI: Computer-Administered Instruction
CAI: Computer-Aided Inspection
CAI: Computer-Aided Instruction
CAI: Computer Analog Input
CAI: Computer-Assisted Instruction
CAK: Command AcKnowledge
CAL: Column Address Line
CAL: Common Assembly Language
CAL: Computer-Aided Learning

Computer-Aided Learning

CAL: Computer Animation Language
CAL: Computer Assembler Language
CAL: Computer-Assisted Learning
CAL: Conversational Algebraic Language
CAM: Computer Address Matrix
CAM: Computer-Aided Management
CAM: Computer-Aided Manufacturing
CAM: Containment Atmospheric Monitoring
CAN: CANcel Character
CAP: Computer-Aided Planning
CAP: Computer-Aided Production
CAP: Computer-Aided Programming
CAP: Computer Analysts and Programmers of England
CAP: Computer-Assisted Production
CAP: Consumer Analysts and Programmers
CAP: Continuous Audit Program
CAP: Council to Advanced Programming
CAP: Cut-And-Paste
CAR: Check Authorization Record
CAR: Computer-Aided Retrieval
CAR: Computer-Assisted Research
CAR: Computer-Assisted Retrieval
CAS: Column Address Select
CAT: Compile And Test
CAT: Computer-Aided Teaching
CAT: Computer-Aided Testing
CAT: Computer-Aided Tomography
CAT: Computer-Aided Translation
CAT: Computer-Aided Typesetting
CAT: Computer-Assisted Testing
CAT: Computer-Assisted Tomography
CAT: Computer-Assisted Training
CBA: Concrete Block Association
CBB: Check Box Button
CBC: Chain Block Character
CBE: Computer-Based Education
CBI: Common Batch Identification
CBI: Compound Batch Identification
CBI: Computer Based Instruction
CBI: Conditional Branch Instruction
CBL: Cold Boot Load
CBL: Computer Based Learning
CBS: Character-Based System
CBT: Computer Based Teaching
CBT: Computer Based Training
CBU: Coefficient of Beam Utilization
CCA: ConCurrent Access
CCB: Character Control Block
CCB: Command-Control Block

CCC: Canadian Computer Conference
CCC: Computerized Card Catalog
CCC: Correction Code Check
CCD: Computer Control Display
CCG: Current Connect Group
CCH: Computerized Criminal History
CCK: Cursor Control Keys
CCL: Common Command Language
CCL: Common Control Language
CCO: Computer Controller Operation
CCP: Certified Computer Programmer
CCP: Communications Control Package
CCP: Coordinated Commentary Programming
CCR: Commitment, Concurrency and Recovery
CCR: Computer Character Recognition
CCR: Computer Clean Room

Computer Clean Room

CCS: Coded Character Set
CCS: Commitment Control System
CCS: Conversational Compiling System
CC&S: Central Computer & Sequencing
CCV: Common Control Vector
CDA: Command and Data Acquisition
CDB: Current Data Bit
CDC: Call Directing Character
CDC: Configuration Data Control
CDC: Control Data Corporation (USA)
CDC: Count Down Counter
CDE: Certification in Data Education
CDE: Contents Directory Entry
CDF: Course Data File
CDI: Command-Driven Interfaces
CDI: Compact Disk Interactive
CDI: Contents DIrectory Entry
CDI: Control Data Institute
CDK: Control Development Kit
CDL: Common Display Logic
CDL: Compiler Description Language
CDL: Computer Description Language
CDM: Central Data Management

CDP:	Centralized Data Processing		CIA:	Computer Industry Association
CDP:	Certification in Data Processing		CIA:	Control Interval Access
CDP:	Commercial Data Processing		CIB:	Console Input Buffer
CDP:	Current Directory Path		CIC:	Computer Instruction Code
CDR:	Conceptual Design Requirement		CIC:	Corporate Information Center
CDR:	Critical Design Review		CID:	Center for Information and
CDS:	Cataloged Data Set			Documentation
CDS:	Code Dependent System		CIF:	Central Information File
CDS:	Command Driven Software		CIF:	Computer-Integrated Factory
CDS:	Compatible Duplex System		CIF:	Controller Information Fields
CDS:	Concatenated Data Sets		CIL:	Character Inter-Leaving
CDS:	Conceptual Design Study		CIL:	Computer Interpreter Language
CDS:	Consecutive Data Set		CIL:	Condition Incident Log
CDS:	Control Data Set		CIM:	Command Interrupt Mode
CDV:	Check Digit Verification		CIM:	Computer Integrated Manufacturing
CDW:	Computer Data Word		C/IM:	Conceptual /Internal Mapping
CD1:	Clocked-Data 1		CIN:	Chemical Industry Notes
CEA:	Character Engineering Abstracts		CIO:	Chief Information Officer
CEC:	Code Extension Character		CIO:	Code-Independent Operation
CEC:	Computers, Electronics and Control		CIP:	Centralized Information Processing
CEI:	Computer Extended Instruction		CIP:	Complex Information Processing
CEO:	Comprehensive Electronic Office		CIS:	Character Instruction Set
CEP:	Civil Engineering Package		CIS:	Code Independent System
CEP:	Computer Entry Punch		CIS:	Code Insensitive System
CER:	Character Error Rate		CIS:	Computer Information Systems
CET:	Cumulative Elapsed Time		CIS:	Control Indicator Set
CFA:	Continuous Forms Attachment		CIS:	Control Interval Split
CFG:	Context-Free Grammar		CIS:	Cue Indexing System
CFL:	Context-Free Language		CIS:	Current Information Selection
CFP:	Continous-Form Paper		CIS:	Customer Information System
			CIS:	Custom Integrated System
			CIT:	Computer Illustrated Text
			CJE:	Converted Journal Entry
			CJI:	Conditional Jump Instruction
			CKT:	Cryptographic Key Translation
			CLA:	CLear and Add
			CLA:	Computer Law Association
			CLA:	Computer Lessors Association
			CLD:	Central Library and Documentation

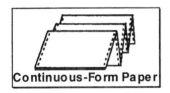

Continuous-Form Paper

CFP:	Creation Facilities Program			Branch (ILO)
CFS:	Continuous Form Stacker		CLE:	Conservative Logic Element
CFU:	Current File User		CLI:	Command Language Interface
CGI:	Computer Generated Image		CLI:	Command-Line Interface
CGI:	Computer Generated Imagery		CLP:	Command Line Parameters
CGL:	Computer Generated Letter		CLP:	Control Language Program
CGM:	Computer Graphics Metafile		CLP:	Current Line Pointer
CGS:	Cap-Gemini-Sogetti		CLR:	Combined Line and Recording
CGS:	Circuit Group Congestion Signal		CLR:	Computer Language Research
CGU:	Character Generator Utility		CLS:	CLear and Subtract
CHI:	Computer Human Interaction		CLS:	Command Line Switch
CHI:	Computer-Human Interface		CLS:	Common Language System
chk:	check		CLT:	Computer Language Translator
CHP:	CHannel Pointer			
CHT:	Collection, Holding, and Transfer			

CLV:	Control Language Variable	CPL:	Core Performance Log
CMA:	Case Management Application	CPL:	Current Privilege Level
CMA:	Computer Management Association	cpm:	circle per minute
CMC:	Code for Magnetic Character	CPM:	Critical Path Method
CME:	Computer Measurement and Evaluation	CP/M:	Control Program for Micro-Computers
CMF:	Comprehensive Management Facility	CPO:	Computer Program Origin
		cpp:	characters per pica
CMG:	Computer Measurement Group	CPP:	Command Processing Program
CMI:	Coded Mark Inversion	CPP:	Computer Professionals for Peace
CMI:	Computer Managed Instruction	CP-R:	Control Program - Real-Time
CML:	Common Mode Logic	CPS:	Cards Per Second
CML:	Computer Managed Learning	cps:	characters per second
CMM:	Computer Music Module	CPS:	Control Program Support
CMR:	Common-Mode Rejection	CPS:	Conversational Programming System
CMS:	Compiler Monitor System	CPS:	Conversion Program System
CMS:	Computer Management System	CPS:	Cooperative Processing System
CMS:	Conversational Monitor System	CPS:	Counts Per Second
CMY:	Cyan Magenta Yellow	CPS:	Cycles Per Second
CNC:	Computer Numerical Control	CPT:	Chief Programmer Team
CNF:	City-Named Fonts	CPT:	Critical Part Technique
COC:	Coded Optical Character	CP-V:	Control Program - FiVe Technique
COF:	COnFusion Signal	CRA:	Catalog Recovery Area
COG:	Computer Operations Ground	CRA:	Camera-Ready Art
COI:	Central Office of Information (UK)	CRB:	Complimentary Return to Bias
COI:	Cine Oriented Image	CRC:	Camera Ready Copy
COL:	Computer Oriented Language	CRE:	Controlled Residual Element
CON:	CONtroller	CRV:	CRyptography Verification
COP:	Computer Optimization Package	CSA:	Canadian Standards Association
COS:	Cassette Operating System	CSA:	Computer Services Association (UK)
COS:	Commercial Operating System	CSA:	Computer Systems Analyst
COS:	Compatible Operating System	CSA:	Current Segment Approach
COS:	Concurrent Operating System	CSC:	Computer Society of Canada
COW:	Character Oriented Window	CSC:	Computer-Supported-Cooperative
CPA:	Critical Path Analysis	CSC:	Computing System Catalog
CPB:	Computer PhoBia	CS&C:	Capitals and Small Capitals
CPC:	Computer Program Component	CSD:	Character Spacing Display
CPC:	Computer Programming Concept	CSD:	Cold Shut Down
CPC:	Cycle Program Control	CSD:	Computerized Standard Data
CPC:	Cycle Program Counter	CSD:	Conceptual System Design
CPD:	Consolidated Programming Document	CSF:	Critical Success Factor
		CSG:	Context Sensitive Grammar
CPE:	Central Processing Element	CSG:	Constructive Solid Geometry
CPE:	Concurrent Program Execution	CSI:	Command String Interpreter
CPF:	Control Program Facility	CSL:	Code Selection Language
CPG:	Computer Processing Group	CSL:	Computer Sensitive Language
CPH:	Characters Per Hour	CSL:	Content Sensitive Language
cpi:	characters per inch	CSL:	Control and Simulation Language
CPI:	Computer Prescribed Instruction	CSM:	Computer System Manual
CPL:	Combined Programming Language	CSM:	Copy Screen Mode
CPL:	Common Program Library	C/SM:	Client /Server Model
CPL:	Common Programming Language	CSS:	Character Start Stop

48

CSS:	Computer Special System	DAF:	Destination Address Field
CSS:	Computer System Security	DAF:	Destination Address File
CSS:	Containment Spray System	DAI:	Direct Access Information
CSS:	Control Storage Save	DAL:	Data Address Line
CSS:	Core Support Structure	DAL:	Direct Address Line
CSS:	Customer Service System	DAM:	Descriptor Attribute Matrix
CSV:	Comma-Separated Variables	DAM:	Digital to Analog Multiplier
CS0:	Control Signal Zero	DAM:	Direct Access Memory
CS1:	Control Signal One	DAM:	Direct Access Method
CTB:	Code Table Buffer	DAM:	Document Assembly/Merge
CTL:	Checkout Test Language	DAP:	Data Access Protocol
CTL:	Compiler Target Language	DAP:	Deformation of Aligned Phases
CTP:	Command Translator & Programmer	DAP:	Digital Assembly Program
CTR:	Computing, Tabulating, Recording	DAP:	Direct Access Protocol
CTR:	ConTRol Key	DAQ:	Data AcQuisition
CTS:	Cable Turning Section	DAR:	Damage Assessment Routine
CTS:	Carpal Tunnel Syndrome	DAS:	Data Access Security
CTS:	Computer TypeSetting	DAS:	Data Administration System
CTS:	Control Transfer Statement	DAS:	Data Analysis System
CTS:	Conversational Terminal System	DAS:	Data Automation System
CUA:	Computer Users Association	DAS:	Digital Analog Simulator
CUD:	Control Unit Description	DAT:	Desk-Top Analysis Tool
CUG:	Closed User Group	DAT:	Director of Advanced Technology
CUI:	Character-Based User Interface	DAT:	Disk Allocation Table
CUV:	Current Use Value	DAT:	Dynamic Address Translation
CU1:	Customer Use 1	DAV:	DAta Valid
CU2:	Customer Use 2	DBA:	Data Base Administration
CU3:	Customer Use 3	DBA:	Data Base Administrator
CWA:	Closed World Assumption	DBA:	Data Base Application
CWA:	Control Word Address		
CWL:	Control Word Line		
CWP:	Communicating Word Processor		
CWP:	Current Word Pointer		
CWS:	Compiler Writing System		
CZE:	Computer Zone Equal		
CZU:	Computer Zone Unequal		

Data Base Application

dba:	decibel adjusted
DBA:	Dynamic Buffer Allocation
DBC:	Data Base Call
DBD:	Data Base Description
DBE:	DataBase Engine
DBF:	DataBase Facility
DBF:	Data Base File
DBG:	Data Base Generator
DBI:	Data Base Integrity
DBI:	Double Byte Interleaved
DBL:	Data Base Language
DBL:	Data Base Logging
DBM:	Data Base Management
DBM:	Data Base Manager

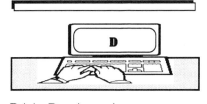

DAA:	Data Access Arrangement
DAA:	Direct Access Arrangement
DAB:	Display Attention BITs
DAC:	Data ACcepted
DAC:	Data Acquisition and Control
DAC:	Design Augmented by Computer
DAD:	Drag-And-Drop
DAF:	Data Acquisition Facility

DBM: Data Base Module
DBP: Data Base Position
DBP: Dynamic Branch Prediction
DBR: Data Base Record
DBR: Data Base Reorganization
DBR: Data Base Representation
DBR: Data Base Retrieval
DBS: Data Base System
DBS: Dictionary-Board System
DBT: DataBase Transaction
DBU: Differential BackUp
DBV: Daily Backup Volume
DC1: Device Control One
DC2: Device Control Two
DC3: Device Control Three
DC4: Device Control Four
DCA: Destination Computer Address
DCA: Digital Command Assembly
DCA: Digital Computer Association
DCB: Data Control Block
DCB: Device Control Block
DCC: Data Code Conversion
DCC: Data Country Code
DCC: Device Control Character
DCD: Data Carrier Detect
DCD: Dynamic Computer Display
DCF: Discounted Cash Flow
DCF: Dual Cluster Feature
DCF: Dynamic Control Function
DCG: Display Character Generator
DCL: Digital Command Language
DCL: Digital Computer Laboratory
DCL: Display Control ModuLe
DCM: Diagnostic Control Manager
DCM: Display Control Module
DCO: Digital Central Office
DCP: Data Collection Platform
DCP: Design Change Package
DCP: Design Criteria Plan
DCP: Digital Computer Programming
DCR: Data Collection Routine
DCS: Data Character Set
DCS: Data Collection Station
DCS: Data Control Services
DCS: Data Control Staff
DCS: Dedicated CAD Systems
DCS: Design Control Specifications
DCS: Digital Command System
DCS: Direct-Couple Operating System
DCS: Distributed Computer System
DCS: Document Control System

DCT: Data Circuit Transparency
DCT: Device Characteristics Table
DCT: Discrete Cosine Transform
DCU: Data Conversion Utilities
DCU: Disk Compression Utility
DCW: Data Control Word
DDA: Data Differential Analyzer
DDA: Digital Differential Analyzer
DDA: Digital Display Area
DDB: Distributed DataBase
DDC: Direct Data Capture
DDD: Display Decoder Driver
DD/D: Data Dictionary Directory
DDE: Decentralized Data Entry
DDE: Direct Data Entry
DDE: Distributed Data Entry
DDF: Database Definition File
DDG: Digital Data Generator
DDG: Digital Display Generator
3DG: 3-Dimensional Graphics

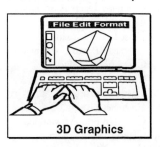

3D Graphics

DDI: Dynamic Display Image
DDL: Data Definition Language
DDL: Data Description Language
DDL: Document Description Language
DDM: Data Demand Module
DDM: Digital Display Make-Up
DDM: Distributed Data Management
DDP: Distributed Data Processing
DDS: Data Display Station
DDS: Data Description Specification
DDS Dedicated Data Set
DDS: Digital Display Scope
DDS: Direct Dependent Segment
DDS: Document Delivery Service
DDS: Dummy Data Set
DDT: Dynamic Debugging Technique
DEA: Data Encryption Algorithm
DEA: Data Entry Application
DEB: Data Event Block
DEB: Data Extent Block
DED: Data Elementary Dictionary

DED:	Double Error Detection	DLL:	Dynamic Link Library
DEE:	Digital Events Evaluator	DL/1:	Data Language /1
DEF:	Data Extension Frame	DLP:	Data Listing Programs
DEF:	Data Entry Facility	DLS:	Display Layout Sheet
DEK:	Data Encrypting Key	DLT:	Decision Logic Table
DEL:	DELete	DMC:	Direct Memory Channel
DEL:	Direct Exchange Line	DME:	Data Mode Escape
DEP:	Data Edit Program	DME:	Differential Manchester Encoding
DEP:	Data Entry Panel	DMH:	Device Message Handler
DEP:	Digital Encryption Processor	DML:	Data Manipulation Language
DE/Q:	Design Evaluation/Qualification	DMO:	Data Management Office
DES:	Data Encryption Standard	dmp:	dump
DES:	Data Encryption Subroutine	DMQ:	Direct Memory Queue
DFC:	Data Flow Control	DMS:	Data-based Management System
DFC:	Design Field Change	DMS:	Data Management Service
DFC:	Diagnostic Flow Charts	DMS:	Data Management System
DFC:	Disk File Check	DMS:	Documentation of Molecular
DFC:	Disk File Controller		Spectroscopy
DFD:	Data Flow Diagram	DMV:	Daisy, Monitor, Valid
DFI:	Defect Free Interface	DNL:	Do Not Load
DFL:	Display Formatting Language	DOB:	Disbursed Operating Base
DFM:	Data and File Manager	DOC:	Decimal to Octal Conversion
DFO:	Direct File Organization	DOC:	Direct Operating Cost
DFS:	Default Format Statement	DOL:	Display Oriented Language
DFS:	Disk File Storage	DOR:	Digital Optical Reading
DFS:	Disk Filing System	DOR:	Digital Optical Recording
DFS:	Distributed File Server	DOS:	Disk Operating System
DFS:	Distributed Free Space	DOS:	Distributed Office Systems
DFT:	Diagnostic Function Test	DPA:	Data Processing Activities
DFU:	Data File Utility	DPA:	Data Processing Analyst
DGA:	Dual Graphics Adapter	DPA:	Data Protection Act
DGS:	Data Gathering System	DPA:	Double Precision Arithmetic
DHS:	Data Handling System	DPB:	Data Processing Branch
DIB:	Data Inspection Board	DPC:	Data Processing Center
DID:	Datamation Industry Directory	DPC:	Data Processing Cycle
DID:	Digital Information Display	DPC:	Direct Program Control
DIF:	Data Interchange Format	DPD:	Data Processing Department
DIN:	Data Identification Number	DPD:	Data Processing Division
DIO:	Data Input/Output	DPF:	Disabled Page Fault
DIO:	Direct Input/Output	DPI:	Digital Pseudorandom Inspection
DIP:	Document Image Processing	DPI:	Dots Per Inch
DIQ:	Device Input Queue	DPL:	Database Programming Languages
DIR:	Deutsche Information Retrieval	DPL:	Descriptor Privilege Level
DIR:	DIRectory	DPM:	Data Processing Manager
DIS:	Data Input Station	DPM:	Data Processing Mode
DIS:	Digital Integration System	DPP:	Direct Positive Process
DIS:	Draft International Standard	DPS:	Data Preparation Staff
DIS:	Dynamic Impedance Stabilization	DPS:	Data Processing Standard
DIU:	Digital Interchange Utility	DPS:	Data Processing Station
DLF:	Down Loadable Fonts	DPS:	Data Processing System
DLL:	Data Link Layer	DPS:	Disk Programming System
		DPS:	Distributed Presentation Services

DPS:	Double Page Spread	DSM:	Dynamic Scattering Mode
DQC:	Data Quality Control	DSN:	Data Set Name
DQL:	Data-Ease Query Language	DSO:	Data Set Organization
DQO:	Draft-Quality Output	DSO:	Direct System Output
DQP:	Draft-Quality Print	DSP:	Data Set Profile
DRA:	Digital Read-In Assembly	DSP:	Digital Signal Processing
DRC:	Data Recording Control	DSP:	Distributed System Program
DRC:	Data Reduction Compiler	DSP:	Dye Sublimation Printing
DRC:	Design Rule Checking	DSR:	Data Set Requirement
DRI:	Data Reduction Interpreter	DSS:	Data Set Security
DRI:	Document Retrieval Index	DSS:	Decision Support Software
DRO:	Destructive Read-Out	DSS:	Decision Support System
DRO:	Digital Read-Out	DST:	Data Service Task
DRQ:	Data ReQuest	DST:	Device Service Task
DRR:	Document Release Record	DSV:	Digital Sum Variation
DRS:	Data Retrieval System	DTA:	Data Transfer Area
DRS:	Distributed Resource System	DTB:	Decimal To Binary
DRS:	Document Resource System	DTC:	Desk Top Computing

DRT: Data Recovery Tool
DRT: Device Reference Table
DRW: Disk Request Word
DRW: DRaW Format
DSA: Directory Service Agent
DSA: Direct Store Access
DSA: Dynamic Storage Allocation
DSB: Data Set Block
DSC: Device Selection Character
DSD: Data Set Definition
DSD: Data Set Deletion
DSD: Data Structure Diagram
DSE: Data Set Extension
DSE: Data Systems Engineering
DSF: Data Sensitive Fault
DSF: Default Specification File
DSF: Device Support Facilities
DSF: Disk Storage Facility
DSF: Display Station Field
DSF: Double Sided Floppy
DSG: Data Set Group
DSH: Data Set Header
DSI: Data Stream Interface
DSI: Digital Speech Interpolation
DSI: Direct Source Input
DSK: Data Set Key
DSL: Data Set Label
DSL: Data Simulation Language
DSL: Data Structures Language
DSL: Digital Simulation Language
DSM: Daily Space Management
DSM: Data Services Managers
DSM: Disk Storage Module
DSM: Disk System Management

desk top computing

DTC: Device Type Code
DTF: Define The File
DTI: Department of Trade
& Industry (UK)
DTI: Direct Trader Input
DTL: Desk Top Level
DTM: Data Transfer Mode
DTO: Desk Top Organizers
DTP: Data Transfer Phase
DTP: Desk Top Publishing

Desk Top Publishing

DTR: Data Terminal Ready

DTR: Data Transfer Rate
DTS: Data Transfer State
DTS: Dynamic Transient
     Segment Register
DUA: Directory User Agent
DUN: Default User Name
DUO: Datatron Users Organization
DUP: Disk Utility Program
DVF: Dump Viewing Facility
DVI: Digital Video Interactive
DWQ: Device Work Queue
DWS: Data Word Size
DXF: Data EXchange Format

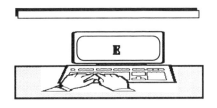

EAP: Emulator Application Program
EAU: Erase All Unprotected
EBR: Electron Beam Recording
EBR: Electronic Beam Recording
ECB: Electronic Code Book
ECB: Event Control Block
ECC: Error Check and Control
ECC: Error Checking and Correction
ECC: Error Checking Code
ECC: Error Correcting Code
ECD: Enhanced Color Display
ECD: Estimated Completion Date
ECI: European Cooperation in Informatics
ECL: Executive Control Language
E/CM: External/Conceptual Mapping
ECO: Electronic Central Office
ECO: Electronic CheckOut
ECS: ElectroChemical Society
ECS: Error Condition Statement
ECS: Error Control Software
ECS: Error Correcting System
ECS: Extended Character Set
ECS: Extended Core Storage
ECT: Environment Control Table
EDA: Electronic Design Automation
EDA: Electronic Differential Analyzer
EDA: Electronic Digital Analyzer
EDA: Error Data Analysis
EDB: Educational Data Bank
EDB: Extensional DataBase
EDC: Error Detection and Correction

EDC: Error Detection Code
EDD: Electronic Data Display
EDD: Externally Described Data
EDF: Extendable Disk File
EDF: External Data File
EDF: Externally Described File
EDI: Elementary Data Items
EDL: Emulation Design Language
EDM: Electronic Distance Measurement
EDM: Engineering Data Management
EDP: Educational Data Processing
EDP: Electronic Data Processing
EDS: Electronic Data Switching
EDS: Electronic Data System
EDS: Environmental Data Service
EDS: Exchangeable Disk Storage
EDX: Event Driven EXecutive
EEA: Electronic Engineering Association
EED: Electronic EavesDropping
EEI: Essential Elements of Information
EEM: Electronic Engineer's Master
EEP: Exact End Position
EFA: Extended Field Attribute
EFD: Engineering Flow Diagram
EFF: Electronic Frontier Foundation
EFF: Expandable File Family
EFI: Error Free Interval
EFR: Electronic Filing and Retrieval
EFS: Extended Function Store
EFS: External Function Store
EFT: Electronic Financial Transaction
EFT: Electronic Funds Transfer
EIA: Electronic Industries Association
EIB: Electronics Installation Bulletin
EIS: Electronic Information Service
EIS: Environment Information System
EIS: Executive Information Services
EIS: Executive Information System
EIS: Extended Instruction Set
ELC: Eye Legible Copy
ELF: Engine Load Facility
ELF: Extensible Language Facility
ELM: Error Log Manager
ELP: English Language Programs
ELS: Entry Level System
ELS: Error Likely Situation
ELT: Error Log Table
EMA: Enterprise Management Architecture
EMD: Embedded Microcomputer Division
EMH: Expedited Message Handling
EML: Emulator Machine Language
EMM: Expanded Memory Manager

EMP: Electro-Magnetic Pulse Radiation
EMP: Electronic Market Place
EMQ: External Message Queue
EMT: EMulator Trap
ENC: Edge Notched Card
ENQ: ENQuiry Character
eoa: end Of address
eob: end Of block
eoc: end Of chain
eoc: end Of conversion
eoc: end Of cycle
eod: end Of data
eod: end Of document
eoe: end Of extent
eof: end Of file
eoi: end-Of-information
eoj: end-Of-job
eol: end-Of-letter flag
EOL: End-Of-Line
EOL: End Of List
EOL: Expression Oriented Language
eom: end Of message
EON: End-Of-Number
EOP: End Of Program
EOP: End-Of-Page
EOP: End OutPut
EOQ: End-Of-Query
eor: end Of record
eor: end Of reel
eor: end Of run
EOS: Electro-Optical Systems
EOS: End-Of-Segment
EOT: End Of Office Terminals
eot: end Of tape
eot: end Of task
EOT: End-Of-Test
EOT: End-Of-Text
eov: end Of Volume
EOW: End-Of-Word
EPA: Electronic Publishing Abstracts
EPA: Enhanced Performance Architecture
EPA: Event Process Array
EPA: External Page Address
EPC: Editorial Processing Center
EPL: Encoder Programming Language
EPP: External Program Parameter
EPS: Electronic Payment System
EPS: Electronic Publishing Service
EPS: Encapsulated PostScript File
EPS: Encapsulated PostScript Format
EPS: Even Parity Select

EPS: External Page Storage
EPT: End-User Productivity Tool
EPT: Executive Process Table
ERA: Electronic Representatives Association
ERA: ERAse
ERB: Extended Response Byte
ERF: Extended Response Field
ERM: Error Recovery Manager
ERM: Extended Relational Model
ERP: Error Recovery Procedure
err: error
ERT: Expected Run-Time
ESA: Externally Specified Address
ESC: ESCape Code/Character
ESD: External Symbol Dictionary
ESF: Extended Super Frame
ESM: Electronic Support Measures
ESM: Electronic Warfare Support Measu
ESP: Enhanced Service Provider
ESR: Electronic Send Receive
ESS: Effective Search Speed
ESS: Electronic Spread Sheet

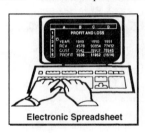
Electronic Spreadsheet

ESS: Executive Support System
ESS: Expert-System Shell
ESS: Explanation Sub-System
ESS: Event Scheduling System
ESV: Error Statistics by Volume
ETC: Embedded Text Control
E-to-E: Electronic -to -Electronic
ETL: Educational Technology Language
ETL: Ending Tape Label
ETR: Expected Time of Response
ETT: Expected Test Time
EUC: End User Computing
EUD: End-User Development
EVA: Error Volume Analysis
EWA: Erase /Write Alternate
EWM: Electronic Work Monitoring
EWM: Electronic Write Monitoring
EXF: EXternal Function
EXR: EXception Request

FAC: Function Authority Credentials
FAD: Face Attribute Definition
FAM: File Archive Manager
FAP: File Access Point
FAP: Failure Analysis Program
FAP: Financial Analysis Program
FAP: Floating Point Arithmetic Package
FAP: FORTRAN Assembly Program
FAR: Failure Analysis Report
FAS: File Access Store
FAS: Flexible Access System
FAT: File Allocation Table
FAT: Formula Assembler Translator
FBA: Fixed-Block Architecture
FBB: Four Bit Byte
FBP: FAST BUS Protocol
FBS: Financial Blackboard System
FBU: Full BackUp
FCA: Frequency Control Analysis
FCB: File Control Block
FCB: Forms Control Buffer
FCB: Function Control Block
FCC: Face Change Character
FCC: Frame Check Character
FCG: Facsimile Character Generation
FCI: Free Control Interval
FCI: Functional Configuration Identification
FCL: Format Control Language
FCP: File Control Program
FCP: Four-Color Process
FCS: File Control Service
FCS: Fixed Currency Symbol
FCS: Four-Color Separation
FDB: Field Descriptor Block
FDB: File Data Block
FDC: Facsimile Data Converter
FDC: Field Data Code
FDC: Functional Design Criteria
FDI: Foreground Display Image
FDL: Forms Description Language
FDP: Field Developed Program
FDR: Fast Dump Restore
fdr: feeder
FDR: File Data Register
FDS: File Description Statement
FDS: Flat-File Database System

FDS: Font Data Set
FDS: Format Description Statement
FDS: Full Development System
FDT: Formal Description Technique
FDT: Functional Description Table
FDU: Form Description Utility
FDV: Fault Defect Verification
FEA: Finite Element Analysis
FEC: Feedback Error Control
FEC: Fetch-Execute Cycle
FEC: Forward Error Control
FEC: Forward Error Correction
FEG: Form Environment Group
FEM: Finite Element Model
FEN: Frequency-Emphasizing Network
FES: Foreign Exchange Service
FES: Forms Entry System
FFC: Form Feed Character
FFC: Fully Formed Character
FFD: Flat-File Database
FFD: Fully Functional Dependent
FFP: Fast FORTRAN Processor
FFR: Forward File Recovery
FFS: Flash File System
FFT: Fast Fourier Transform
FGL: Fourth Generation Language
4GL: 4th Generation Language
5GL: Fifth Generation Language
1GL: First Generation Language

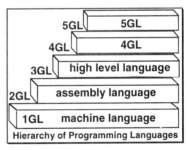

Hierarchy of Programming Languages

FHF: Fixed Head File
FHP: Fixed Header Prefix
FIB: File Information Block
FIB: FORTRAN Information Bulletin
FID: Format IDentification
FID: International Federation for Documents
FIG: FIGures Shift
FIO: File Input/Output
FIO: Formatted Input/Output
FIP: Finance Image Processing
FIS: Field Information System
FIS: Financial Information System

FIS:	Floating Instruction Set	FTR:	Full Text Retrieval
FIU:	Federation of Information Users	FTR:	Functional Test Requirement
FLC:	Foreign-Language Characters	FTS:	Fast Time Scale
FLF:	Fixed Length Field	FTS:	Frequency and Timing Subsystem
FLI:	First-Line Indent	FTZ:	Fernmeld Technisches Zentralamt
FLI:	Frame Level Interface	FUS:	FORTRAN Utility System
FLO:	Fixed-Length Operations	FVU:	File Verification Utility
FLP:	FLoating Point	FWA:	First Word Address
FLR:	Fixed-Length Record	FWL:	Fixed Word Length
FLS:	Field Level Sensitivity	FWP:	First Word Pointer
FLS:	Field Level Specifications		
FLS:	File Level Specifications		
FLT:	Fault Locating Test		
FMD:	Field Macro Diagram		
FMD:	Function Management Data		
FML:	File Manipulation Language		
FMS:	File Management System		
FNB:	File Name Block		
FNF:	First Normal Form		

FPA:	Fixed Point Arithmetic
FPA:	Floating Point Arithmetic
FPC:	Four-Phase Commit
FPD:	Flat-Panel Display
FPD:	Full-Page Display
FPF:	Full Procedural File
FPI:	Formatted Program Interface
FPL:	Financial Planning Language
FPO:	Fixed-Point Operator
FPR:	File Protect Ring
FPS:	Focus Projection and Scanning
FQL:	Formal Query Language
FRD:	Functional Requirements Document
FRF:	Field Reference Field
FRF:	File Reference Function
FRL:	Frame Representation Language
FRM:	Free Running Mode
FRM:	Full Recording Mode
FRR:	Functional Recovery Routines
FSA:	Field Search Argument
FSD:	Flat Screen Display
FSI:	Functional Subsystem Interface
FSL:	Formal Semantic Language
FSN:	Full Screen Naming
FSP:	Full-Screen Processing
FSS:	Functional Sub-System
FST:	File Status Table
FSV:	Floating-Point Status Vector
FTA:	Fast Turn Around
FTE:	Field Table Entry
FTF:	File Transfer Facility
FTN:	FORTRAN
FTP:	File Transfer Program

GAL:	Generalized Assembly Language
GAM:	Graphic Access Method
GAP:	General Assembly Program
GAP:	Graphics Application Program
GAP:	Groupe d'Analyse et de Prevision
GAS:	Global Address Space
GAT:	Generalized Algebraic Translator
GBF:	Geographic Base File
GBS:	General Business System
gch:	gigacharacters
GCI:	Graphic Command Interpreter
GCP:	Graphing and Charting Package
GCR:	Group Coded Recording
GCS:	Graphics Compatibility System
GDA:	Global Data Administrator
GDA:	Global DAtabase
GDE:	Generalized Data Entry
GDF:	Graphics Data File
GDF:	Group Distribution Frame
GDG:	Generation Data Group
GDI:	Generalized Data Base Interface
GDI:	Graphic Data Interface
GDL:	Graphic Display Library
GDM:	Global Data Manager
GDP:	Generalized Data Base Processor
GDP:	Graphic Display Program
GDS:	Group Data Set
GDS:	Graphic Data System
GDS:	Graphic Design System
GDS:	Grumman Data System
GDT:	Global Descriptor Table
GEC:	Graphic Escape Character
GEL:	General Emulation Language
GEM:	Graphics Environment Manager

GEM:	Graphical Environment Manager	GTF:	Generalized Trace Facility
GFN:	Gray Font Names	GTP:	Graphic Transform Package
GFP:	Generalized File Processor	GUD:	Global UpDate
GHC:	Gating Half-Cycle	GUI:	Graphical User Interface
GHz:	Giga-Hertz	GUS:	Guide to Use of Standards
GID:	Group IDentifier (UNIX)	GVS:	Guest Virtual Storage
GIF:	Graphics Interchange Format	GWE:	GeoWorks Ensemble
GIL:	General-Purpose Interactive Language		
GIM:	Generalized Information Management		
GIR:	Generalized Information Retrieval		
GIS:	Generalized Information System		
GIS:	Geographical Information System		
GKS:	Graphic Kernel System		
GML:	Generalized Mark-Up Language		
GML:	Graphic Machine Language		
GMT:	Generalized Multi-Tasking	HAB:	Home Address Block
GOL:	General Operating Language	HAG:	Home Address Gap
GOL:	Goal Oriented Language	HAJ:	Hyphenation And Justification
GOR:	Gained Output Ratio	HAL:	Highly Automated Logic
GOS:	Grade Of Service	HAM:	Hierarchical Access Method
GOS:	Graphics Operating System	HAM:	Host Access Method
GPA:	General-Purpose Analysis	HAM:	Hybrid Access Method
GPB:	Global Parameter Buffer	HAP:	Host Application Program
GPD:	Gas Plasma Display	HBS:	High Byte Strobe
GPD:	General Protocol Driver	HCF:	Host Command Facility (IBM)
GPD:	Graphic Performance Display	HCF:	Host Conversational Function
GPL:	General Purpose Language	HCL:	Hard Copy Log
GPL:	General Purpose Library	HCP:	Host Command Processor
GPL:	Generalized Programming Language	HCT:	Hard Copy Task
GPM:	General-Purpose Macrogenerator	HDB:	Hierarchical DataBase
GPM:	General-Purpose Module	HDM:	Hierarchical Development
GPP:	General-Purpose Program		Methodology
GPS:	General Problem Solver	HDN:	HexaDecimal Number
GPS:	Graphic Programming Services	hdr:	header
GPS:	General Programming Subsystem	HDR:	High Data Rate
GPX:	Generalized Programming EXtended	HDR:	Horizontally Displayed Records
GQL:	Graphic Query Language	HDS:	Hybrid Development System
GRF:	Geographic Reference File	HER:	Human Error Rate
GRR:	Group Resource Record	HEX:	HEXadecimal
GRS:	General Register Stack	HFB:	Help File Builder
GRS:	General Reporting System	HFS:	Hierarchical File System
GRS:	Generalized Retrieval System	HFS:	Horizontal Fragmentation Scheme
GRS:	Guest Real Storage	HHC:	Hand-Held Calculator
GSE:	Graphics Screen Editor	HIP:	Host-Initiated Program
GSI:	Graphic Structure Input	hir:	hierarchy
GSL:	Generalized Simulation Language	HIS:	Honeywell Information Systems
GSM:	General System Module	HIS:	Hospital Information System
GSM:	Graphics System Module	HLI:	Host Language Interface
GSP:	General Simulation Program	HLL:	High Level Language
GSP:	Graphics Subroutine Package	HLM:	High Level Message
GSS:	Graphic Support Software	HMI:	Happy Mac Icon
GSS:	Graphics Symbol Set	HMI:	Horizontal Motion Index

HMK: Host Master Key
HMS: Hospitality Management System
HOF: Head Of Form
HOL: High-Order Language
HOL: Human-Oriented Language
HOP: Hybrid Operating Program
HOS: Higher Order Software
HPC: Hand-Printed Characters
HPL: High Performance Language
HPQ: Hold Page Queue
HRS: Host Real Storage
HRS: Host-Resident Software
HSB: Hue, Saturation, Brightness
HSD: High Speed Data
HSD: High Speed Displacement
HSM: Hierarchical Storage Manager
HSR: Host System Responses
HSS: High-Speed Skip
HSS: High-Speed Storage
HTB: Hexadecimal To Binary
HTF: Host Transfer File
HTL: High Threshold Logic
HTS: Head Track Selector
HUD: Head Up Display
HVP: High Video Pass
HVS: Host Virtual Storage
HWI: HardWare Interpreter

IAC: Information Analysis Center
IAC: Inter-Application Communication
IAC: International Algebraic Compiler
IAD: Initial Address Designator
IAD: Integrated Automatic Documentation
IAE: Integral Absolute Error
IAF: InterActive Facility
IA5: International Alphabet Number 5
IAG: IFIP Administrative Data
        Processing Group
IAI: African Informatics Institute
IAI: Institut Africain D'Informatique
IAL: International Algebraic Language
IAL: International Algorithmic Language
IAL: Investment Analysis Language
IAM: Index Address Mark
IAM: Initial Address Message

IAM: Innovation Access Method
IAM: Interactive Algebraic Manipulatic
IAP: Industry Applications Program
IAP: Institution of Analyst
        & Programmers
IAS: Immediate Access Store
IAS: Instruction Address Stop
IAS: Interactive Application System
IBC: Intermediate Block Check
IBF: Input Buffer Full
IBG: Inter-Block Gap
IBI: Inter-Governmental Bureau for
        Informatics
IBI: International Bureau for Informati
IBM: International Business Machines
        (Computer Company)
IBS: Intelsat Business Services
IBU: Incremental BackUp
ICB: Interrupt Control Block
ICC: International Computation
        Center (Italy)
ICC: International Control Center
ICD: Interface Control Document
ICD: Interface Control Drawings
ICD: International Code Designer
ICF: Integrated Catalog Facility
ICF: Integrated Control Facility
ICG: Interactive Computer Graphics
ICL: International Computers Limited
ICL: Interpretive Coding Language
ICR: Independent Component Release
ICS: Inland Computer Service
ICS: Institute of Computer Science
ICS: International Computer Symposiun
ICS: Inventory Control System
ICT: Institute of Computer Technology
ICV: Initial Chaining Value
ICW: Initial Condition Word
ICW: Interface Control Word
IDA: Integrated Data Access
IDA: Integrated Data Analysis
IDA: Integrated Digital Access
IDA: Intelligent Data Access
IDA: Interactive Data Analysis
IDA: Interactive Debugging Aid
IDB: Integrated Data Base
IDB: Intentional DataBase
IDD: Integrated Data Dictionary
IDE: Integrated Drive Electronics
IDE: Interaction Data Entry
IDE: Interactive Data Entry
IDF: Image Description File

IDF:	Inline Data File	IFT:	International Foundation for Telemetering
IDF:	Integrated Data File	IGL:	Interactive Graphics Language
IDI:	Improved Data Interchange	IGS:	Information Group Separator
IDI:	Initial Domain Identifier	IGS:	Interactive Graphics System
IDI:	Intelligent Dual Interface	IGS:	Interchange Group Separator
IDL:	Information Description Language	IIA:	Information Industries Association
IDL:	Instruction Definition Language	IIO:	Intelligent Input/Output
IDL:	Intelligent Data Language	IIP:	Intergovernmental Informatics Program (UNESCO)
IDL:	Intermediate Data Description Language	IIS:	Institute of Information Scientists (USA)
IDM:	Integrated Database Management	IIS:	Intelligent Interface Standard
IDO:	Interactive Distribution and Order System	IIS:	Interactive Instructional System
IDO:	Isolated Digital Output	IJQ:	Input Job Queue
IDP:	Industrial Data Processing	IJS:	Input Job Stream
IDP:	Initial Domain Part	IJS:	Interactive Job Submission
IDP:	Integrated Data Processing	ILB:	Initial Load Block
IDP:	Integrated Digital Processing	ILC:	Instruction Length Code
IDP:	Interactive Data Base Processor	ILC:	Instruction Location Counter
IDP:	Inter-Digit Pause	ILD:	Internal Library Definition
IDP:	International Data Processing	ILO:	Individual Load Operation
IDR:	Industrial Data Reduction	ILP:	Intermediate Language Program
IDR:	Information Descriptor Record	ILS:	Integrated Link Software
IDS:	Input Data Set	ILS:	Integrated Logistic Support
IDS:	Integrated Data Store	IMA:	Input Message Acknowledgement
IDU:	Interactive Database Utilities	IMA:	Invalid Memory Address
IDU:	Interactive Data Utilities	IMC:	Instruction Marker Control
IDV:	Input Data Validation	IMC:	Interactive Module Controller
IED:	Information Engineering Directorate	IMD:	Inter-Modulation Distortion
IEF:	Instruction Execution Function	IMG:	IMaGe File Format
IER:	Inline Exit Routine	IMH:	Internodal Message Handler
IER:	Installation Exit Routine	IMI:	Intermediate Machine Instruction
IER:	Invalid Exclusive Reference	IML:	Information Manipulation Language
IET:	Input Execution Time	IML:	Initial Machine Load
IEW:	Information Engineering Workbench	IML:	Initial Microcode Load
IFA:	Information Flow Analysis	IML:	Initial Microprogram Load
IFA:	Integrated File Adapter	IMM:	Intelligent Memory Manager
IFC:	Information Flow Control	IMM:	Interaction Multi-Mode
IFC:	InterFace Clear	IMP:	Information Management Package
IFD:	Instantaneous Frequency Discriminator	IMP:	Integrated Manufacturing Planning
IFD:	International Federation for Documentation	IMP:	Intrinsic Multi-Processing
		IMS:	Information Management System
IFF:	Image/Interchange File Format	IMS:	Integrated Manufacturing System
IFI:	Inter-Fault Interval	IMS:	Integrated Message Services
IFM:	Interactive File Manager	IMS:	Inventory Management System
IFP:	Integrated Family of Programs	inc:	increment
IFS:	Information Feedback System	INR:	Interference-to-Noise Ratio
IFS:	Installable File System	int:	interrupt
IFS:	Interactive File Sharing	INX:	INdeX Character
IFS:	Interchange File Separator	IOB:	Input/Output Block
		IOB:	Inter-Organization Board (UN)

IOC:	Input/Output Control	IRC:	Information Retrieval Center
IOE:	Integrated Operating Environment	irc:	inter-record Constraints
IOF:	Input/Output Fronted	irc:	intra-record Constraints
IOI:	Input-Output Interface	IRD:	Information Resource Dictionary
IOI:	Input/Output Interruption	IRF:	Input Register Full
IOL:	Input/Output List	IRG:	Inter-Record Gap
IOQ:	Input/Output Queue	IRH:	Index Record Header
IOR:	Input-Output Read	IRI:	Instituto per la Ricostruzione
IOS:	Input-Output Statement		Industriale (Italy)
IOS:	Input-Output Supervisor	IRL:	Information Retrieval Language
IOS:	Input-Output Symbol	IRM:	Information Resource Management
IOS:	Interactive Operating System	IRM:	Intensive Recording Mode
IOT:	Input/Output Transfer	IRO:	Inquiry/Response Operation
IOU:	Input-Output Unit	IRP:	Inventory and Requirements Plannir
IOX:	Input-Output EXecutive	IRQ:	Interrupt ReQuest Level/Line
IPA:	Information Processing Architecture	IRS:	Information Retrieval Systems
IPA:	International Pharmaceutical Abstract	IRS:	Inquiry and Reporting System
IPC:	Industrial Process Control	IRS:	Interchange Record Separator
IPC:	Information Processing Center	IRT:	Index ReTurn Character
IPC:	Information Processing Code	IRV:	International Reference Version
IPC:	Internal Parity Checking	IRV:	Interrupt Request Vector
IPF:	Information Processing Facility	IRW:	Indirect Reference Word
IPF:	Information Productivity Facility	ISA:	Information Science Abstracts
IPG:	Information Policy Group	ISC:	Ideal Standard Cost
IPL:	Information Processing Language	ISC:	Integrated Storage Control
IPL:	Initial Program Load	ISD:	Information Structure Design
IPL:	Initial Program Loader	ISD:	International Software Database
IPL:	Interrupt Priority Level	ISE:	Institute for Software Engineering
IPM:	Impulse Per Minute	ISF:	Index Sequential Files
IPM:	Infinite Pad Method	ISG:	Inter Sub-Block Gap
IPM:	Interruptions Per Minute	ISI:	Information Structure Implementatio
IPN:	Initial Process Name	ISI:	Institute For Scientific Information
IPO:	Input Process and Output	ISI:	Inter-Symbol Interference
IPO:	Installation Productivity Option	ISK:	Instruction Space Key
IPP:	Information Publishing Program	ISL:	Information Search Language
IPP:	Integrated Plotting Package	ISL:	Information System Language
IPR:	Isolated Pacing Response	ISL:	Instructional Systems Language
IPS:	Image Processing Software	ISL:	Interactive Simulation Language
IPS:	Impulse Per Second	ISM:	Information System Manager
IPS:	Index Pointer Segment	ISM:	Information Systems for Managemer
IPS:	Information Processing System	ISN:	Initial Sequence Number
IPS:	Information Providers	ISN:	Input Sequence Number
ips:	instructions per second	ISN:	Internal Sequence Number
IPT:	Improved Programming Techniques	ISO:	Indexed Sequential Organization
IPT:	Interactive ProtoTyping	ISO:	Information System Office
IQA:	Institute of Quality Assurance	ISO:	International Standards Organization
IQE:	Interruption Queue Element	ISP:	Internally Stored Program
IQF:	Interactive Query Facility	ISR:	Information Storage and Retrieval
IQL:	Interactive Query Language	ISS:	Image Storage Space
IRA:	Input Reference Axis	ISS:	Index Sequential Storage
IRB:	Interruption Request Block	ISS:	Index Source Segment
		ISS:	Information Storage System

ISS:	Input SubSystem
ISS:	Integrated Support System
ISS:	Intelligent Support System
IST:	Information Science and Technology
IST:	Interrupt Service Task
IST:	Internal STandard
ISU:	Ideographic Sort Utility
ISV:	Independent Software Vendor
ISV:	Interval Service Value
ISZ:	Increment and Skip on Zero
ITB:	Intermediate Text Block
ITC:	Integrated Transaction Controller
ITC:	Intelligent Transaction Controller
ITC:	Inter-Data Transaction Controller
ITC:	International Telemetering Conference
ITP:	Information Transfer Phase
ITF:	Interactive Terminal Facility
ITG:	InTer-Record Gap
ITL:	Intermediate Transfer Language
ITP:	Interactive Transactional Program
ITS:	Index Target Segment
ITS:	Intelligent Tutoring System
IUB:	Instruction Used BIT
IUI:	Intuitive User Interface
IUP:	Independent Utility Program
IUP:	Installed User Program
IVG:	Interrupt Vector Generation
IVP:	Installation Verification Procedure
IVT:	Interrupt Vector Table
IV & V:	Independent Verification & Validation
IWP:	International Word Processing Organizations
IWQ:	Input Work Queue
IWS:	Instruction Work Stack
IXC:	Inter EXchange Control
IXM:	IndeX Manager

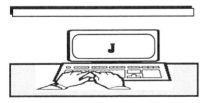

JAB:	Job Analysis and Billing
JAF:	Job Accounting Facility
JAI:	Job Accounting Interface
JAS:	Job Analysis System

JAT:	Job Accounting Table
JCB:	Job Control Block
JCL:	Job Control Language
JCM:	Job Cylinder Map
JCN:	Jump On CoNdition
JCP:	Job Control Processor
JCP:	Job Control Program
JCR:	Job Control Record
JCR:	Job Control Rights
JCS:	Job Control Statement
JCT:	Job Control Table
JDL:	Job Description Language
JDL:	Job Description Library
JDM:	Journal of Data Management
JDS:	Job Data Sheet
JEF:	Japanese Processing Extended Feature
JES:	Job Entry Sub-System
JES:	Job Entry System
JET:	Journal Entries Transfer
JFN:	Job File Number
JFT:	Job File Table
JIB:	Job Information Block
JIC:	Joint Information Center
JIF:	Job Input File
JIP:	Joint Input Processing
JIS:	Job Information System
JIS:	Job Input Stream
JMA:	James Martin Associates
jmp:	jump
JMQ:	Job Message Queue
JND:	Just Noticeable Difference
JNT:	Joint Network Team
JOF:	Job Output File
JOL:	Job Organization Language
JOS:	Job Output Stream
JPA:	Job Pack Area
JQE:	Job Queue Entry
JQM:	Job Queue Management
JSA:	Japanese Standards Association
JSD:	Jackson System Development
JSF:	Job Services File
JSI:	Job Step Initiation
JSL:	Job Specification Language
JSM:	Jackson Structured Method
JSP:	Jackson Structured Programming
JSP:	Joint Study Program
JSR:	Jump to Sub-Routines
JST:	Job Support Task
JTM:	Job Transfer & Manipulation
JUG:	Joint Users Group
JUN:	Jump UNconditionally

KAS: Knowledge Acquisition Subsystem
KBE: KeyBoard Entry
KBS: KeyBoard Shortcuts
kbs: kilobyteS
KBS: Knowledge Based System

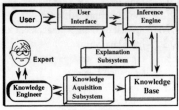

Knowledge Based System

kch: kiloCharacter
KCL: Keystation Control Language
KCS: Kanji Character Set
KCS: Kansas City Standard
KCS: KiloCharacters Per Second
KDA: Keyed Direct Access
KDC: Key Distribution Center
KDE: Keyboard Data Entry
KEG: KEy Gap
KEP: Key Entry Processing
KHz: Kilo HertZ
KIC: Kernel Input Controller
KIL: Keyed Input Language
KIM: Keyboard Input Matrix
KIS: Keyboard Input Simulation
KMF: Key Management Facility
KPC: Keyboard/Printer Control
KPH: Keystrokes Per Hour
KPO: Key Punch Operator
KPS: Knowledge Processing System
KRL: Knowledge-Representation Language
KSA: Keyed Sequential Access
KSH: Key Strokes per Hour
KSR: Keyboard Select Routing
KSR: Keyboard Send Receive
KSV: Key Stroke Verification
KTL: KEY-EDIT Terminal Language

LAE: Left Arithmetic Element
LAF: Long Address Form
LAF: Look-And-Feel
LAG: Load And Go Assembler
LAL: Logical Access Level
LAM: Laser Accessed Method
LAM: Look At Me Signal
LAM: Loop Adder and Modifier
LAM: Loop Adder and Multiplier
LAP: Lesson Assembly Program
LAP: Link Access Procedure
LAP: List Assembly Program
LAS: Local Address Space
LBC: Left Bounded Context
LBG: Load Balancing Group
LBO: Line Build-Out
LBT: Low Bit Test
LCA: Life-Cycle Approach
LCB: Logic Control Block
LCC: Line Control Character
LCD: Line Control Discipline
LCL: Linkage Control Language
LCL: LoCaL
LCM: Lock Compatibility Matrix
LCM: Loosely Coupled Multiprocessing
LCO: Local Central Office
LCO: Local Copy Operation
LCP: Language Conversion Program
LCP: Link Control Procedure
LCP: Local Control Point
LCP: Logical Construction of Programs
LCS: Large Core Store
LCS: Library Character Set
LCS: Load Character Set
LCS: Loop Control System
LCT: Latest Completing Time
LCT: Level Control Table
LCT: Log Control Table
LCT: Logical Channel Termination
LDA: LoaD in Accumulator
LDA: Local Data Administrator
LDA: Locate Drum Address
LDA: Logical Device Address
LDB: Large Data Base
LDB: Logical Data Base
LDC: Local Display Controller

LDF:	Logic Data Field	LML:	Load Module Library
LDI:	Local Data Interface	LML:	Logical Memory Level
LDI:	Logical Data Independence	LMS:	Level Measuring Set
LDL:	Logical Data Base Level	LMS:	Library Member Subtype
LDP:	Language Data Processing	LMS:	List Management System
LDR:	Line Display Range	LMT:	Library Migration Table
LDR:	Low Data Rate	LMT:	Logical Mapping Table
LDS:	Line Data Set	LMT:	Logon Mode Table
LDS:	Line Delete Symbol	LNE:	Line Number Editing
LDS:	Local Distribution Service	LOB:	Line Of Balance
LDS:	Log Data Set	loc:	location
LDS:	Logical Data Structuring	LOC:	LOcation Counter
LDT:	Language Dependent Translator	LPA:	Link Pack Area
LDT:	Local Descriptor Table	LPC:	Linear Predictive Coding
LDT:	Logical Data Transfer	LPC:	Longitudinal Parity Check
LDT:	Logic Design Translator	LPD:	Language Processing and Debugging
LEC:	Link Escape Character		
LED:	Light Emitting Display	LPE:	Layer Primitive Equation
LEF:	Line Expansion Function	LPG:	Language de Programmation et de Gestion
LES:	Logical Editing Symbols		
LES:	Logical Escape Symbol	LPG:	Listing Program Generator
LFC:	Local Form Control	LPH:	Laser Print Header
LFM:	Local File Manager	LPI:	Lines Per Inch
LFM:	Logical File Member	LPL:	Last Priority Level
LFN:	Logical File Name	LPL:	Linear Programming Language
LFR:	Label Format Record	LPL:	List Processing Language
LFS:	Local Format Storage	LPL:	Lotus Programming Language
LGA:	Lower Gate Alphabet	LPL:	Lower Print Line
LGN:	Logical Group Number	lpm:	lines per minute
LHS:	List Handling Statement	LPN:	Logical Page Number
LHS:	Loop Handling System	LPS:	Linear Programming System
LIA:	Label Information Area	LPS:	Lines Per Second
LIA:	Loop Interface Address	LPT:	Largest Processing Time First
LIC:	Last In Chain	LQP:	Letter Quality Print
LIM:	Language Interpretation Module	LRA:	Logical Record Access
LIM:	Line Interface Module	LRG:	Low-Resolution Graphic
LIM:	Lotus/Intel/Microsoft	LRI:	Logical Record Interface
LIR:	Logon Interpret Routine	LRL:	Logical Record Length
LIT:	Load Initial Table	LRL:	Logical Record Location
LIX:	Legal Information EXchange	LSA:	Logical Storage Address
LJE:	Local Job Entry	LSA:	Logic State Analyzer
LLC:	Low Level Code	LSB:	Least Significant Bit
LLG:	Logical Line Group	LSB:	Least Significant Byte
LLL:	Low Level Language	LSC:	Least Significant Character
LLL:	Low Level Logic	LSD:	Language for Systems Development
LLP:	Low-Level Programming	LSD:	Least Significant Digit
LLS:	Linked List Search	LSD:	Link State Database
LMB:	Left Most BIT	LSE:	Language Support Environment
LMD:	Library Macro Definition	LSE:	Language Symbolique D'Enseignement
LME:	Layer-Management Entity		
LMF:	Licensing Management Facility	LSF:	Logging Service Facility
LMI:	Local Memory Image		

LSF: Logic Short Fault
LSL: Link and Selector Language
LSM: Line Select Module
LSP: Local Store Pointer
LSS: Language for Symbolic Simulation
LSS: Looped Surged Suppresser
LST: Latest Starting Time
LTA: Logical Transient Area
LTA: Logic Timing Analyzer
LTB: Logical Twin Backward Pointer
LTF: Logical Twin Forward Pointer
LTH: Logical Track Header
LTP: Language Translator Program
LTP: Local Transaction Procedure
LTP: Local Transaction Program
LUB: Logical Unit Block
LUF: Limiting System Utilization Factor
LUF: Lowest Usable Frequency
LUN: Logical Unit Number
LVA: Local Virtual Address
LVR: Longitudinal Video Recording
LWA: Last Word Address
LWA: Library Work Area
LWA: Load Work Area
LWA: Log Write-Ahead
LWE: Lower Window Edge

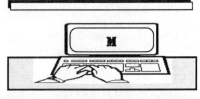

MAC: Maintenance Allocation Chart
MAC: Measurement and Analysis Center
MAC: Memory Access Controller
MAC: Multi-Access Computing
MAH: Memory Arena Header
MAI: Machine-Aided Indexing
MAI: Multiple Access Interface
MAI: Multiple Address Instruction
MAL: Macro-Assembly Language
MAL: Memory Access Logic
MAL: Memory Address Location
MAL: Meta-Assembly Language
MAL: Micro-Assembly Language
MAM: Memory Allocation Manager
MAO: Mini Access Office
MAP: Macro-Assembly Program
MAP: Maintenance Analysis Procedures

MAP: Mathematical Analysis Without Programming
MAP: Memory Allocation and Protection
MAP: Microprocessor Application Project
MAP: Multiple Allocation Procedure
MAR: Machine Aided Retrieval
MAR: MAchine Retrieval System
mas: macro-assembler
MAS: Memory-Address Space
MAS: Multi-Aspect Signaling
MAT: Machine Aided Translation
MAT: Memory Access Table
MAT: Memory Address Test
MAT: Memory Address Translation
MBC: Multiple Block Code
MBF: Monotonic Boolean Function
MCA: Multi-Channel Analyzer
MCC: Magnetic Card Code
MCC: Master Control Code
MCC: Multiple Copy Control
MCD: Monitor Console Routine Dispatcher
MCF: Magnetic Card File
MCF: Major Class Field
MCF: Major Control Field
MCF: Minor Class Field
MCG: Man-Computer Graphics
mch: megacharacter
MCL: Micro-Program Control Logic
MCP: Master Control Program
MCP: Multilanguage Code Page
MCR: Machine Configuration Record
MCR: Magnetic Character Recognition
MCR: Mass Configuration Record
MCR: Master Control Routine
MCS: Maintenance Control System
MCS: Master Control System
MCS: Medical Computer Services
MCS: MegaCycles Per Second
MCS: Micro-Program Certification System
MCS: Multinational Character Set
MCS: Multi-Programmed Computer System
MDA: Multi-Dimensional Access
MDA: Multi-Dimensional Analysis
MDB: Manual Device Backup
MDB: Master Data Bank
MDC: Maintenance Data Collection
MDC: Modification Detection Code
MDC: Multiple Device Controller
MDD: Multi-Dimensional Database
MDE: Master DOS Environment
MDF: Main Distribution Frame

MDF: Micro-Computer Development Facilities
MDI: Menu-Driven Interface

MDI: Multiple Document Interface
MDK: Multimedia Development Kit
MDL: Macro Data Language
MDL: Macro Description Language
MDP: Minimum Delay Programming
MDR: Miscellaneous Data Record
MDS: Maintenance Data System
MDS: Management Decision System
MDS: Management Display System
MDS: Microprocessor Development System
MDS: Mixed Data Set
MDS: Modern Data Systems
MDS: Modular Data System
MDT: Mean Down Time
MDT: Merchant Deposit Transmittal
MDT: Modified Data Tag
MEA: Memory Inspection Ending Address
MEF: Mandatory Entry Field
meg: mega-byte
MEP: Machine Execution Priority
MEP: Micro-Electronics Education Program (UK)
MFD: Master File Directory
MFE: Multi-Function Equipment
MFT: Multi-Programming Fixed Tasks
MGG: Matrix Generator Generator
MGL: Matrix Generator Language
MGP: Macro Generating Program
MGP: Multiple Goal Programming
MHS: Message Handling System
MHZ: MegaHertZ
MIB: Management Information Base
MIC: Machine Information Code
MIC: Magnetic Ink Character
MIC: Mean Information Content
MIC: Message Identification Code
MIC: Middle In Chain
MIE: Management Information Element
MIF: Master Index File

MIH: Missing Interruption Handler
MIL: Micro-Implementation Language
MIL: Module Interconnection Language
MIO: Multiple Input/Output
M/IO: Management/ Input Output
MIP: Manual Input Processing
MIP: Manual Input Program
MIP: Matrix Inversion Program
MIS: Machine Instruction Set
MIS: Management Information Service
MIS: Management Information System
MIS: Marketing Information System
MIW: Micro-Instruction Word
MJD: Management Job Description
MJP: Multiple Job Processing
MKC: Master Key Concept
MKH: Multiple Key Hashing
MKR: MarKeR
MKR: Multiple Key Retrieval
MLA: Matching Logic and Adder
MLD: Machine Language Debugger
MLD: Member List Display
MLI: Machine Language Instruction
MLP: Machine Language Program
MLS: Machine Literature Searching
MLS: Multi-Language System
MMA: Multi-Media Applications
MMA: Multiple Module Access
MMC: Main Memory Control
MMC: Meet Me Conference
MMC: Memory Management Controller
MML: Man-Machine Language
MMR: Magnetic Memory Record
MMR: Main Memory Record
MMS: Manufacturing Monitoring System
MMS: Mass Memory Store
MNR: Maximum Number of Records
MOC: Management-Oriented Computing
MOC: Memory Operating Characteristic
MOC: Mnemonic Operation Code
MOL: Machine-Oriented Language
MOP: Maintenance/Operator Panel
MOP: Multiple Online Processing
MOP: Multiple Online Programming
MOP: Multiple Open Publications
MOS: Macintosh Operating System
MOS: Management Operating System
MOS: Manufacturing Operating Systems
MOS: Micro-Program Operating System
MOS: Multi-processing Operating System
MOS: Multi-programming Operating System

MOS: Multi-Tasking Operating System	MSL: Mathematical Sub-Program Library
MPC: Micro-Program Control	MSO: Multi-Stage Operations
MPD: Multi-Lingual Product Description	MSP: MicroSoft Painting
MPE: Maximum Permitted Error	MSR: Magnetic Sound Recording
MPI: Macro Processing Instruction	MSR: Mark Sense Reading
MPI: Missing Page Interruption	MSR: Mechanized Storage and Retrieval
MPL: Macro-Procedure Language	MSR: Modified Subfile Record
MPL: Micro-Programming Language	MST: Master Scheduler Task
MPM: Multi-Programming Monitor	MSV: Mass Storage Volume
MP/M: Multiprogramming Control Program for Microprocessors	MTE: Machine Transaction Entry
	MTE: Multiple Terminal Emulator
MPO: Memory Protect Over-ride	MTF: Message Transfer Facility
MPP: Message Processing Program	MTN: Money Transaction Number
MPS: Macro-Processing System	MTO: Master Terminal Operator
MPS: Mathematical Programming System	MTS: Major Time Slice
MPS: Modified Partition Support	MUD: Master User Directory
MPS: MultiProcessing System	MUG: Multi-User Game
MPS: MultiProgramming System	MUR: Management Update and Retrieval System
MPT: Memory Processing Time	
MPT: MultiProcessing Time	MUS: Multi-Programmable Utility System
MPX: MultiProgramming EXecutive	MVD: Multi-Sync Video Display
MQL: Mean Queue Length	MVM: Minimum Virtual Memory
MRA: Materials Requirement Analysis	MVP: Multiple Virtual Processing
MRB: Modification Review Board	MVS: Multiple Virtual Storage (IBM)
MRC: Machine Readable Code	MVS: Multiple Virtual System
MRC: Margin-Release Control	MVT: Multi-Programming with Variable Number of Task (IBM)
MRC: Memory Request Controller	
MRD: Machine-Readable Data	MWD: MegaWorD
MRD: Memory ReaD	MWE: Management Work Element
MRG: Medium-Resolution Graphics	MWS: Multi-Work Station
MRI: Machine Readable Information	
MRI: Magnetic Resonance Imaging	
MRI: Memory Reference Instruction	
MRL: Machine Representation Language	
MRO: Multi-Region Operation	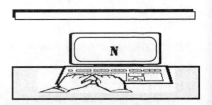
MRP: Manufacturing Resources Planning	
MRP: Material Requirement Planning	
MRP: Memory Resident Program	
MRP: Multiple-Related Protocols	NAL: New Assembly Language
MRR: Multiple Response Resolution	NAM: Non Addressable Memory
MRS: Management Reporting System	NAR: No Action Required
MSB: Most Significant Bit	NAS: Nested Address Space
MSB: Most Significant Byte	NAT: No Action Taken
MSC: Macro Selection Compiler	NAV: Norton Anti-Virus
MSC: Mass Storage Control	NBS: National Bureau of Standards
MSC: Most Significant Character	NBS: Numeric BackSpace Character
MSD: Most Significant Digit	NCC: National Computer Center (UK)
MSF: Mass Storage Facility	NCI: National Computer Institute
MSF: Mono Spaced Font	NCI: National Computing Industries
MSI: Mass Sequential Insertion	NCI: Netherlands Center for Informatics
MSL: Machine Specification Language	NCI: Non-Coded Information
MSL: Map Specification Library	NCI: Northeast Computer Institute

NCL: Nested Command List
NCL: Numeric Control Language
NCP: Network Control Program
NCS: National Computer Systems
NCS: Netherlands Computer Society
NCS: Nonloadable Character Set
NCV: No Core Value
NDA: Nonpageable Dynamic Area
NDC: National Data Corporation
NDF: Non-Deterministic FORTRAN
NDF: Numeric Data Field
NDM: Normal Disconnected Mode
NDQ: Nonreusable Disk Queuing
NDR: Non-Destructive Read
NDS: Non-Destructive Storage
NDT: Non-Destructive Testing
NDT: Normal Data Transfer
NES: Non-Erasable Storage
NES: Non-Executable Statement
NGT: Nominal Group Technique
NIA: No Input Acknowledge
NIF: Not In File
NIP: Nucleus Initialization Program
NLA: Normalized Load Access
NLA: Normalized Local Address
NLC: New Line Character
NLE: Non-Linear Encoding
NLI: Natural-Language Interface
N/LI: Normal/Low Intensity
NLK: Num Lock Key
NLP: Natural Language Processing
NLQ: Near-Letter Quality
NLQ: Not-Letter-Quality
NMF: New Master File
NMO: Number of Critical
        Micro-Operations
NMR: Normal Mode Rejection
NMS: New MaSter File
NNN: Non-Normalized Number
NOF: NCR Optical Font
NOI: No Operation Instruction
NOM: Null Output Message
NOP: No OPeration
NOP: Not Otherwise Provided For
NOR: 'Not OR'
NPA: Numerical Production Analysis
NPC: Non-Printable Characters
NPC: Non-Printing Characters
NPL: Natural Processing Language
NPL: New Programming Language
NPL: Non-Procedural Language

NPP: Negative Positive Process
NPR: Non-Procedural Reference
NPR: Non-Processor Request
NR/D: Not Required but Desired
NRI: Non-Reflective Ink
NRR: Non-Resident Routine
NRS: Name Registration Scheme
NRZ: Non-Return to Zero Recording
NSA: National Standards
        Association (USA)
NSI: Next Sequential Instruction
NSO: National Standards
        Organization (USA)
NSP: Non-Shareware Program
NSP: Numeric SPace
NSP: Numeric Subroutine Package
NSW: National Software Works
NTE: Navy Teletypewriter Exchange
NTF: No Trouble Found
NTP: Nonrequesting Terminal Program
NTQ: Near Typeset Quality
Nul: Null Character
NUM: NUMeric
NVR: Nonspecific Volume Request
NVS: Non-Volatile Storage
NZR: Non-Zero Return
NZT: Non-Zero Transfer

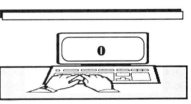

OAC: Office Automation Conference
OAC: Operations Analysis Center
OAF: Origin Address Field
OAG: Operand Address Generator
OAM: Operand Address Mode
OAR: Operations Analysis Report
OAR: Operator Authorization Record
OAS: Office Automation System
OAT: Operating Acceptance Test
OBB: Operation Better Block
OBF: Operational Base Facility
obj: object
OBP: On-Board Processing
OBP: Online Batch Processing
OBR: Optical Bar Recognition
OBS: OnLine Business Systems
OCB: Override Control BITS

OCB:	Over-the-Counter Batch	OFB:	Output FeedBack
OCC:	Object Code Compatibility	OFI:	OnLine Free Form Input
OCC:	Operator Control Command	OFI:	Originating Financial Institution
OCF:	On-Board Computational Facility	OFN:	Open File Number
OCF:	Operator Console Facility	OFR:	Open File Report
OCG:	Optical Code Generation	OGC:	Operator Guidance Code
OCG:	Optimal Code Generation	OGI:	Operator Guidance Indicator
OCI:	Office of Computer Information (USA)	OGL:	Overlay Generation Language
		OIA:	Office Information Architecture
OCL:	Operation Control Language	OIA:	Operator Information Area
OCL:	Operational Check List	OIC:	OnLine Instrument and Control Program
OCL:	Operator Control Language		
OCL:	Operational Control Level	OIC:	Only In Chain
OCL:	Optical Connector Losses	OID:	Octal IDentifier
OCL:	Overall Connection Loss	OIE:	Optical Incremental Encoder
OCO:	Operations Control Operator	OIL:	Only Input Lines
OCP:	Operating Control Procedure	OIP:	Operational Improvement Program
OCP:	Operational Checkout Procedure	OIS:	Office Information System
OCP:	Output Control Program	OIS:	Operating Information System
OCP:	Oxford Concordance Program	OLA:	One Level Address
OCR:	Optical Character Recognition	OLA:	OnLine Address
OCS:	Office Computing System	OLB:	OnLine Batch
OCS:	Operation Control Statement	OLC:	Open-Loop Control
OCS:	Overall Control Subsystem	OLC:	Operation Load Code
oct:	octal	OLE:	Object Linking & Embedding
OCT:	Operator Control Table	OLE:	Overlay Linkage Editor
ODA:	Octal Debugging Aid	OLF:	Out-Line Fonts
ODA:	Operational Data Analysis	OLH:	OnLine Help
ODA:	Operational Design and Analysis	OLL:	Output Logic Level
ODA:	Output Display Area	olo:	off-line Operation
ODC:	OnLine Data Capture	olo:	online Operation
ODC:	Output Data Control	OLP:	OnLine Processing
ODD:	Operator Distance Dialing	OLP:	OnLine Programming
ODD:	Outward Data Dissemination	OLQ:	OnLine Query
ODG:	Off-Line Data Generator	OLS:	Off-Line Storage
ODM:	Outboard Data Manager	OLS:	OnLine Service
ODP:	Offline Diagnostic Program	OLS:	OnLine Storage
ODP:	Open Distribution Processing	OLS:	OnLine System
ODP:	Optical Data Processing	OLT:	OnLine Test
ODP:	Original Document Processing	OLX:	OnLine EXecutive
ODR:	Optical Data Recognition	OMF:	Object Module Formats
ODR:	Original Data Record	OMF:	Old Master File
ODS:	Output Data Set	OMF:	Order Materials For
ODT:	Object Definition Table	OMG:	Object Management Group
ODT:	Octal Debugging Technique	OMI:	Operations Maintenance Instructions
ODT:	Open Desk Top	OMI:	Organization for Micro-Information
OEA:	Operator Error Analysis	OML:	Object Module Library
OEA:	Order Entry Application	OMR:	Object Management Rights
OEB:	Odd-Even-Bit	OMR:	Optical Mark Reading
OEF:	Origin Element Field	OMR:	Optical Mark Recognition
OER:	Object Existence Rights	ONI:	Operator Number Identification
OET:	Objective End Time	OOI:	Object-Oriented Images

OOK:	On-Off Keying	OSS:	Operation Systems Support
OOL:	Operator Oriented Language	OS/2:	Operating System/2
OOM:	Object-Oriented Model	OTC:	Objective, Time, and Cost
OOP:	Object-Oriented Programming	OTC:	Offline Terms Code
OPA:	One-Pass Assembly	OTE:	Operational Test & Evaluation
OPA:	Operator Priority Access	OT&E:	Operational Test & Evaluation
OPC:	Operation Planning and Control	OTF:	Optical Transfer Function
opd:	operand	OTF:	Optical Type Font
OPE:	Optimized Processing Element	OTG:	Option Table Generation
OPI:	Optional Pause Instruction	OTG:	Option Table Generator
opl:	operational	OTL:	OnLine Task Loader
OPL:	Organizer Programming Language	OTR:	Optical TRacking
OPM:	Operations Per Minute	OTS:	Object Time System
opr:	operand	OTS:	Off-The-Shelf
opr:	operator	OTS:	Optical Transport System
OPR:	Optical Page Reading	OTT:	Online Tutorial Text
OPR:	Optical Pattern Recognition	OUD:	Operational Unit Data
OPS:	OnLine Process Synthesis	ovr:	verflow
OPS:	OnLine Process Synthesizer	OWL:	Object Windows Library
OPS:	Operational Paging System	OWQ:	Output Work Queue
ops:	operations		
ops:	Operations per Second		
opt:	optimization		
OPT:	Optimized Production Technology		
opt:	optimizer		
opt:	optional		
OQL:	OnLine Query Language		
OQL:	Outgoing Quality Level		
ORE:	Overall Reference Equivalent		
ORR:	Operational Ready Rate		
OSA:	Onion Skin Architecture		

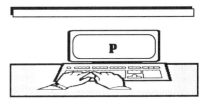

OSB:	Operational Status Bit	PAB:	Primary Application Block
OSC:	Output Stream Control	PAC:	PACkaged Application Software
OSD:	OnLine System Driver	PAC:	Performance Analysis and Control
OSD:	Operational Sequence Diagram	PAC:	Point-And-Click
OSF:	Open Software Foundation	PAC:	Prestel Administration Center
OSF:	Open Systems Foundation	PAC:	Primary Address Code
OSI:	Office of Scientific Intelligence	PAC:	Program Authorized Credentials
OSI:	Operating System Interface	PAC:	Project Accountability Chart
OSL:	Onion Skin Language	PAD:	Press-And-Drag
OSL:	Operand Specification List	PAD:	Program Analysis for Documentation
OSL:	Operating System Language	PAF:	Page Address Field
OSM:	Operating System Manual	PAF:	Peripheral Address Field
OSM:	Operating System Monitor	PAG:	Process Access Group
OSN:	Output Sequence Number	PAI:	Paging Activity Index
OSP:	Operating System Program	PAI:	Programmer Appraisal Instrument
OS/P:	Operating Systems for People	PAK:	Program Attention Key
OSQ:	Ordered Seek Queuing	PAL:	Pedagogic Algorithmic Language
OSR:	Optical Scanning Recognition	PAL:	Precision Artwork Language
OSS:	Office Support System	PAL:	Process Assembly Language
OSS:	Open Systems Standard	PAL:	Process Audit List
OSS:	Operating Systems Supervisor	PAL:	Program Application Library
		PAL:	Program Assembly Language
		PAL:	Programmer Assistance and Liaison
		PAM:	Primary Access Method

par:	parameter
PAP:	Primary Application Program
PAR:	Program Analysis and Review
PAR:	Program Appraisal Review
PAS:	Packaged Application Software
PAS:	Parallel Associative Storage
PAS:	Phase Address System
PAS:	Phase Array System
PAS:	Physical Address Space
PAS:	Point-And-Shoot
PAS:	Primary Access Service
PAS:	Private Address Space
PAS:	Program Address Storage
PAT:	Peripheral Allocation Table
PAT:	Prediction Analysis Technique
PAT:	Program for Advanced Technology
PAT:	Programmer Aptitude Test
PAT:	PseudoAdder Tree
PAV:	Program Activation Vector
PAX:	Parallel Architecture EXchange
PBC:	Pure Block Code
PBD:	Precise Block Diagram
PBN:	Physical Block Number
PBO:	Push Button Operations
PBS:	Picture Building System (IBM)
PCA:	Process Control Analyzer
PCB:	Page Control Block
PCB:	Process Control Block
PCB:	Program Control Block
PCC:	Prime Compression Character
PCC:	Print Control Character
PCC:	Program Control Counter
PCC:	Punch Card Code
PCD:	Page Cache Disable
PCD:	Partition Control Description
PCD:	Personal Computer Director
PCD:	Program Control Document
PCE:	Procedure Control Expression
PCE:	Processing & Control Element
PCE:	Program Cost Estimate
PCF:	Program Complex File
PCF:	Program Control Facility
PCG:	Programmable Character Generator
pch:	punch
PCI:	Pre-Connection Inspection
PCI:	Process Control Interface
PCI:	Program Check Interruption
PCI:	Program-Controlled Interruption
PCI:	Protocol Control Information
PCI:	Punch Card Interpreter
PCL:	Print Control Language
PCL:	Printer Command Language

PCL:	Printer Control Language
PCL:	Process Control Language
PCM:	Parallel Conversion Method
PCM:	Print Contrast Mark
PCO:	Program Controlled Output
PCP:	Peripheral Control Pulse
PCP:	Primary Control Program
PCP:	Process Control Program
PCP:	Program Change Proposal
PCR:	Procedure Change Request
PCR:	Program Change Request
PCS:	Page Composition Software
PCS:	Print Contrast Signal
PCS:	Power Conditioning Subsystem
PCS:	Power Conversion System
PCS:	Print Contrast Scale
PCS:	Print Contrast Signal
PCS:	Process Control System
PCS:	Production Control System
PCS:	Project Control System
PCT:	Partition Control Table
PCT:	Planning and Control Techniques
PCT:	Processing Control Table
PCT:	Program Control Table
PCU:	Punch Card Utility
PCW:	Program Control Word
PCX:	PiCture EXchange
PCX:	Process Control EXecutive
PDA:	Pageable Dynamic Area
PDA:	Physical Device Address
PDA:	Probability Discrete Automata
PDA:	Problem Determination Aid
PDB:	Physical DataBase
PDB:	Program Definition Block
PDC:	Program Decision Control
PDC:	Programmable Data Controller
PDD:	Processor Description Database
PDD:	Program Described Data
PDD:	Program Description Document
PDD:	Program Design Data
PDF:	Packed Decimal Format
PDF:	Program Data File
PDF:	Program Development Facility
PDF:	Program Described File
PDG:	Program Documentation Generator
PDI:	Physical Data Independence
PDI:	Picture Description Instruction
PDL:	Page Definition Language
PDL:	Page Description Language
PDL:	Picture Description Language
PDL:	Procedure Definition Language
PDL:	Process Design Language

70

PDL:	Program Design Language
PDL:	Programmable Data Logger
PDL:	Programmed Digital Logic
PDL:	Push Down List
PDM:	Practical Data Manager
PDM:	Prerecorded Data Medium
PDM:	Preset Destination Mode
PDM:	Print Down Module
PDM:	Pull-Down Menu
PDO:	Program Directive-Operations
PDP:	Panel Definition Program
PDP:	Problem Determination Procedure
PDP:	Program Definition Phase
PDP:	Program Development Plan
PDQ:	Programmed Data Quantizer
PDR:	Preliminary Data Report
PDR:	Preliminary Design Review
PDR:	Price Description Record
PDR:	Priority Data Reduction
PDR:	Processing Data Rate
PDR:	Program Drum Recording
PDS:	Page Data Set
PDS:	Partitioned Data Set File
PDS:	Passed Data Set
PDS:	Personnel Data System
PDS:	Photo-Digital Store
PDS:	Physical Data Set
PDS:	Physical Data Structure
PDS:	Premises Distribution System
PDS:	Primary Display Sequence
PDS:	Print Data Set
PDS:	Procedures Development Simulator
PDS:	Professional Development Series
PDS:	Program Data Set
PDS:	Program Data Source
PDS:	Program Development System
PDS:	Programmable Data Station
PDS:	Protected Dynamic Storage
PDS:	Public Domain Software
PDT:	Program Development Time
PDT:	Program Development Tools
PDX:	Program Development EXecutive
PEA:	Push Effective Address
PEC:	Program Element Code
PED:	Personnel Equipment Data
PEK:	Phase-Exchange Keying
PEL:	Picture ELement
PEL:	Production Error Log
PEM:	Performance Enhancement Module
PEM:	Program Element Monitor
PEM:	Program Execution Monitor

PEN:	Parity ENable
PEP:	Paperless Electronic Payment
PEP:	Partitioned Emulation Programming
PEP:	Professional Education Program
PEP:	Program Evaluation Procedure
PER:	Post-Execution Reporting
PER:	Program Error Report
PER:	Program Event Recording
PER:	Program Event Request
PER:	Program Execution Request
PES:	Program Execution System
PET:	Process Evaluation Tester
PET:	Program Evaluator and Tester
PET:	Program Execution Time
PFA:	Paper Feed Aperture
PFA:	Production Flow Analysis
PFC:	Program Flow Chart
PFF:	Page Fault Frequency
PFI:	Physical Fault Insertion
PFK:	Program Function Key
PFM:	PerFormance Monitor
PFM:	Physical File Member
PFN:	Permanent File Name
PFP:	Programmable Function Panel
PFS:	Path Fault Secure
PFS:	ProFessional Series
PFS:	Programmable Frequency Standard
PFS:	Protected Free Storage
PFT:	Page Frame Table
PFT:	Program Fetch Time
PGC:	Programmed Gain Control
pgm:	program
PGP:	Presentation Graphics Program
PGR:	Presentation Graphic Routines
PGS:	Pacing Group Size
PGS:	Program Generation Sub-System
PGS:	Program Generation System
PGT:	PaGe Table
PGT:	Program Global Table
PHR:	PHysical Record
PHS:	Pattern Handling Statement
PIA:	Programmable Industrial Automation
PIC:	PICture Format
PIC:	Position Independent Code
PIC:	Priority Interrupt Controller
PIC:	Program Interrupt Control
PID:	Process ID Number
PIE:	Program Interrupt Entry
PIF:	Partially Inverted File
PIF:	Program Information File
PII:	Programmed Input Instructions
PIL:	Page Interchange Language

PIL:	Priority Interrupt Level	PMA:	Priority Memory Access
PIL:	Processing Information List	PMA:	Priority Memory Address
PIM:	Personal Information Manager	PMA:	Protected Memory Address
PIN:	Program Identification Number	PMC:	Pseudo Machine Code
PIO:	Parallel Input Output	PMD:	Post Mortem Dump
PIO:	Process Input-Output	PMF:	Payroll Master File
PIO:	Processor Input-Output	PMF:	Performance Monitor Function
PIO:	Program Input-Output	PMF:	Print Management Facility
PIP:	Peripheral Interchange Program	PMI:	Program Management Instruction
PIP:	Phased Implementation Plan	PML:	Programmable Macro Level
PIP:	Probabilistic Information Processing	PMP:	Performance Management Package
PIP:	Problem Input Preparation	PMP:	Photo Manipulation Program
PIP:	Project on Information Processing	PMP:	Preprocessed Macro Program
PIQ:	Parallel Instruction Queue	PMP:	Primary Memory Prime
PIR:	Print Intercept Routine	PMS:	Pantone Matching System
PIR:	Program Incident Report	PMS:	Parallel Multi-Spoolers
PIS:	Privileged Instruction Simulation	PMS:	Performance Management System
PIS:	Process Interrupt Signal	PMS:	Performance Measurement System
PIS:	Prototype Information System	PMS:	Process Management System
PIS:	Provider-Initiated Services	PMS:	Program Management System
PIT:	Processing Index Terms	PMS:	Project Management Software
PIT:	Program Instruction Tape	PMT:	PhotoMechanical Transfer
PIT:	Programmable Interface Translator	PMT:	Prepare Master Tape
PIT:	Programmable Interrupt Timer	PMW:	Project Manager Workbench
PIT:	Programmable Interval Timer	PNC:	Program Numerical Control
PIT:	Programmed Input Transfer	PND:	Present Next Digit
PIU:	Path Information Unit	PNS:	Positional Numbering System
PIX:	PIcture EXchange Format	POD:	Program Operation Description
PKA:	Public Key Algorithm	POF:	Programmed Operator Facility
PKC:	Public Key Cryptosystem	POI:	Program Of Instruction
pkg:	package	POI:	Program Operator Interface
PLA:	Page Layout Program	POL:	Problem-Oriented Language
PLA:	Print Load Analyzer	POL:	Procedure-Oriented Language
PLC:	Program Level Change	POL:	Process-Oriented Language
PLC:	Programming Language Committee	POM:	Program Operation Mode
PLD:	Partial Line Down	POP:	Programmed Operators and
PLD:	Physical Logical Description		Primitives
PL/E:	Programming Language/Edit	POP:	Program Operating Plan
PLF:	Page Length Field	POR:	Problem-Oriented Routine
PL/1:	Programming Language/1	POS:	Pink Operating System
PLL:	Phased-Locked Loop	POS:	Plant Operating System
PLM:	Programming Logic Manual	POS:	Point Of Sale
PLM:	Pulse Length Manual	POS:	Pregenerated Operating System
PL/M:	Programming Language for	POS:	Primary Operating System
	Microprocessor	POS:	Programmable Option Select
PLO:	Paper-Less Office	POS:	Program Order Sequence
PLP:	Presentation Level Protocol	POT:	Picture Object Table
PLP:	Procedural Language Processor	POT:	Programmed Output Transfer
PLR:	Program Library Release	PPA:	Professional Programmers
PLU:	Partial Line Up		Association
PLU:	Programmer Logical Unit	PPB:	Planning Programming Budgeting
PMA:	Physical Memory Address	PPC:	Parallel Poll Configure

PPC: Production Planning and Control
PPC: Program Planning and Control
PPD: Parallel Poll on this Device
PPE: Problem Program Efficiency
PPE: Problem Program Evaluator
PPE: Program Performance Evaluation
PPF: Program Preparation Facilities
PPI: Program Position Indicator
PPL: Polymorphic Programming Language
PPL: Print Positions Per Line
PPL: Program Production Library
PPM: Pages Per Minute
PPP: Programmed Production Planning
PPR: Playback Print Rate
PPS: Parallel Processing System
PPS: Patchboard Programming System
PPS: Programmed Processor System
PPS: Project Planning and Control System
PPT: Periodic Programs Termination
PPT: Primary Program Operator
Interface Task
PPT: Programmer Productivity Techniques
PPT: Program Production Time
PPU: PreProcessor Utility
PQA: Protected Queue Area
PQR: Productivity, Quality and Reliability
PQT: Preliminary Qualification Test
PRA: Page Replacement Algorithm
PRA: Primary Rate Access
PRA: PRint Alphanumerically
PRC: Partial Response Coding
PRC: Primary Return Code
PRC: PRinter Control
PRC: Programmed Route Control
PRC: Program Request Count
PRC: Program Request Credentials
PRD: Program Requirements Data
PRD: Program Requirements Document
PRF: Permanent Requirements File
PRG: Principal Register Group
PRH: Print Record Header
PRI: Physical Record Interface
pri: priority
PRI: Processing Research Institute
PRI: Pulse Repetition Interval
PRN: PRiNt
PRN: PRint Numerically
PRN: Print Record Number
pro: procedure
PRS: Program Requirements Summary
prt: print
PRT: Program Reference Table

PRV: Permanently Resident Volume
PSA: Primary Space Allocation
PSA: Program Statement Analyzer
PSB: Program Specification Block
PSC: PostScript Clone
PSC: Program Schedule Chart
PSC: Program Sequence Control Structure

Program Sequence Control Structure

PSC: Program Status Chart
PSC: Pure Serial Code
PSD: Peripheral Software Drivers
PSD: Program Status Documents
PSD: Program Status Doubleword
PSF: Program Sensitive Fault
PSI: Programmed Self-Instruction
PSI: Program Status Information
PSL: Processor Status Longword
PSL: Program Support Library
PSM: Programming Support Monitor
PSN: Print Sequence Number
PSO: Pilot Systems Operator
PSO: Primary System Operator
PSP: Planned Standard Programming
PSP: Pre-Sending Pause
PSP: Program Segment Prefix
PSR: Procedure Start Request
PSR: Program Status Report
PSR: Program Support Representative
PSS: Parallel Search Storage
PSS: Planned Systems Schedule
PSS: Programmable Store System
PST: Partition Specification Table
PST: Program Structure Technology
PSV: Program Status Vector
PSW: Program Status Word
PTB: Page Table Base
PTB: Parse Table Builder Utility

PTB:	Physical Translation Block	QCR:	Queue Control Record
PTC:	Paper Tape Code	QCS:	Quality Control System
PTC:	Punched Tape Code	QDT:	Queued Driven Task
ptd:	rinted	QED:	Quick EDitor
PTD:	Print-To-Disk	QIO:	Queued Input Output
PTD:	Programmable Threshold Detector	QIT:	Quality Information and Test
PTE:	Page Table Entry	QJN:	Qualified Job Name
PTE:	Page Translation Exception	QL/1:	Query Language One
PTE:	ProTect Error	QLP:	Query Language Processor
PTF:	Payroll Transaction File	QLR:	Queued Logon Request
PTF:	Program Temporary Fix	QMF:	Query Management Facility
PTI:	Program Transfer Interface	QON:	Qualified Object Name
PTL:	Process and Test Language	QPM:	Quality Program Manager
ptr:	pointer	QPS:	Queued Printing Services
PTR:	Programmer Trouble Report	Q&RA:	Quality & Reliability Assurance
PTS:	Program Test System	QRI:	Qualitative Requirements Informatio
PTS:	Pure Time Sharing	QRM:	Quiet Recording Mode
PTX:	Plus TwX	QRT:	Queue Run Time
PUB:	Physical Unit Block	QSL:	Queue Search Limit
PUD:	Physical Unit Directory	QTE:	QuickTime Extension
PUL:	Program Update Library	QTH:	Queued Transaction Handling
PUM:	Pop-Up Menu		
PUP:	Programmer User Profile		
PUT:	Program Update Tape		
PVR:	Process Variable Record		
PVS:	Program Validation Services		
PVT:	Parameter Variable Table		
PVT:	Performance Validation Test		
PVV:	PIN Verification Values		
PWB:	Programmer's WorkBench		
PWF:	PreWired Functions		
PWI:	Public Windows Interface		
PWO:	Partial Write Operation		
PWR:	Processor WRite		
PWS:	Programmer Work Station		
PWT:	Page Write Through		
PZC:	Point of Zero Charge		

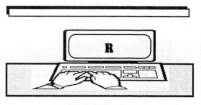

RAA: Real Address Area
RAC: Read Address Counter
RAD: Random Access Data
RAF: Random Access File
RAF: Record Address File
RAF: Requirements Analysis Form
RAI: Random Access and Inquiry
RAL: Random Access Loop
RAL: Row Address Line
RAM: Random Access Method
RAM: Reliability, Availability and
      Maintainability
RAP: Resident Assembly Program
RAP: Response Analysis Program
RAP: Review and Analysis Program
RAR: Rapid Access Recording
RAS: Random Access Storage
RAS: Rapid Access Storage
RAS: Real Address Storage
RAS: Resource Access Security
RAW: Read After Write
RAX: Random Access
RBA: Relative Byte Address

QAM: Queued Access Method
QAM: Quick Access Memory
QBD: Quasi Bi-Directional
QBE: Query-By-Example
QCB: Queue Control Block
QCF: Quick Cell Facility
QCM: Quantitative Computer Management

RBC:	Reflected Binary Code	REX:	Real-Time EXecutive Routine
RBD:	Reliability Block Diagram	REX:	Real-Time EXecutive System
RBE:	Remote Batch Entry	RFA:	Remote File Access
RBF:	Remote Batch Facility	RFB:	Reliability Functional Block
RBM:	Real-Time Batch Monitor	RFD:	Ready For Data
RBM:	Record-Based Model	RFD:	Record Format Descriptor
RBM:	Relative Batch Monitor	RFG:	Report Format Generator
RBM:	Remote Batch Module	RFI:	Request For Information
RBP:	Registered Business Programmer	RFP:	Request For Programming
RBP:	Remote Batch Processing	RFP:	Request For Proposal
RBS:	Rule Based System	RFQ:	Request For Quotation
RCB:	Resource Control Block	RFS:	Random Filing System
RCC:	Read Channel Continue	RFS:	Real File Store
rcd:	reCord	RFS:	Remote File Sharing (AT &T)
RCI:	Read Channel Initialize	RFS:	Remote File Store (AT &T)
RCI:	Remote Control Interface	RFS:	Report Forwarding System
RCL:	Reloadable ControL Storage	RFT:	Request For Test
RCP:	Resident Control Program	RGL:	Report Generator Language
RCR:	Required Carrier Return Character	RHA:	Records Holding Area
RCS:	Remote Control Software	RHI:	Right Hand Indent
RCS:	Repetition Control Structure	RHP:	Retail Host Program
RCT:	Read Cycle Time	RIB:	Renderman Interface Byte Stream
RCW:	Return Control Word	RIC:	Read-In Counter
RDA:	Register Display Assembly	RID:	Review Item Disposition
RDA:	Reliability Design Analysis	RIH:	Read InHibit
RDA:	Run-Time Debugging Aid	RIL:	Representation Independent
RDB:	Recreatable Data Base		Language
RDB:	Relational DataBase	RIM:	Read-Indirect Mode
RDC:	Reliability Data Center	RIM:	Read-In Mode
RDC:	Remote Distribution Center	RIM:	Read Interrupt Mask
RDE:	Remote Data Entry	RIM:	Resource Interface Module
RDF:	Record Definition Field	RIO:	Relocatable Input Output
RDF:	Remote Diagnostic Facility	RIO:	Remote Input Output
RDF:	Reverse Direction Flow	RIP:	Random InPut Sampling
RD/I:	Research, Development	RIP:	Rest In Position Printing Code
	and Innovation	RIP:	Rest In Proportion
RDL:	Random Dynamic Load	RIS:	Recorded Information Service
RDL:	Report Definition Language	RIS:	Record Input Subroutine
RDP:	Relational Database Processor	RIS:	Revolution Indicating System
RDR:	Receive Data Ready	RJE:	Remote Job Entry
RDS:	Random Data Set	RJO:	Remote Job Output
RDT:	Resource Definition Table	RLC:	Recording Level Control
rec:	record	RLC:	Run Length Code
ref:	reference	RLD:	ReLocation Dictionary
REJ:	REJect	RLI:	Recording Level Indicator
REM:	REMarks	RLL:	Relocating Linking Loader
REN:	Remote ENable	RLL:	Run Length Limited Encoding
REN:	REName	RLM:	Resident Load Module
RER:	ReEntrant Routine	RLS:	Record Level Specifications
RER:	Residual Error Rate	RMA:	Random Multiple Access
RER:	Retail Exit Routines	RMA:	Reliability, Maintainability,
RES:	REStore		Availability

RMA:	Return Material Authorization Number	RPS:	Records Per Second
RMB:	Right Most BIT	RPS:	Records Per Sector
RMC:	Rack-Mount Control	RPS:	Remote Printing System
RMF:	Resource Management Facility	RPS:	Remote Processing Service
RMF:	Resource Measurement Facility	RPS:	Remote Processing System
RML:	Relational Machine Language	RPS:	Requirements Planning System
RMM:	Read Most Mode	RPS:	Resident Program Storage
RMO:	Read Modified Operation	RPT:	Records Per Track
RMP:	Re-Entry Measurements Program	rpt:	repeat
RMS:	Random Mass Storage	RPT:	RePeaT Character
RMS:	Record Management System	RPT:	Request Programs Termination
RMS:	Recovery Management Support	RPU:	Regional Processing Unit
RMS:	Remote Manipulator System	R&QA:	Reliability & Quality Assurance
RMS:	Root Mean Square	R&QC:	Reliability & Quality Control
RMT:	Real-Time Multi-Tasking System	RQE:	Reply Queue Element
RMT:	ReMoTe	RRA:	Remote Record Access
RMW:	Read Modify Write	RRG:	Resource Request Generator
RNC:	Request Next Character	RRN:	Relative-Record Number
RNR:	Receive Not Ready	RRR:	Run-Time Reduction Ratio
ROA:	Return On Assets	RRS:	Reference Retrieval Systems
ROF:	Remote Operator Facility	RRT:	Relative Retention Time
ROI:	Rate On Investment	RSA:	Real Sector Access
ROP:	Read-Only Protection	RSC:	Record Separator Character
ROS:	Read-Only Storage	RSC:	Remote Store Controller
ROS:	Real-Time Operating System	RSD:	Responsible System Designer
ROS:	Resident Operating System	RSE	Real Systems Environment
RPB:	Remote Programming Box	RSE:	Record Selection Expression
RPB:	Required Page Break	RSE:	Request Select Entry
RPC:	Regional Processing Center	RSF:	Remote Support Facility
RPC:	Registered Protective Circuit	RSI:	Rationalization, Standardization and Integration
RPC:	Row Parity Check	RS&I:	Rules, Standards & Instructions
RPE:	Required Page-End Character	RSL:	Requirements Statement Language
RPE:	Resource Planning And Evaluation	RSM:	Real Storage Management
RPG:	Raster Pattern Generator	RSN:	Real Soon Now
RPG:	Report Program Generator	RSO:	Real System Operator
RPI:	Read, Punch and Interpret	RSO:	Regional Standards Organization
RPI:	Rows Per Inch	RSP:	Record Selector Program
RPL:	Remote Program Loader	RSP:	Required SPace
RPL:	Requester Privilege Level	RSS:	Relational Storage System
RPL:	Request Parameter List	RSS:	Remote Shutdown System
RPL:	Robot Programming Language	RSS:	Repeated Selection Sort
RPL:	Running Program Language	RST:	Read Symbol Table
RPM:	Rate Per Minute	RST:	Remote STation
RPN:	Real Page Number	rst:	reSet
RPN:	Reverse Polish Notation	RSX:	Real-Time Resource-Sharing EXecutive
RPO:	Raster Pattern Overlay		
RPO:	Reserved Page Option	RSX:	Resource Sharing EXecutive (DEC)
RPQ:	Request Price Quotation		
RPS:	Raster Pattern Storage	RTA:	Real-Time Analyzer
RPS:	Real-Time Processing System	RTA:	Real-Time Application
RPS:	Real-Time Programming System	RTA:	Resident Transient Area

RTB: Real-Time BASIC
RTB: Response/Throughput Bias
RTC: Real-Time Command
RTC: Remote Terminal Controller
RTD: Read Tape Decimal
RTD: Real-Time Display
R&TD: Research & Technological
       Development
RTE: Real-Time Executive
RTE: Remote Terminal Emulator
RTE: Request To Expedite
RTE: Run Time Error
RTF: Real-Time FORTRAN
RTF: Rich Text Format
RTI: Real-Time Interface
RTI: Referred To Input
RTI: ReTurn from Interrupt
RTI: Road Transport Informatics
RTJ: ReTurn Jump
RTL: Read Through Locks
RTL: Real-Time Language
RTL: Real-Time Library
RTM: Real-Time Management
RTM: Recovery Termination Manager
RTM: Register-Transfer Module
rtn: return
RTO: Real-Time Operation
RTO: Referred To Output
RTP: Real-Time Processing
RTP: Remote Transaction Program
RTP: Requirement and
       Test Procedures
RTP: Run-Time Package
RTR: Real-Time Reliability
RTR: Response Time Reporting
RTS: Real-Time Simulation
RTS: Real-Time Subroutines
RTS: Real-Time System
RTS: Reliable Transfer Service
RTS: Relocatable Task Set
RTS: Remote Testing System
RTV: Run Time Variable
RTW: Run Through Work
RTX: Real-Time EXecutive
RTZ: Return To Zero
RUC: Reporting Unit Code
RUD: Recently Used Directory
RUM: Resource Utilization Monitor
RUN: Rewind and UNload
RUT: Resource Utilization Time
RVA: Reactive Volt-Ampere Meter

RVA: Relative Virtual Address
RVI: ReVerse Interrupt
RVR: Runway Visual Range
RVT: Reliability Verification Tests
RVT: Resource Vector Table
RWD: ReWinD
RWI: Read-Write-Initialize
RWM: Random Walk Method
RWO: Routine Work Order
RWS: Read/Write Storage
RWT: Read/Write Tested
RWX: Read Write EXecute
RZL: Return to Zero Level
RZM: Return to Zero Mark
RZ(P): Polarized Return-To-Zero

SAA: Service Action Analysis
SAA: Servo-Actuated Assembly
SAA: System Application Architecture
SAB: Stack Access Block
SAB: System Advisory Board
SAC: Semi-Automatic Coding
SAC: Serving Area Concept
SAC: Storage Access Control
SAD: Store Address Director
SAD: Structured Analysis and Design
SAD: System Analysis Drawing
SAE: Stand-Alone Executive
SAF: Segment Address Field
SAF: Specification Approval Form
SAF: Structural Adjustment Facility
SAG: Screen Anti-Glare
SAG: Standard Address Generator
SAG: Systems Analysis Group
SAI: Single Address Instruction
SAL: Service Action Log
SAL: Specialized Application Language
SAL: Structured Assembly Language
SAL: Symbolic Assembly Language
SAL: Systems Assembly Language
SAM: Semi-Automatic Mathematics
SAM: Service Attitude Measurement
SAM: Sequential Access Method (IBM)
SAM: Simulation of Analog Methods
SAM: Software Acquisition Management

SAM:	Sort And Merge	SCI:	Society of Computer Intelligence
SAM:	Symbolic and Algebraic Manipulation	SCI:	Stacker Control Instruction
SAM:	System Activity Monitor	SCI:	System Control Interface
SAM:	System Analysis Module	SCL:	Sequential Control Logic
SAO:	Select Address and Operate	SCL:	Supervisory Control Language
SAO:	Single Association Object	SCL:	System Control Language
SAO:	Systems Analysis Office	SCM:	Service Command Module
SAP:	Secondary Application Program	SCM:	Shorthand Customer Module
SAP:	Service Access Point	SCM:	Single Conditioning Module
SAP:	Share Assembly Program	SCM:	Software Configuration Management
SAP:	Structural Analysis Program	SCP:	Supervisory Control Program
SAP:	Symbolic Address Program	SCP:	Symbolic Conversion Program
SAR:	Search-And-Replace	SCP:	System Control Program
SAS:	Self Adapting System	SCR:	Software Change Report
SAS:	Sequential Access Storage	SCR:	System Change Request
SAS:	Serial Access Storage	SCS:	Selection Control Structure
SAS:	Spool Access Support	SCS:	Sequence Control Structure
SAS:	Statistical Analysis System	SCS:	Shared Computer System
SBA:	Shared Batch Area		
SBA:	Strategic Business Area		
SBC:	Serialized Block Code		
SBD:	Structured Block Diagram		
SBI:	Single Byte Interleaved		
SBK:	Sequential By Key		
SBM:	Semantic Binary Model		
SBM:	Space Block Map		
SBP:	Sequential Batch Processing		
SBS:	SuBScript		
SBT:	Six-BIT Transcode	SCS:	Simulation-Control Subsystem
SCA:	Sequence Control Area	SCS:	SNA Character String
SCA:	Sneak Circuit Analysis	SCS:	Society for Computer Simulation
SCA:	Source Code Address	SCS:	Southern Computer Service
SCA:	System Control Area	SCS:	Store Controller Storage
SCB:	Segment Control Bit	SCS:	Switch Control Statement
SCB:	Stack Control Block	SCT:	Special Characters Table
SCB:	Stream Control Block	SCT:	Step Control Table
SCB:	String Control Byte	SDA:	Screen Design Aid
SCC:	Self Checking Codes	SDA:	Source Data Acquisition
SCC:	Self Correcting Code	SDA:	Source-Data Automation
SCC:	Sequential Control Counter	SDA:	Supply Data Approval
SCC:	Source Code Compatibility	SDA:	System Data Analyzer
SCC:	Standards Council of Canada	SDA:	System Design Aid
SCD:	Service Computation Data	SDB:	Segment Descriptor Block
SCD:	Store Controller Data	SDB:	Software Development Board
SCD:	System Contents Directory	SDC:	Shopfloor Data Collection
SCE:	Situation Caused Error	SDC:	Shopfloor Data Control
SCF:	System Control Facility	SDC:	Simple Delivery Control
SCF:	System Control File	SDC:	Software Development Cycle
SCG:	Stroke Character Generator	SDC:	Software Distribution Center
sch:	schedule	SDC:	System-Defined Catalog
sch:	scheduler	SDD:	Software Design Description

SDD:	Stored Data Description	SEA:	Static Error Analysis
SDD:	System Design Description	SEA:	Systems Effectiveness Analyzer
SDD:	System for Distributed Databases	SEB:	Storage Expansion Blank
SDE:	Society for Data Educators	SED:	Spelling Error Detection
SDE:	Software Development Environment	SED	Split Edit Display
SDE:	Source Data Entry	SEF:	Software Engineering Facility
SDE:	Students for Data Education	SEF:	Standard External File
SDF:	Screen Definition Facility	seg:	segment
SDF:	Software Development Facility	SEG:	Special Effects Generator
SDF:	Summary Data Field	SEG:	Standardization Evaluation Group
SDH:	Synchronous Digital Hierarchy	SEI:	Single-Ends Inputs
SDI:	Selective Dissemination of Information	SEI:	Systems Engineering and Integration
SDI:	Source Data Information	sel:	select
SDI:	Static Display Image	SEL:	Digital SELectors
SDI:	Strategic Defense Initiative	SEL:	Self-Extensible Programming Language
SD-I:	Standardization DIrectory	SEL:	System Error Log
SDK:	Software Development Kit	SEM:	Standard Estimating Module
SDK:	System Design Kit	SEN:	Scanning ENcoding
SDL:	Software Design Language	SEN:	Software Error Notification
SDL:	Software Development Language	SEP:	Systematic Evaluation Program
SDL:	Specification and Description Language	seq:	sequence
		seq:	sequential
SDL:	System Descriptive Language	ser:	serial
SDL:	System Design Language	SES:	System External Storage
SDM:	Semantic Data Models	SET:	Schedule Engineering Time
SDM:	Standardization Design Memoranda	SET:	Self-Extending Translator
SDM:	Station Debugged Module	SET:	Software Engineering Terminology
SDM:	Stored Data Manager	SET:	Standard Exchange and Transfer
SDM:	Symbolic Description Map	SEU:	Source Entry Utility
SDM:	Systems Development Methodology	SEW:	Software Engineering Workbench
SDP:	Source Data Processing	SFA:	Segment Frequency Algorithm
SDR:	Statistical Data Recorder	SFC:	Sectored File Controller
SDR:	System Definition Record	SFC:	Spool File Class
SDR:	System Design Review	SFC:	System Flow Chart
SDS:	Scientific Data Systems	SFD:	Simple Formattable Document
SDS:	Secondary Display Sequence	SFD:	Software Functional Description
SDS:	Sequential Data Set	SFD:	Start Frame Delimiter
SDS:	Simulation Data Subsystems	SFE:	Smart Front-End
SDS:	Software Development Specifications	SFI:	Stored Format Instruction
		SFO:	Sequential File Organization
SDS:	Software Development System	SFO:	Start Field Order
SDS:	Software Distribution Services	SFS:	Symbolic File Support
SDS:	Sparse Data Scan	Sft:	Shift
SDS:	Subsystem Definition Statement	SFT:	Spool File Tag
SDS:	Swap Data Set	SGA:	Shareable Global Area
SDS:	System Data Set	SGD:	Self-Generating Dictionary
SDT:	Syntax-Directed Translation	SGP:	Statistical Gathering Program
SDT:	System Down Time	SGP:	Statistical Generation Program
SDU:	Source Data Utility	SGS:	Status Group Select
SDV:	Soft Dollar Value	SGT:	SeGment Table
SDW:	Segment Descriptor Word	SHA:	Software Houses Association (UK)

SHC:	Syllable Hyphen Character	SLE:	Sequential Logic Element
SHL:	Studio to Head-End Link	SLI:	System Load and Initialization
SHL:	System Handshake Logic	SLM:	Second Level Message
SHS:	System Help Support	SLM:	Single Lock Manager
SHS:	System Hold Status	SLM:	Storage Load Module
SHY:	Syllable HYphen	SLO:	Segment Limits Origin
SIA:	Software Industry Association	SLP:	Segmented Level Programming
SID:	Society for Information Displays (USA)	SLP:	Single Link Procedure
		SLP:	Source Language Processor
SIF:	Spooled Input File	SLP:	Symbolic Language Program
SIF:	Storage Interface Facility	SLS:	Second Level Statement
SIF:	System's Information File	SLS:	Second Level Storage
SIG:	Special Interest Group	SLS:	Storage Location Selection
SIL:	Scanner Input Language	SLS:	Source Library System
SIL:	Store Interface Link	SLU:	Service Level Update
SIL:	System Information Library	SLU:	Source Library Update
SIM:	Set Initialization Mode	SMC:	SysteMs Science and Cybernetics
SIM:	Set Interrupt Mask	SMF:	Storage Mapping Function
sim:	simulator	SMF:	Systems Management Facilities
SIN:	Symbolic INtegrator	SMG:	Super Master Group
SIO:	Simultaneous Interface Operation	SMG:	System Management Group
SIO:	Serial Input Output	SMI:	Structure of Management Information
SIO:	Start Input Output	SMI:	System Management Interrupt
SIP:	Self Interpreting Program Generator	SMK:	System Monitor Kernel
SIP:	Symbolic Input Program	SML:	Source Module Library
SIR:	Selective Information Retrieval	SML:	Spool Multi-Leaving
SIR:	Semantic Information Retrieval	SML:	Symbolic Machine Language
SIR:	Simultaneous Impact Rate	SMM:	Start of Manual Message
SIR:	Statistical Information Retrieval	SMM:	System Management Mode
SIR:	Stratified Indexing and Retrieval	SMM:	System Management Monitor
SIR:	Symbolic Input Routine	SMP:	Sort Merge Program
SIS:	Shorter Interval Scheduling	SMP:	Symmetric Multi-Processing
SIS:	Simulation Interface Subsystem	SMP:	System Management Protocol
SIS:	Scientific Information System	SMP:	System Modification Program
SIS:	Scientific Instruction Set	SMR:	Series Mode Rejection
SIS:	Software Integrated Schedule	SMR:	Shift-Out Modular Redundancy
SIS:	Special Interest Sub-group	SMR:	Single Mode Rejection
SIS:	Standard Instruction Set	SMS:	Self-Monitoring System
SIS:	System Interrupt Supervisor	SMS:	Storage Management System
SIT:	Software Integration Test	SMS:	System Monitor Session
SIT:	System Integration Test	SNI:	Selective Notification of Information
SJF:	Shortest Job First	SNT:	System Name Table
SJP:	Stacked Job Processing	SOB:	Start Of Block
SKU:	Stock Keeping Unit	SOC:	Simulation Operations Center
SLA:	Synchronous Line Adapter	SOC:	Span Of Control
SLC:	Shift Left and Count Instructions	SOC:	Start Of Conversion
SLC:	Software Life Cycle	SOD:	Serial Output Data
SLC:	System Life Cycle	SOD:	System Operational Design
SLD:	Second Level Directory	SOE:	Significant Operating Experience
SLD:	Single Line Display	SOF:	Spooled Output File
SLD:	Source Language Debug	SOF:	Start-Of-Format
SLE:	Segment Limits End	SOF:	Structured Oriented FORTRAN

SOI:	Specific Operating Instruction	SPR:	System Parameter Record
SOI:	Standard Operating Instruction	SPS:	String Process System
SOL:	Simulation Oriented Language	SPS:	SuPersCript Character
SOL:	System Oriented Language	SPS:	Symbolic Programming System
SOP:	Simulation Operations Plan	SPT:	Shadow Page Table
SOP:	Special Operating Procedure	SPT:	Structured Programming Technique
SOP:	Standard Operating Procedure	SPT:	Symbolic Program Translator
SOR:	Statement Of Requirement	SPT:	System Parameter Table
SOS:	Save Often, Sweetie	SQA:	Software Quality Assurance
SOS:	Share Operating System	SQA:	System Queue Area
SOS:	Start Of Significance	SQI:	Software Quality Initiative
SOS:	Symbolic Operating System	SQL:	Structured Query Language
SOT:	Start Of Text	SQP:	Standard Quality Print
SOT:	Syntax Oriented Translator	SRA:	Self-Relative Address
SOW:	System Output Writer	SRA:	Self-Relative Addressing
SPA:	Scratch Pad Area	SRA:	Systems Requirements Analysis
SPA:	Software Publishers' Association (USA)	SRB:	Service Request Block
		src:	source
SPA:	Systems Programmed Application	SRC:	Stored Response Chain
SPC:	Small Peripheral Controller	SRC:	Strategic Review Committee
SPC:	Software & Publication Center (IBM)	SRC:	System Reference Code
SPC:	Software Publishing Corporation	SRD:	Secondary Receive Data
SPC:	Statistical Process Control	SRD:	Software Requirements Document
SPC:	Stored Program Concept	SRE:	Single Region Execution
SPC:	Stored Program Control	SRE:	Stored Reference Equivalent
SPC:	Stored Programmed Command	SRF:	Secondary Record Format
SPD:	Software Product Description	SRF:	Software Recording Facility
SPE:	Serial Poll Enable	SRF:	Software Recovery Facility
SPE:	Single Processing Element	SRF:	System Recorder File
SPE:	Signal Processing Element	SRF:	System Resident File
SPF:	Standard Program Facility (IBM)	SRF:	System Response Field
SPF:	Structured Programming Facility	SRI:	Stored Record Interface
SPG:	Sort Program Generator	SRL:	Scheme Representation Language
SPI:	Self-Paced Instruction	SRL:	Square Root Limiter
SPI:	Single Programming Initiator	SRL:	Structured Return Loss
SPI:	Software Products International	SRM:	System Resource Manager (IBM)
SPK:	Storage Protection Key	SRN:	System Reference Number
SPL:	Simulation Programming Language	SRP:	Self-Relocating Program
SPL:	Software Programming Language	SRP:	Shared Resource Processing
SPL:	Source Program Library	SRQ:	Service ReQuest
SPL:	Spaceborne Programming Language	SRR:	Secondary Receive Ready
SPL:	Special Purpose Language	SRR:	Serially Reusable Resource
SPL:	Structured Programming Language	SRR:	Software Requirement Review
SPL:	System Program Loader	SRR:	System Requirement Review
SPL:	System Programming Language	SRS:	Software Requirements Specification
SPM:	Software Project Management	SRT:	Segmentation Register Table
SPM:	Source Program Maintenance	SRT:	Selective Repeat Technique
SPM:	System Planning Manual	SRV:	System Residence Volume
SPO:	Separate Partition Option	SSA:	Save System Allocation
SPO:	System Program Office	SSA:	Segment Search Arguments
SPP:	Special-Purpose Program	SSA:	Skip Sequential Access

SSB:	Scanning Spot Beam	SUM:	System Utilization Monitor
SSD:	Structured Systems Design	SUP:	Set Up Program
SSE:	Start Stop Envelope	sup:	supervisor
SSG:	Symbolic Stream Generator	SUP:	System Utility Program
SSI:	Storage-to-Storage Instruction	SUS:	Start-Up Screen
SSL:	Scientific Subroutine Library	SUW:	Synchronized Unit of Work
SSL:	Software Specific Language	SVP:	Software Verification Plan
SSL:	Source Statement Library	SVR:	Software Verification Report
SSL:	Storage Structure Language	SVR:	Specific Volume Request
SSL:	System Specification Language	SWA:	Scheduler Work Area
SSM:	Soft System Methodology	SWA:	System Work Area
SSN:	Segment Stack Number	SWE:	Status Word Enable
SSO:	Single Step Operation	SWI:	SoftWare Interrupt Instruction
SSP:	Scientific Subroutine Package	SWL:	Software Writer's Language
SSP:	Spread Sheet Program	SWM:	SoftWare Monitor
SSP:	Store Support Procedure	SWS:	SoftWare Services
SSP:	Subsystem Support Program	SWT:	Structured Walk Through
SSP:	System Service Program	sym:	symbol
SSP:	System Support Program	sym:	system
SSR:	Software Specification Review	sys:	system
SSR:	System Status Report		

SSS: Sequential Scheduling System
SSS: Software System Services
SSS: Software Support System
SSS: Software System Support
SSS: Sort Sequence Specification
SST: Sibling Segment Type
SST: System Scheduler Table
SST: System Segment Table
STA: Spanning Tree Algorithm
STC: STart Conversion
STD: Science and Technology for
        Development (EEC)
std: standard
STE: Segment Table Entry
STF: Supervisory Time Frame
stk: stack
STM: Static Test Mode
STO: Segment Table Origin
STP: Space Test Program
STP: SToP Character
sts: status
STS: Storage Tab Setting
STS: Structural Transition Section
S/TS: Simulator/Test Set
STT: Seek Time per Track
STT: Single Transition Time
STX: Start of TeXt
STW: Software Test Workshop
SUB: SUBroutine
SUB: SUBstitute Character
SUM: Single-User Multi-Tasking

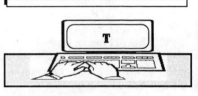

TAA: Typical Address Access Time
TAB: TABular Language
TAC: Translator Assembler Compiler
TAD: Terminal Address Designator
TAD: Transaction Applications Driver
TAD: Turn Around Document
TAE: Tough Applications Enabler
TAF: Time And Frequency
TAF: TransAction Facility
TAG: Technical Advisory Group
TAL: Tandem Application Language
TAL: Terminal Application Language
TAL: Transaction Application Language
TAM: Terminal Access Method
TAN: TrAnsaction Number
TAP: Terminal Access Protocol
TAP: Terminal Applications Package
TAP: Test Assistance Program
TAP: Time sharing Assembly Program
TAS: Tag-Along Sort
TAS: Test And Set
TAT: Turn Around Time
TBD: Test Bed Debugger
TBI: Time Between Inspections

TBS:	Traditional Business Systems	TIF:	Tagged Image File
TCB:	Transaction Control Block	TIF:	Tagged Image Format
TCE:	Terminal Control Element	TIF:	Tape Inventory File
TCL:	Terminal Command Language	TIF:	Terminal Independent Format
TCL:	Terminal Control Language	TIM:	Table Input to Memory
TCL:	Time and Cycle Log	TIP:	Technical Information Program
TCL:	Transaction Control Language	TIO:	Test Input Output
TCM:	Tightly Couple Multiprocessing	TIQ:	Task Input Queue
TCN:	Throughput Class Negotiation	TLA:	Time Line Analysis
TCP:	Tape Conversion Program	TLC:	Task Level Controller
TCP:	Task Control Program	TLS:	Tape Librarian System
TCP:	Terminal Control Program	TLU:	Table Look-Up
TCS:	Transaction Command Security	TML:	Tutorial & Message Library
TCS:	Transaction Control System	TMO:	TiMe Out
TCT:	Terminal Control Table	TMP:	Terminal Monitor Program
TCT:	Transaction Control Table	TMS:	Table Management System
TCT:	Translator and Code Treatment Frame	TMS:	Tape Management System
TDA:	Top-Down Approach	TMS:	Text Management System
TDD:	Top-Down Design	TMS:	Test Mode Select
TDD:	Top Down Development	TNF:	Third Normal Form
TDE:	Total Data Entry	TNZ:	Transfer on Non-Zero
TDF:	Transnational Data Flows	TOF:	Top Of File
TDG:	Test Data Generator	TOF:	Top Of Form
TDI:	Test Data Input	TOL:	Test Oriented Language
TDL:	Terminal Display Language	TOM	Tear-Off Menu
TDL:	Transaction Definition Language	TOM:	Type Over Mode
TDL:	Transformation Definition Language	TOP:	Transaction-Oriented Processing
TDM:	Top Down Method	TOS:	Tape Operations System
TDM:	Tray Delivery Mechanism	TOS:	Text Oriented Software
TDO:	Test Data Output	TOS:	Type Of Service
TDP:	Teradata Director Program	TOT:	Transfer Overhead Time
TDP:	Test Data Package	TPA:	Transient Program Area
TDP:	Top Down Programming	TPA:	Transitory Program Area
TDS:	Target Data Set	TPA:	Two-Pass Assembler
TDS:	Temporary Data Set	TPC:	Transaction Processing Council
TDS:	Transaction Distribution System	TPC:	Transverse Parity Check
TDT:	Top Down Testing	TPD:	Transaction Processing Description
TDT:	Typed Data Transfer	TPE:	Transaction Processing Executive
TDW:	Terminal Debugger Windows	TPG:	Technology Planning Group
TEA:	Task Execution Area	TPL:	Table Producing Language
TED:	Text EDitor	TPL:	Terminal Processing Language
TEI:	Terminal Endpoint Identifier	TPL:	Terminal Programming Language
TEL:	Task Execution Language	TPL:	Test Procedure Language
TEP:	Terminal Error Program	TPL:	Traditional Programming Language
TES:	Text Editing System	TPL:	Transaction Processing Language
TFA:	Transaction Flow Auditing	TPR:	Transaction Processing Routine
TFM:	Time File Management	TPS:	Terminal Polling System
TFR:	Transaction Formatting Routines	TPS:	Terminal Programming System
TFS:	Tape File Supervisor	tps:	transaction per Sec
TGL:	Third Generation Languages	TPS:	Transaction Processing System
TIC:	Terminal's Identification Code	TPS:	Transaction Program Support
TID:	Tuple IDentifier	TPS:	Turbo Pascal for Windows

TQM: Total Quality Management
TQP: Typeset Quality Print
TQS: Transaction Query Subroutine
tra: transfer
TRC: Tape Record Coordinator
TRC: Technical Review Committee
TRC: Telemetry & Remote Control
trf: transfer
TRH: Transaction Record Header
TRL: True Run List
TRM: Terminal Response Mode
TRP: Text and Retrieval Program
TRQ: Task Ready Queue
TRR: Transaction Routing Routines
TRS: Tape Resident System
TRS: Time Reference System
trs: transpose text
TRW: Tape Request Word
trx: transaction
TSA: Traditional Systems Approach
TSB: Terminal Status Block
TSC: Terminal Server Configuration
TSC: Total Systems Concept
TSC: Totally Self Checking
TSE: Terminal Source Editor
TSE: Time Sharing Executive
TSE: Translation Specification Exception
TSI: Task Set Installation
TSI: Text Screen Image
tsk: task
TSL: Test Source Library
TSL: Time Series Language
TSL: Time Sharing Library
TSM: Terminal Server Manager
TSM: Terminal Specific Module
TSM: Terminal Support Module
TSM: Time Shared Monitor
TSM: Tutorial Sample Mode
TSO: Time Sharing Option
TSP: Task-Scheduling Priorities
TSP: Temperature Sensitive Parameter
TSR: Terminate and Stay
       Resident Program
TSS: Task State Segment
TSS: Time Sharing System
TSS: Time Sharing Subsystem
tst: test
TST: Transaction Step Task
TSX: Time Sharing EXecutive
TTD: Temporary Text Delay
TTE: Terminal Table Entry

TTE: Translation Table Entry
TTF: Terminal Transaction Facility
TTM: Transparent Text Mode
TTM: Tutorial Text Mode
TTP: Tape To Print
TTS: Transaction Tracing System
TTX: TeleTeX
TUT: Transistor Under Test
TWA: Transaction Work Area
TWS: Translator Writing System

UAC: Uninterrupted Automatic Control
UAE: Unrecoverable Application Errors
UAE: User Agent Entity
UAF: Unit Authorization File
UAF: User Action Frame
UAF: User Authorization File
UAK: Unique Alternate Key
UAL: Unit Authorization List
UAP: User Area Profile
UAT: User Accounting Table
UBC: User Buffer Controller
UBI: Unconditional Branch Instruction
UBS: Unit BackSpace Character
UCA: Upper Control Area
UCB: Unit Control Block
UCF: Utility Control Facility
UCS: Universal Call Sequence
UCS: Universal Character Set
UCS: User Control Store
UCS: Utility Control Statement
UCW: Unit Control Word
UDB: User Data Buffer
UDC: Universal Decimal Classification
UDC: Universal Digital Control
UDE: Universal Data Entry
UDL: Uniform Data Language
UDS: Unload Data Set
UDS: User Data Set
UDS: Utility Definition Specification
UEQ: User Exit Queue
UER: User Exit Request
UFD: User File Directory
UFI: User Friendly Interface
UFM: User-To-File Manager

84

UFO: User Files OnLine
UFP: Utility Facilities Program
UGT: User Group Table
UHS: User Hold Status
UIA: User Input Area
UIC: User Identification Code
UID: User IDentifier (UNIX)
UIG: User Instruction Group
UIL: UNIVAC Interactive Language
UIO: Universal Input/Output
UIS: Universal Instruction Set
UIS: User Interface System
UJI: Unconditional Jump Instruction
ULB: Universal Logic Block
UL1: User Language 1
UMS: Unbalanced Merge Sort
UMS: Universal Multi-Programming
System
UOR: Updated-Only Recovery
UOS: UNIX Operating System
UPA: User Program Area
UPC: Universal Peripheral Control
UPI: Unformatted Program Interface
UPL: Universal Programming Language
UPL: Upper Print Line
UPL: User Programming Language
UPP: Universal PROM Programmer
UPS: Universal Processing System
UPT: User Process Table
UQT: User Queue Table
URA: User Requirements Analysis
URC: Unit Record Control
URL: User Requirement Language
URM: Updated-Record Mark
USC: User Service Class
USF: Uniformly Spaced Font
USF: User Task Set¹
USI: User System Interface
USL: UNIX Software Laboratories
USP: Usage Sensitive Pricing
USR: User Service Routine
USS: Unformatted System Services
UST: User Symbol Table
UTA: User Transfer Address
UTI: Unconditional Transfer Instruction
UTP: User Transient Program
UTS: Unbound Task Set
UUA: UNIVAC Users Association
UWA: User Working Area

VAA: Virtual Address Area
VAD: Value-Added Dealer
VAL: Velocity Acceleration Language
VAM: Virtual Access Method
VAP: Value-Added Process
VAR: Value-Added Reseller
var: variable
var: variation
VAS: Value-Added Service
VAS: Virtual Address Space
VAT: Virtual Address Translator
VAU: Vertical Arithmetic Unit
VAX: Virtual Address EXtended
VBI: Vertical Blanking Interval
VCF: Virtual Call Facility
VCP: Virtual Control Panel
VCS: Vision Control System
VDD: Vertical Drop Distance
VDD: Visual Display Data
VDI: Video Display Input
VDI: Visual Display Input
VDL: Virtual Database Level
VDP: Vertical Data Processing
VDR: Vertically Displayed Records
VEC: Videotex Enquiry Center
VER: Valid Exclusive Reference
ver: verify
VFC: Variable File Channel
VFD: Vacuum Fluorescent Display
VFG: Variable Function Generator
VFL: Variable Field Length
VFM: Variable Field Marks
VFM: Variable Format Messages
VFS: Vertical Fragmentation Scheme
VFS: Video Frame Store
VFS: Virtual File Store
VFU: Vocabulary File Utility
VGA: Video Graphics Array
VHA: Very High Accuracy
VHR: Very High Reduction
VIA: Videotex Industry Association
VIC: Virtual Interaction Controller
VIE: Virtual Interactive Environment
VIO: Video Input/Output
VIO: Virtual Input/Output
VIP: Variable Information Processing

VIP: VIdeo Programming
VIP: Visual Information Projection
VIS: Vector Instruction Set
VIS: Verification Information System
VLF: Variable Length Field
VLO: Variable-Length Operations
VLR: Variable-Length Record
VMA: Vertical Market Applications
VMC: Vertical MicroCode
VME: Virtual Mode Extensions
VMT: Variable Microcycle Timing
VOS: Virtual Operating System
VPA: Valid Peripheral Address
VPE: Vector Processing Element
VPF: Vector Parameter File
VPF: Vector Processing Facility
VPT: Virtual Processing Time
VPU: Ventura Publisher Users
VPZ: Virtual Processing Zero
VRC: Vector to Raster Converter
VRS: Voice Recognition System

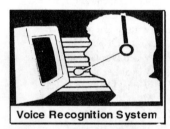

Voice Recognition System

VRX: Virtual Resource EXecutive (NCR)
VSA: Value Systems Analysis
VSA: Virtual StorAge
VSC: Variable Speed Control
VSE: Virtual-Storage Extended (IBM)
VSI: Virtual Storage Interrupt
VSN: Volume Serial Number
VSP: Volume Switch Procedure
VSS: Vector Symbol Set
VTA: Variable Transfer Address
VTC: Vertical Tabulation Character
VTK: Vertical Tabulator Key
VTL: Void-Transaction Log
VTP: Verification Test Plan
VWA: Vertical Wrap Around
VWS: Variable Word Size
VWT: Virtual Wait Time

WAC: Working Address Counter
WAF: Word Address Format
WAK: Wait AcKnowledge
WAK: Write Access Key
WAR: Write After Read
WBP: White Box Process
WBS: Work Breakdown Schedule
WCC: Wild Card Character
WCC: Write Control Character
WCF: WorkLoad Control File
WCL: Word Control Logic
WCS: Writable Control Storage
WCS: Writable Control Store
WCT: Write Cycle Time
WDB: Word Driver BIT
WDB: Working Data Base
WDC: World Data Center
WDF: Working Data File
WDS: Work Data Set
WFW: Windows For Workgroups
WfW: Windows of Workshop
WGC: Work Group Computing
WGS: Working Group Standards
Win: Window
WIT: Women into Information Technolo
WLR: Wrong Length Record
WMF: Windows Metafile Format
WOB: White On Black
WOS: Word Organized Storage
WPB: Write Printer Binary
WPC: Word Processing Center
WPG: WordPerfect Graphic
WPI: World Patent Index
WPM: Words Per Minute
WPO: Word Perfect Office
WPS: Word Processing System
WPW: Word Perfect Works
WRE: WRite Enable
WTO: Write-To-Operator
WUS: Word UnderScore Character
WWB: Writers Work Bench

XAM: EXternal Address Modifier
XBC: EXternal Block Controller
XBT: Cross Bar Tandem
xec: execute
XEC: EXtended Emulator Control
xeq: execute
XES: Xerox Engineering System
XFC: EXtended Function Code
XMP: EXperimental Mathematics
      Programming
XOP: EXtended OPeration
XOR: EXclusive OR
XOS: Xerox Operating System
XPT: EXternal Page Table

ZAI: Zero Address Instruction
ZBA: Zero-Bracket Amount
ZBB: Zero-Base Budgeting
ZIF: Zero Insertion Force
ZLA: Zero Level Address
ZRE: Zero Rate Error
ZWC: Zero Word Count
ZZC: Zero-Zero Condition

YAP: Yield Analysis Pattern
YEC: Youngest Empty Cell
YMS: Yield Measurement System
YSF: Yield Safety Factor

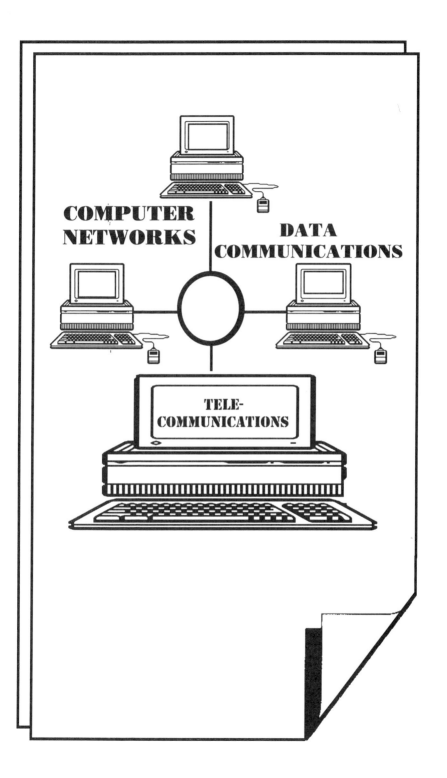

COMPUTER
NETWORKS

DATA
COMMUNICATIONS

TELE-
COMMUNICATIONS

AAC: Abbreviated Address Calling
AAD: Automatic Answering Device
AAO: Arbitrated Access Opportunity
AAR: Automatic Alternative Routing
AAS: Advanced Antenna System
AAT: Arbitrated Access Timer
AAV: Add Attribute Value
ABC: Automatic Bandwidth Control
ABF: All-Routes Broadcast Frame
ABM: Asynchronous Balanced Mode
ABN: Australian Bibliographic Network
ABR: Affinity- Based Routing
ABR: Answer Bid Ratio
ABW: Advise By Wire
ACA: Adaptive Channel Allocation
ACA: Adjacent Channel Attenuation
ACA: American Communications
     Association
ACA: Asynchronous Communications
     Adapter
ACA: Automatic Communication
     Association
ACB: Adapter Control Block
ACB: Asynchronous Communications Base
ACB: Automatic Call Back
ACC: Access Channel Control
ACC: Asynchronous Communications
     Control
ACC: Automatic Carrier Control
ACD: Automatic Call Distribution
ACD: Automatic Call Distributor
ACE: Asynchronous Communication
     Element
ACF: Advanced Communication Facility
ACF: Advanced Communication Function
ACF: Alternate Communications Facility
ACF: Automatic Call Forwarding
ACI: Adjacent Channel Interference
ACK: ACKnowledge
ACM: Access Control Methods
ACM: Associative Communications
     Multiplexer
ACM: Asynchronous Communication
     Control Module
ACO: Automatic Call Origination
ACP: ACtion Point

ACP: Asynchronous Communications P
ACR: Air-field Control Radar
ACR: Antenna Coupling Regulator
ACS: Access Control Store
ACS: Acknowledged Connectionless
     Service
ACS: Advanced Communications Servic
ACS: Advanced Communications Syste
ACS: Advice Call Subscriber
ACS: Alternating Current Synchronous
ACS: Automated Communications Set
ACT: Advanced Communications
     Technology
ACT: Advisory Committee on
     Telecommunications
ACU: Access Control Unit
ACU: Auto-Call Unit
ACU: Automatic Calling Unit
ADB: Adjacency DataBase
ADC: Analog to Digital Conversion
ADC: Asynchronous Data Channel
ADF: Added Digit Framing
ADI: Application Data Interchange
ADL: Automatic Data Link
ADL: Automatic Data Logger
ADM: Asynchronous Disconnected Mode
ADR: Automatic Digital Relay
ADS: Arbitrated Digital Signature
ADT: Analog Data Transmission
ADT: Asynchronous Data Transceiver
ADT: Asynchronous Data Transfer
ADT: Automatic Data Transfer
ADT: Automatic Detection and Tracking
ADU: Automatic Dialing Unit
ADX: Asymmetric Data EXchange
ADX: Automatic Data EXchange
ADX: Automatic Digital EXchange
AEI: Application Entity Invocation
AEP: Asynchronous Entry Point
AER: Alternate Extended Route
AER: Asynchronous Exit Routine
AES: Application Environment Service
AFC: Amplitude Frequency Characteristi
AFC: Area Frequency Coordinator
AFC: Automatic Field Control
AFC: Automatic Frequency Control
AFI: Authority and Format Identifier
AFS: Audio Frequency Shift
AGC: Automatic Gain Control
AGV: Automatic Guided Vehicle Control
AHR: Alternate Hierarchical Routing

AHT:	Average Holding Time	ARR:	Address Recall Register
AIM:	Asynchronous Interface Module	ARR:	Alternative Re-Routing
AIS:	Alarm Inhibit Signal	ARR:	Anti-Repeat Relay
AIS:	Automatic Intercept Systems	ARR:	Automatic Re-Routing
AIX:	Advanced Interactive EXecutive	ARS:	Audio Response System
ALD:	Asynchronous Limited Distance	ARS:	Automatic Route Selection
ALD:	Asynchronous Line Driver	ARS:	Automatic Route Setting
ALE:	Adaptive Line Enhancement	ART:	Audio Response Terminal
ALE:	Analog Local Exchange	ART:	Automated Request Transmission
ALE:	Automatic Line Equalization	ART:	Automatic Reporting Telephone
ALI:	Asynchronous Line Interface	ARU:	Audio Response Unit
ALM:	Asynchronous Line Module	ARX:	Automatic Retransmission EXchange
ALM:	Asynchronous Line Multiplexer	ASA:	American Standards Association
ALS:	Adjacent Link Station	ASA:	ASynchronous Adapter
ALU:	Asynchronous Line Unit	ASA:	Asynchronous/Synchronous Adapter
AMA:	Asynchronous Multiplexer Adapter	ASE:	Application Service Element
AMA:	Automatic Message Accounting	ASI:	American Standards Institute
AMC:	Automatic Message Counting	ASK:	Amplitude Shift Keying
AMC:	Autonomous Multiplexer Channel	ASM:	Asynchronous Sequential Machine
AME:	Amplitude Modulation Equivalent	ASN:	Abstract Syntax Notation
AMH:	Application Message Handling	ASN:	Autonomous System Number
AMI:	Alternative/Alternate Mark Inversion	ASP:	Acoustic Signal Processor
AML:	Amplitude Modulated Link	ASR:	Airborne Surveillance Radar
AMR:	Address Mask Request	ASR:	Airport Surveillance Radar
AMR:	Automatic Message Registering	ASR:	Answer Seizure Ratio
AMR:	Automatic Message Routing	ASR:	Automatic Send and Receive
ANA:	Auxiliary Network Address	ASR:	Automatic Speech Recognition
ANC:	All Number Calling	ASS:	Analog Switching Subsystem
ANL:	Ambient Noise Level	AST:	Address Synchronizing Track
ANL:	Automatic Noise Limiter Circuit	ASU:	Acknowledgement Signal Unit
ANS:	Automatic Noise Suppression	ASU:	Acknowledge Signal Unit
AOL:	America OnLine	ATB:	All Trunks Busy
AOS:	Administrative Operator Station	ATC:	Arbitration Timing Control
APC:	Automatic Phase Control	ATD:	Asynchronous Time Division
APD:	Amplitude Probability Distribution	ATE:	Artificial Traffic Equipment
API:	Application Process Invocation	ATE:	Automatic Telephone Exchange
API:	Automatic Priority Interrupt	ATL:	Audio Telecommunication Line
APT:	Automatic Picture Transmission	ATM:	Asynchronous Transfer Mode
APU:	Asynchronous Processing Unit	ATR:	Anti-Transmit-Receive
ARA:	Automatic Route Advance	ATR:	Automatic Traffic Recorder
ARB:	All-Routes Broadcast	ATR:	Automatic Transmit-Receive
ARD:	Answering Recording and Dialing	ATS:	Acknowledge Time Slot
ARL:	Adjusted Ring Length	ATS:	Application Technology Satellite
ARM:	Asynchronous Response Mode	ATT:	Alternate Transmit Time
ARM:	Audio Response Message	AT&T:	American Telephone &
ARM:	Automated Route Management		Telegraph Company
ARP:	Address Resolution Protocol	ATU:	Antenna Tuning Unit
ARQ:	Answer-Return Query	ATU:	Arab Telecommunication Union
ARQ:	Automatic Repeat ReQuest	AUD:	Asynchronous Unit Delay
ARQ:	Automatic ReQuest for Repetition	AVA:	Azimuth Versus Amplitude
arq:	automatic retransmission request	AVC:	Automatic Volume Control
		AVD:	Alternative Voice And Data

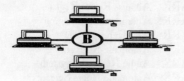

BAL: BrAnch Linkage
BAS: Basic Activity Subset
BBB: BaseBand Bus
BBB: BroadBand Bus
BBB: Building BackBones
BBC: BroadBand Coaxial Cable
BBC: BroadBand Conductor
BBC: BroadBand Control
BBM: BaseBand Mode
BBM: BaseBand Modem
BBM: BroadBand Mode
BBN: BaseBand Network
BBN: BroadBand Network
BBR: BroadBand Radiated
BBS: BaseBand Signaling
BBS: Bulletin Board Service
BBS: Bulletin Board System (USA)
BCA: Bisynchronous Communications
     Adapter
BCC: Baseband Coaxial Cable
BCC: Block Calls Cleared
BCC: Block Check Character
BCC: Block Check Code
BCC: Block Control Character
BCC: Broadband Coaxial Cable
BCH: Block Calls Held
BCI: Bit Count Integrity
BCN: Broadcast Communication Network
BCP: Batch Communications Program
BCP: Bisynchronous Communications
     Processor
BCS: Basic Communications Support
BCS: Binary CommunicationS
BCS: Bridge Control System
BDC: Broadband Data Channel
BDE: Basic Data Exchange
BDE: Branch Data Exchange
BDF: Building Distribution Frame
BDN: Bell Data Network
BDR: Bi-Duplexed Redundancy
BDS: Bulk Data Switching
BDT: Bureau de Development des
     Telecommunications
BEB: Binary Exponential Backoff
BEC: Backward Error Control
BEN: Bus ENable

BER: Bit Error Rate
BEX: Broadband EXchange
BFF: Buffered Flip-Flop
BFL: Busy FLash
BFN: Beam-Forming Network
BIC: Bridge Input Circuit
BIX: Binary Information EXchange
BIX: Byte Information EXchange
BLA: BLocking Acknowledgement
BLN: Bus Local Network

Bus Local Network

BLO: BLOcking Signal
BLS: Band Limited Signal
BMC: Block Multiplexer Channel
BMC: Burst Multiplexer Channel
BMC: Byte Multiplexer Channel
BNA: Burroughs Network Architecture
BNC: Baby "N" Connector
BNC: Branch Network Controller
BNN: Boundary Network Node
BNS: Business Network Service
BNT: Bus Network Topology

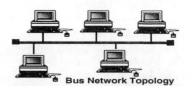

Bus Network Topology

BNV: Bottle-Neck Vulnerability
BOP: Bit-Oriented Protocol
BOT: Bit-Oriented Transmission
BPA: Band Pass Amplifier
BPA: Bridge Protocol Architecture
BPC: Basic Peripheral Channel
BPC: Binding Post Chamber
BPE: BiPolar Encoding
BPE: Bridge Protocol Entity

BPF: BandPass Filter
BPS: ByPass State
BRA: Basic Rate Access
BRF: Baud Rate Factor
BRG: Baud Rate Generator
BRI: Basic Rate Interface
BRR: Baud Rate Reduction
BRS: Break Request Signal
BSA: Binary Synchronous Adapter
BSB: British Satellite Broadcasting
BSC: Basic Message Switching Center
BSC: Binary Symmetric Channel
BSC: Binary Synchronous Communication
BSC: Binary Synchronous Control
BSC: Block Sum Check
BSE: Broadcast Satellite Experiment
BSI: Bit Sequence Independence
BSI: British Standards Institute
BSL: Basic Switching Level
BSM: Backward Set-Up Messages
BSM: Bit Serial Mode
BSN: Backward Sequence Number
BSP: Byte Stream Protocol
BSR: Buffered Send/Receive
BSS: Basic Synchronized Subset
BSS: Broadcast Satellite Services
BST: Bit-Serial Transmission
BST: Broadcast Standard Technique
BST: Byte Serial Transmission
BSY: Binary SYnchronous
BTE: Bi-Directional Transceiver Element
BTI: British Telecom International
BTM: Bit-Serial Transmission Medium
BTR: Broadcast and Television Receivers
BTS: British Telecom Switching System
BTT: Best-Try Transmission
BTU: Basic Transmission Unit
BTX: Bildschirm TeXt
BWM: Backward Wave Magnetron
BWO: Backward Wave Oscillator
BXB: British Cross Bar

CAB: Communication Adapter Board
CAI: Common Air Interface

CAM: Communications Access Manager
CAM: Communications Access Method
CAP: Cable Access Point
CAP: Charging and Accounting Plan
CAR: Centralized Adaptive Routing
CAS: Call Accepted Signal
CAS: Channel-Attached Station
CAS: Communicating Application
         Specification
CAS: Communicating Application Standard
CAT: Computer-Assisted Teleconferencing
CAT: Credit Authorization Telephones
CAW: Channel Address Word
CAX: Community Automatic EXchange
CBC: Chain Block Cipher
CBC: Cipher Block Chaining
CBN: Core Backbone Network
CBS: Central Battery Signaling
CBX: Centralized Branch EXchange
CBX: Computer Controlled Branch
         EXchange
CBX: Computerized Branch EXchange
CCA: Carrier-Controlled Approach
CCA: Common Communications Adapter
CCA: Computer Communications
         Architecture
CCA: Conceptual Communications Area
CCB: Communication Control Block
CCB: Communications Control Batches
CCC: Call Control Character
CCC: Central Communications Controller
CCC: Command Control
         & Communications
CCC: Computer Communications Console
CCE: Communication Control Equipment
CCF: Common Communications
         Format (ISO)
CCF: Communications Control Field
CCH: Connections per Circuit Hour
CCH: Coordination Committee for
         Harmonization
CCL: Communication Control Language
CCM: Call Count Meter
CCM: Communications Control Module
CCM: Communications Control
         Multi-Channel
CCN: Centralized Computer Network
CCN: Common Carrier Network
CCO: Context Control Object
CCO: Crystal-Control Oscillator
CCP: Call Connected Packet
CCP: Call Control Procedure

CCP: Channel Control Processor
CCP: Communications Control Package
CCP: Communications Control Panel
CCP: Communications Control Processor
CCP: Communications Control Program
CCP: Cross Connection Point
CCR: Customized Communications Routine
CCS: Call Control Signal
CCS: Common Channel Signaling
CCS: Communications Control System
CCS: Conversational Compiling System
CCT: Communications Control Team
CCT: Computerized Communications Terminal
CCU: Communications Control Unit
CCW: Channel Command Word
CCW: Channel Control Word
CDA: Compound Document Architecture
CDC: Call Directing Code
CDC: Channel Data Check
CDC: Computer Display Channel
CDF: Combined Distribution Frame
CDL: Carrier Detect Level
CDM: Code-Division Multiplexing
CDN: Corporate Data Network
CDO: Community Dial Office
CDP: Communications Data Processing
CDR: Call Data Recording
CDR: Call Detail Recording
CDR: Command Destruct Receiver
CDR: Current Directional Relay
CDS: Cell Directory Server
CDT: Connectionless Data Transfer
CDT: Connectionless Data Transmission
CDV: Check Digit Verification
CDX: Control Differential Transmitter
CEA: Communications-Electronics Agency
CEF: Cable Entrance Facility
CEI: Commission Electrotechnique Internationale
CEI: Communication Electronics Instructions
CEN: Comite Europeen de Normalisation
CEN: European Committee for Standardization
CET: Cold End Termination
CEU: Channel Extension Unit
CEU: Communications Expansion Unit
CFC: Channel Flow Control
CFL: Call FaiLure Signal

CFM: Cipher Feedback Mode
CFR: Cambridge Fast Ring
CHI: Communications Hardware Interface
CHP: CHannel Processor
CHT: Call Holding Time
CIA: Communications Interface Adapter
CIA: Communications Interrupt Analysis
CIB: Channel Interface Base
CIC: Circuit Identification Code
CIC: Communications Intelligence Channel
CIC: Communications Intelligence Corporation
CID: Communication IDentifier
CIM: Communications Interface Monitor
CIM: Computer Input Multiplexer
CIP: Clear Indication Packet
CIP: Communication Interrupt Program
CIS: Code Independent System
CIS: Communication Information System
CIS: Compuserve Information Service
CIS: Contact Interrogation Signal
CIT: Computer Integrated Telephony
CIU: Channel Interface Unit
CIU: Communication Interface Unit
CJP: Communication Jamming Processor
CLA: Carry Look Ahead
CLA: Communications Line Adapter
CLA: Communications Line Analyzer
CLC: Communications Line Control
CLC: Communications Link Controller
CLC: Concentrator Local Connection Module
CLE: Communications Line Expander
CLF: CLear Forward Signal
CLI: Called Line Identification
CLI: Calling Line Identity
CLL: Consolidated Link Layer
CLM: Communications Line Multiplexer
CLM: Concentrator Line Module
CL/1: Connectivity Language/1
CLP: Communications Line Processor
CLR: Circular Linked Ring
CLS: Collect Localization Satellites
CLS: Communication Line Switch
CLT: Communication Line Terminals
CMA: Communications Managers Association
CMC: Code for Magnetic Character
CMC: CoMmunications Channel
CMC: Communications Management Configuration
CMC: Communications Mode Control

CME:	Circuit Multiplication Equipment
CMM:	Communication Multiplexer Module
CMN:	Common Mode Noise
CMO:	Connectionless-Mode Operation
CMP:	Communications Management Processor
CMR:	Communication Monitoring Report
CMS:	Circuit Maintenance System
CMS:	Compiler Monitor System
CMT:	Computer Mediated Teleconferencing
CMT:	Current-Mode Transmission
CMX:	Character MultipleXer
CMX:	Customer MultipleXer
CNA:	Communications Network Architecture
CNE:	Certified Netware Engineers
CNE:	Communications Network Emulator
CNI:	Changed Number Interception
CNL:	Circuit Net Loss
CNM:	Communications Network Manager
CNP:	Communications Network Procedure
CNP:	Communications Network Processor
CNR:	Carrier-to-Noise Ratio
CNR:	Common Network Representation
CNS:	Channelled Narrow Stripe
CNS:	Communication Network Simulator
CNS:	Communication Network System
CNS:	Community Network System
COC:	Character Oriented Communications
COI:	Communications Operation Instruction
COL:	Communications Oriented Language
CO&M:	Centralized Operation & Maintenance
com:	communication switching
COM:	COMmunication Technology
COM:	Connection-Oriented Mode
CON:	CONnect
COP:	COmmunication Processor
COS:	Class Of Service
COS:	Communication Oriented Software
COS:	Communications Operating System
COS:	Connection-Oriented Service
COS:	Cooperation for Open Systems
COT:	Character-Oriented Transmission
COT:	COnTinuity Signal
COT:	Create Occurrence Table
CPM:	Connection Point Manager
CPS:	Call Progress Signal !
CPS:	Complete Packet Sequence
CPU:	Communication Processor Unit
CRA:	Call Routing Apparatus

CRB:	Customer Reconfiguration Bandwidth
CRC:	Carrier Return Character
CRC:	Cycle Redundancy Check
CRC:	Cyclic Redundancy Check
CRE:	Call Reference Equivalent
CRE:	Corrected Reference Equivalent
CRF:	Central Retransmission Facility
CRM:	Concentrator Remote Multiplexer
CRN:	Computer Room Network
CRP:	Call Request Packet
CRS:	Computerized Reservation System
CRS:	Containment Rupture Signal
CRT:	Cost-Related Tariffs
CRU:	Communication Register Unit
CSA:	Call Subscriber Answer
CSA:	Canadian Standards Association
CSB:	Called Subscriber Busy
CSC:	Circuit-Switched Calls
CSC:	Circuit Switched Connection
CSC:	Circuit Switching Center
CSC:	Common Signaling Channel
CSD:	Circuit Switched Data
CSH:	Called Subscriber Held
CSM:	Client-Server Model
CSM:	Communication System Monitoring
CSN:	Circuit-Switched Network
CSN:	Common Sub-Net Node
CSN:	Control Signaling Network
CSO:	Centralized Service Observation
CSP:	Control Switching Point
CS/P:	Communications/Symbol Processor
CSS:	Communication Satellite System
CSS:	Conceptual Signaling & Status Store
CSS:	Cordless Switchboard System
CSU:	Central Switching Unit
CSU:	Channel Service Unit
CSU:	Circuit Switching Unit
CSU:	Communication System User
CSV:	Circuit Switched Voice
CSW:	Channel Status Word
CS0:	Control Signal Zero
CS1:	Control Signal One
CTC:	Channel-To-Channel
CTE:	Channel Translating Equipment
CTE:	Circuit Terminating Equipment
CTE:	Computer Telex Exchange
CTF:	Common Trace Facility
CTI:	Computers in Teaching Initiative
CTM:	Communications Terminal Module
CTS:	Carrier to Test Switch
CTS:	Clear To Send

CTS: Communications Technology Satellite
CTS: Communications Terminal Synchronous
CTS: Computer Telegram System
CTS: Conversational Terminal System
CTS: Conversational Time Sharing
CUA: Common User Access
CUP: Communications User Program
CVC: Carrier Virtual Circuit
CVR: Computer Voice Response
CVT: Communications Vector Table
CWI: Calls Waiting Indicator
CWI: Virtual Route Change Window Indicator
CWP: Communicating Word Processing
CXA: Central EXchange Area
CXR: Carrier Detector

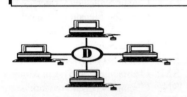

DAA: Direct Access Arrangement
DAC: Data Authentication Code
DAC: Demand Assignment Controller
DAC: Digital to Analog Converter
DAD: Draft ADdendum (ISO)
DAF: Destination Address Field
DAI: Direct Access Information
DAL: Data Access Line
DAM: Data Association Message
DAM: Draft AMendment (ISO)
DAP: Destination Address Parameter
DAP: Direct Access Protocol
DAP: Directory Access Protocol
DAR: Distributed Adaptive Routing
DAR: Dynamic Alternative Routing
DAS: Different Addressing Schemes
DAS: Dual Attachment Station
DAV: Data Above Voice
DAV: Derive Attribute Value
DBA: Dynamic Bandwidth Allocation
DBC: Data Bus Coupler
DBM: Direct Branch Mode
DBP: Deutsche BundesPost Telekom
DBR: Descriptor Base Register
DBS: Direct Broadcast Satellite

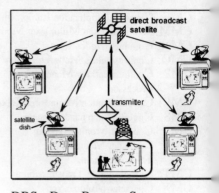

DBS: Direct Broadcast System
DBW: Data BandWidth
DBX: Digital Branch EXchange
DCA: Data Communication Adapter
DCA: Data Communication Administrator
DCA: Defense Communications Agency (USA)
DCA: Destination Computer Address
DCA: Distributed Communications Architecture
DCA: Distributed Computer Architecture
DCA: Document Content Architecture
DCB: Defense Communications Board
DCC: Data Channel Converter
DCC: Data Circuit Concentration
DCC: Data Communication Channel
DCC: Data Communication Controller
DCC: Device Cluster Controller
DCC: Digital Cross-Connect
DCC: District Communications Center
DCD: Data Carrier Detect
DCE: Data Circuit-Terminating Equipment

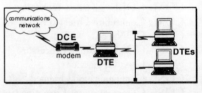

DCE: Data Communication Equipment
DCE: Data Communication Experiment
DCE: Digital Communication Experiment
DCE: Distributed Computer Environment
DCF: Data Communication Facility
DCF: Data Communication Feature
DCH: Data CHannel
DCI: Data Communication Interface
DCI: Direct Channel Interface
DCL: Data Communication Line

DCM:	Data Communications Multiplexer	DIA:	Document Interchange Architecture
DCM:	Direct-Connect Modem	DIB:	Directory Information Base
DCM:	Distributed Computing Model	DID:	Direct Inward Dialing
DCN:	Data Communications Network	DIG:	Digital-Image-Generated
DCN:	Decentralized Computer Network	DIN:	Deutsches Institut fur Normung
DCN:	Distributed Computer Network	DIN:	German Standards Institute
DCP:	Data Collection Platform	DIS:	Distributed Information System
DCP:	Data Communications Processor	DIT:	Directory Information Tree
DCP:	Data Communications Program	DIV:	Data In Voice System
DCP:	Digital Communications Protocol	DKE:	German Electrotechnical Commission
DCP:	Distributed Communication Processor	DLA:	Data Link Adapter
DCR:	Data Conversion Receiver	DLA:	DeadLock Avoidance
DCR:	Digital Conversion Receiver	DLC:	Data Link Control
DCS:	Data Communication Service	DLC:	Digital Leased Circuit
DCS:	Data Communications Subsystem	DLC:	Digital Loop Carrier
DCS:	Data Communication System	DLC:	Duplex Line Control
DCS:	Defense Communications System	DLE:	Data Link Escape
DCS:	Defined Context Set	DLE:	Digital Local Exchange
DCS:	Digital Command Signal	DLF:	Data Link Function
DCS:	Digital Communication System	DLL:	Data Link Level
DCS:	Digital Control Signal	DLL:	Dial Long Lines
DCS:	Distributed Computer System	DLM:	Data Line Monitor
DCS:	Dual Cable System	DLM:	Data Linking Module
DCT:	Data Communications Terminal	DLP:	Data Link Protocol
DCU:	Data Communications Unit	DLS:	Delay Line Storage
DDD:	Direct Distance Dialing	DLS:	Digital Line System
DDE:	Dynamic Data Exchange	DLS:	Digital Local Switch
DDI:	Digital Data Interface	DLS:	Distributed Line Sharing
DDI:	Direct DIaling In to PABXs	DLT:	Data Line Translator
DDM:	Difference of Depth of Modulation	DLT:	Data Loop Transceiver
DDN:	Defense Data Network	DMC:	Direct Multiplexed Channel
DDN:	Digital Data Networks	DME:	Differential Manchester Encoding
DDS:	Dataphone Digital Services (AT&T)	DME:	Digital Multiplex Equipment
DDS:	Digital Data Switch	DMI:	Digital Multiplexed Interface
DDS:	Digital Data System	DMR:	Distributed Message Router
DDS:	Direct Digital Signature	DMS:	Data MultiplexerS
DDT:	Digital Data Transmission	DMS:	Digital Multiplex Switching System
DEB:	Digital European Backbone	DMT:	Digital Message Terminal
DEC:	Digital Equipment Corporation (USA)	DMT:	Dispersive Mechanism Test
DEF:	Data Extension Frame	DMX:	Data MultipleXer
DEM:	DEModulator	DNA:	Digital Network Architecture (DEC)
DES:	Data Encryption Standard	DNA:	Distributed Network Architecture
DEU:	Data Exchange Unit	DNC:	Direct Numerical Control
DEX:	Data EXchange	DNS:	Distributed Name Server
DFA:	Distributed Function Architecture	DNS:	Domain Name Server
DFR:	Double Frequency Recording	DNS:	Domain Name System
DFS:	Distributed File System	DNT:	Digital Network Terminator
DGS:	Data Ground Station	DOC:	Department Of Communications
DGT:	Direction General de		(Canada)
	Telecommunications	DOD:	Department Of Defense
DHC:	Dynamic Huffman Coding	DOD:	Direct Outward Dialing
		DOS:	Distributed Office Systems

DOV: Data OverVoice
DPC: Destination Point Code
DPM: Distributed Presentation Management
DPN: Digital Private Network
DPS: Datagram Packet Switching
DRF: Data Received Flag
DRM: Digital RadioMeter
DRP: Distributed Routing Protocol
DRQ: Data Ready Queue
DRS: Data Relay Satellite
DRS: Delay Relay Satellite
DRS: Digital Radar Simulator
DSA: Dial Service Assistance
DSA: Digital Signal Analyzer
DSB: Data Set Block
DSB: Double SideBand
DSC: District Switching Center
DSC: Document Satellite Carrier
DSE: Data Switching Equipment
DSE: Data Switching Exchange
DSE: Digital Signal Encoding
DSE: Direct Switching Exchange
DSI: Digital Speech Interpolation
DSI: Digital Speech Interpretation
DSN: Deep Space Network (NASA)
DSN: Derived Services Network (British Telecom)
DSN: Distributed Service Network
DSP: Data Stream Push
DSP: Digital Signal Processor
DSP: Directory Service Protocol
DSP: Directory System Protocol
DSP: Distributed System Program
DSP: Domain Specific Part
DSR: Data Scanning and Routing
DSR: Data Set Ready
DSR: Data Signaling Rate
DSR: Discriminating Selector Repeater
DSS: Data Switching System
DSS: Digital Signaling System
DSS: Digital Switching Subsystem
DSS: Digital Switching System
DST: Dual Serial Transceiver
DST: Dual Serial Transmitter
DSU: Data Services Unit
DSU: Data Synchronizer Unit
DSX: Digital Signal Cross-Connection
DSX: Distributed System EXecutive (IBM)
DTC: Data Transmission Center

DTC: Data Transmission Channel
DTD: Data Transfer Done
DTE: Data Terminal Equipment

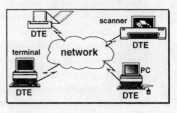

DTE: Data Transmission Equipment
DTF: Data Transfer Facility
DTG: Display Transmission Generator
DTH: Direct To Home
DTI: Data Transmission Interface
DTL: Data Transmission Line
DTM: Delay Timer Multiplier
DTN: Directory Transport Node
DTP: Data Transfer Protocols
DTP: Distributed Transaction Processing
DTR: Data Transfer Rate
DTR: Data Transmission Rate
DTR: Definite-Time Relay
DTR: Demand-Totalizing Relay
DTR: Document Transmittal Record
DTS: Data Transmission Service
DTS: Data Transmission System
DTS: Data Transport System
DTS: Digital Transmission System
DTU: Data Transmission Unit
DTU: Digital Transmission Unit
DUI: Data Unit Identifier
DUL: Dial-Up Line
DUP: Data User Parts
DUT: Dial Up Teleconferencing
DUV: Data Under Voice
DVA: Distance-Vector Algorithm
DVI: Digital Videotex Interactive
DVX: Digital Voice EXchange
DXA: Document EXchange Architecture (Data General Corporation)
DXC: Document EXchange Control
DXL: Digital EXchange Line
DXS: Data EXchange System

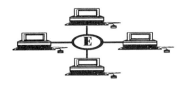

EAR: Electronically Agile Radar
EAS: Extended Area Service
EAT: Enhanced Audio Teleconferencing
EAX: Electronic Automatic EXchange
EBC: Electronic Business Communications
EBM: Extended Branch Mode
EBU: European Broadcasting Union
EBX: Electronic Branch EXchange
ECB: Electronic Code Book
ECB: Error Check Bits
ECB: Event Control Block
ECE: Executive Communications Exchange
ECH: Echo Cancellation Hybrid
ECM: Effective Calls Meter
ECN: Error Code Number
ECP: Error Correcting Part
ECR: Electronic Control Relay
ECR: Error Control Receiver
ECS: Electronic Cable Section
ECS: European Communications Satellite
ECS: European Fixed-Service Satellite
EDC: Error Detecting Code
EDI: Electronic Data Interchange
EDI: Electronic Document Interchange
EDT: Expedited Data Transfer
EEL: Exclusive Exchange Line
EER: Explosive Echo Ranging
EET: Equipment Engaged Tone
EFL: Emitter-Follower Logic
EFS: Electronic Frequency Selection
EFS: Error-Free Seconds
EFT: Electronic Financial Transaction
EFT: Electronic Funds Transfer
EGP: Exterior Gateway Protocol
EHF: Extra High Frequency
EHF: Extremely High Frequency
EIA: Electrical Industries Association
EIA: Electronics Industries Association
EIN: Education Information Network
EIN: European Information Network
ELA: Extended Line Adapter
ELF: Extremely Low Frequency
ELN: Empty Leaf Node
ELR: EaRthed Loop
ELT: Emergency Locator Transmitter

EMA: Electronic Mail Association (USA)
EMB: Electronic Mail Box
EMC: Extended Multiplexer Channel
EMC: External Multiplexer Channel
EMR: Electro-Magnetic Radiation
EMR: Electro-Mechanical Relay
EMS: Electronic Mail System
EMS: Electronic Message Service
EMS: Electronic Message System
ENA: Extended Network Addressing
ENA: Extended Network Architecture
ENE: Enterprise Networking Event
ENG: Electronic News Gathering
ENN: Expand Nonstop Network
ENQ: ENQuiry
ENR: External Number Repetition
ENS: European Nervous System
eoi: end Of identity
eot: end Of transmission
EPA: Enhanced Performance Architecture
EPN: Enterprise-Wide Private Network
ERC: Electronics Research Center (NASA)
ERL: Echo Return Loss
ERN: Explicit Route Number
ERP: Exterior Router Protocol
ERX: Electronic Remote Switching
ESA: European Space Agency
ESH: End System Hello
ESR: Electronic Send Receive
ESS: Echo Suppression System
ESS: Electronic Switching System
ESS: Event Scheduling System
EST: Event-State Table
ETB: End of Transmission Block
ETC: Exchange Terminal Circuit
ETE: End-To-End Basis
ETN: Extra Terrestrial Noise
ETS: Electronic Tandem Switching
ETS: Electronic Telegraph System
ETS: European Telecommunication Standards
ETV: Educational TeleVision
ETX: End-Of-TeXt
EVD: EVent Dispatcher
EWB: Enterprise-Wide Backbone
EWN: Enterprise-Wide Network

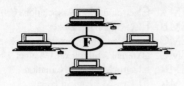

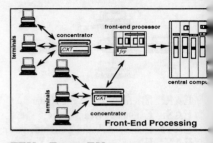

Front-End Processing

FAC: Features for Attaching Communications
FAC: File Access Channel
FAL: File Access Listener
FAL: Frequency Allocation List
FAM: Frequency-Agile Modem
FAP: File Access Protocol
FAP: Frequency Allocation Panel
FAX: FAcsimile
FCA: Frequency Control Analysis
FCC: Federal Communications Commission (USA)
FCN: Fully Connected Network
FCR: France Cables et Radio
FCS: Facsimile Communication System
FCS: Federation of Communication Services
FCS: Frame Check Sequence
FCS: Frequency Check Sequence
FCX: Facsimile Communication System
FDB: Forwarding DataBase
FDC: Facsimile Data Converter
FDC: Frame Dependent Control
FDC: Full Duplex Channel

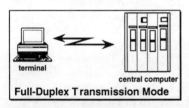

Full-Duplex Transmission Mode

FDC: Full-Duplex Communications
FDC: Fully Distributed Costs
FDF: Flight Data File
FDL: Full Duplex Line
FDM: Frequency Division Multiplexing
FDS: Frequency Division Separator
FDX: Full-DupleX
FEN: Frequency-Emphasizing Network
FEP: Front-End Processor

FEX: Foreign EXchange Telecommunica
FIB: Forwarding Information Base
FIF: Facsimile Information Field
FKT: Fyns Mommunale TelefonselsKab
FLN: Factory Local Network
FLR: Forward-Looking Radar
FLS: Free Line Signal
FMI: Frequency Modulation Intercity
FMT: Form Mode Terminal
FMX: Frame MultipleXer
FNP: Front-End Network Processor
FOC: Fiber Optic Cables
FOC: Fiber Optics Cable Assembly
FOC: Fiber Optics Communications
FOM: Fiber Optics Modem
FOT: Frequence Optimum de Travail
FPM: Frequency Position Modulation
FPP: Fixed Path Protocol
FPP: Fixed Point Protocol
FPS: Fast Packet Switching
FPS: Frames Per Second
FQA: Fully-Qualified Address
FRA: Frame Relay Adapter
FRC: Federal Radio Commission (USA)
FRC: Flat Ribbon Cable
FRC: Functional Redundancy Checking
FRD: Functional Requirements Document
FSA: Finite State Automation
FSA: Fixed Slot Acknowledgement
FSK: Frequency Shift Keying
FSM: Forward Set-Up Messages
FSS: Fast Select Sequence
FSS: Fixed Satellite Services
FSU: Facsimile Switching Unit
FTF: File Transfer Facility
FTP: File Transfer Protocol
FTS: Federal Telecommunications System
FXT: FiXed Time Call

GAD: Gate Alternative Denial
GAV: Get Attribute Value
GBW: Greater Band-Width
GCE: Ground Communication Equipment
GCI: Generalized Communication Interface
GCR: Global Call Reference
GCT: Graphics Communications Terminal
GDF: Group Distribution Frame
GDH: Global Digital Highway
GDN: Government Data Network (UK)
GEC: General Electric Company (UK)
GFI: Group Format Identifier
GFT: Grant Functional Transmission
GHZ: Giga HertZ
GIA: General Industry Applications
GIA: General International Area
GIA: Global Internet Address
GIC: General Input Channel
GIM: Graded Index Multi-Mode
GMR: Ground Mapping Radar
GND: GrouND
GNS: Global Network Services
GOM: Group Occupancy Meter
GPT: GEC Plessey Telecommunications Ltd
GRP: Group Reference Pilot
GSA: Ground Station Antenna
GSC: Group Switching Center
GSM: General Set-Up Messages
GSM: Global System for Mobile Communications
GSM: Groupe Speciale Module
GSR: Global Shared Resource
GTE: Group Translating Equipment
GTS: Global Telecommunication System
GTS: Government Telecommunication Services (UK)
GWS: GetWay Service

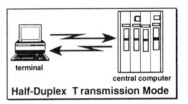

Half-Duplex Transmission Mode

HBH: Hop-By-Hop
HCN: Heterogeneous Computer Network
HCN: Hierarchical Computer Network
HCN: Homogeneous Computer Network
HCP: High-Speed Channel Processor
HCP: Host Communications Processor
HCT: Huffman Code Tree
HCV: High Capacity Voice
HDC: Half Duplex Channel

HDC: Half-Duplex Communications
HDC: High-Speed Data Channel
HDF: Horizontal Distribution Frame
HDO: Half-Duplex Operation
HDT: Half Duplex Transmission
HDX: Half DuPleX
HES: House Exchange System
HEU: Head-End Unit
HFO: High-Frequency Oscillator
HGT: High Group Transmit
HHL: Host-Host Layer
HKC: Hull Kingston Communications
HKT: Hong Kong Telecommunications
HLN: Hybrid Local Network
HNA: Hierarchical Network Architecture
HPF: Highest Probable Frequency
HPR: Hot Potato Routing
HRX: Hypothetical Reference Connection
HSC: High-Speed Concentrator
HSD: High-Speed Data
HSN: High Speed Network
HSP: Hand Shake Procedure
HST: High Speed Transmission
HTC: Helsinki Telephone Company
HTR: Harmonic Telephone Ringer
HTS: Host To Satellite
HUT: High Usage Inter-Toll Trunk
HUT: High-Usage Trunk

IAB:	Internet Activities Board
IAC:	Intelligent Asynchronous Controller
IA2:	International Alphabet Number 2
IA5:	International Alphabet Number 5
IAM:	Intermediate Access Message
IAS:	Interlayer Address Selectors
IBC:	Information Bearer Channel
IBC:	Integrated Block Channel
IBC:	Integrated Broadband Communications
IBM:	International Business Machine
IBW:	Impulse BandWidth
ICA:	Integrated Communication Adapter
ICA:	International Communication Association
ICB:	Incoming Calls Barred
ICC:	Implicit Congestion Control
ICC:	Intelligent Communications Controller
ICC:	International Conference on Communications
ICD:	International Code Designation
ICD:	International Code Designator
ICE:	Integrated Communication Environment
ICF:	Inter-Communication Flip-Flop
ICI:	Intelligent Communications Interface
ICL:	Inter-Communication Logic
ICL:	Intercomputer Communication Link
ICL:	International Computers Limited
ICN:	Integrated Computer Network
ICP:	Initial Connection Protocol
ICP:	Institute das Comunicacoes de Portugal
ICP:	Inter-Connection Protocol
ICS:	In-Channel Signaling
ICS:	Integrated Communication System
ICS:	Interactive Communications Software
ICS:	Inter-Communication System
ICT:	In-Coming Trunk
ICW:	Interrupted Continuous Wave
IDC:	Independent Data Communication
IDC:	Internal Data Channel
IDC:	International Digital Communications Inc.
IDC:	Inward Data Collection
IDD:	International Direct Dialing
IDE:	Interchange Data Elements
IDF:	Image Description File
IDF:	Intermediate Distribution Frame

IDI:	Improved Data Interchange
IDI:	Initial Domain Identifier
IDN:	Integrated Data Network
IDN:	Integrated Digital Network
IDN:	Intelligent Data Network
IDP:	Initial Domain Part
IDQ:	Internodal Destination Queue
IDR:	Intermediate Data Rate
IDU:	IDle Signal Unit
IEC:	International Electrotechnical Commission
IEG:	Information Exchange Group
IFC:	Implicit Flow Control
IFC:	In-Band Flow Control
IFG:	Inter-Frame Gap
IFR:	Instantaneous Frequency Measuring Receiver
IFT:	International Foundation for Telemetering
IGP:	Interior Gateway Protocol
IHL:	In-House Line
IHL:	Internet Header Length
IHN:	Intermediate Host Node
IHY:	I Heard You
IIC:	International Institute of Communications
IIR:	Infinite-Duration Impulse Response
IJC:	Inter-Job Communications
ILD:	Injection Laser Diode
ILF:	Infra Low Frequency
ILS:	International Line Selector
IMC:	Integrated Multiplexer Channel
IMG:	International MailGram
IMN:	Inter-Modulation Noise
IMP:	Interface Message Processor
IMS:	International Message Switching
IMX:	In-Line MultipleXer
IMX:	Inquiry Message EXchange
INA:	Integrated Network Architecture
INF:	InterNet Fragmentation
INF:	IntraNet Fragmentation
INF:	ISDN Numbering Format
INP:	Integrated Network Processor
INP:	Intelligent Network Processor
INT:	INTerrupt Line
IOC:	Input/Output Channel
IOM:	Input-Output Multiplexer
IPC:	Integrated Packet Channel
IPI:	Intelligent Peripheral Interface
IPM:	Impulse Per Minute
IPM:	Internal Polarization Modulation
IPM:	Inter-Personal Messaging

IPS:	Interruptions Per Second
IPX:	Interactive Package EXchange
IPX:	Internet Packet EXchange
IRC:	International Record Carrier
IRE:	Institute of Radio Engineers (USA)
IRF:	Intermediate Routing Function
IRM:	Intelligent Remote Multiplexer
IRN:	Internal Routing Network
IRS:	Intermediate Reference System
IRS:	Inter-Network Routing Service
IRV:	International Reference Version
ISB:	Independent SideBoard Transmission
ISC:	International Switching Center
ISD:	International Subscriber Dialing
ISE:	Integrated Service Engineering
ISF:	Individual Store and Forward
ISH:	Intermediate System Hello
ISL:	Integrated Software Link
ISL:	Inter-Satellite Link
ISL:	Inter-System Link
ISO:	International Standards Organization
ISN:	Information System Network
ISP:	Intermediate Service Part
ISP:	International Standard Profile
ISR:	Information Service Request
ISR:	Interrupt Service Routine
ISR:	Intersecting Storage Ring
ISS:	Ionosphere Sounding Satellite
IST:	Interrupt Service Task
ISU:	Interface Switching Unit
ITA:	International Telegraph Alphabet
ITB:	Intermediate Transmission Block
ITB:	InTermediate Block
ITC:	Information Transfer Channel
ITC:	International Teletraffic Congress (Denmark)
ITC:	Inter-Task Communications
ITE:	Institute of Telecommunications Engineers
ITJ:	International Telecom Japan Inc.
ITL:	Integrated-Transfer-Launch
ITN:	Integrated Teleprocessing Network
ITN:	Interactive TermiNal Facility
ITN:	InTerNetworking
ITP:	Interactive Terminal Protocol
ITS:	Institute for Telecommunications Sciences
ITS:	Invitation To Send
ITT:	Inter-Toll Trunk
ITU:	International Telecommunications Union
IVD:	Integrated Voice Data

IVR:	Integrated Voice Response (UK)
IXC:	Inter-EXchange Channel
IWU:	InternetWorking Unit

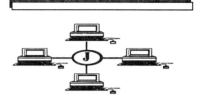

JBS:	Japanese Broadcast Satellite
JCI:	Joint Communications Instructions
JCN:	JunCtioN
JFL:	Joint Frequency List
JFP:	Joint Frequency Panel
JSA:	Japanese Standards Association
JTE:	Junction Tandem Exchange

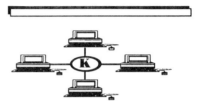

kHz:	kilo-Hertz
KLU:	Key and Lamp Unit
KTS:	Key Telephone System

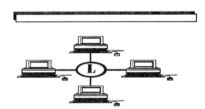

LAA:	LAN Administration Architecture
LAC:	Local Area Concentrator
LAN:	Local Area Network

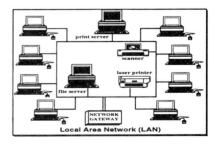

Local Area Network (LAN)

LAP:	Link Access Procedure	LDA:	Local Data Area
LAP:	Link Access Protocol	LDC:	Low-Speed Data Channel
LAS:	Large Astronomical Satellite	LDD:	Local Data Distribution
LAS:	Link Attached Station	LDI:	Link Delay Information
LAS:	Locally Attached Station	LDM:	Limited Distance Modem
LAT:	Link Attached Terminal	LDM:	Linear Delta Modulation
LAT:	Local Area Transport Protocol	LDP:	Link Disconnection Phase
LAT:	Locally Attached Terminal	LDR:	Low Data Rate
LAU:	Line Access Unit	LDT:	Long Distance Transmission
LAU:	Line Adapter Unit	LDU:	Line Drive Unit
LBG:	Lead Balancing Group	LDX:	Long Distance Xerography
LBS:	Line Buffer System	LDX:	Long Distance Xerox
LBS:	Link Bad Signal	LEF:	Line Expansion Function
LBT:	Listen Before Talk	LEN:	Low Entry Networking
LCA:	Line Control Adapter	LEO:	Low Earth Orbiting Satellite
LCA:	Local Communication Adapter		
LCA:	Local Core Alignment		

LEO Satellite

LCB:	Line Control Block
LCB:	Link Control Block
LCC:	Late Choice Call
LCC:	Leadless Chip Carrier
LCC:	Life Cycle Cost
LCC:	Local Calls Cleared
LCC:	Lost Calls Cleared
LCD:	Lost Calls Delayed
LCF:	Logical Channel Fill

LCH:	Lost Calls Held	LES:	Lincoln Experimental Satellite
LCJ:	Low Cost Junction	LEX:	Line EXchange
LCL:	Limited Channel Log-Out	LFC:	Low Frequency Control
LCL:	Linkage Control Language	LFD:	Local Frequency Distribution
LCM:	Last Call Meter	LFM:	Limited File Management
LCM:	Line Concentrator Module	LGN:	Logical Group Number
LCM:	Link Control Module	LGT:	Low Group Transmit
LCM:	Longhaul Customer Modem	LHN:	Long Haul Network
LCN:	Local Computer Network	LHP:	Local Host-ID Part
LCN:	Local Connection Name	LIB:	Line Interface Base
LCN:	Logical Channel Number	LIB:	Line-Item Budget
LCN:	Loosely Coupled Network	LID:	Line Isolation Device
LCO:	Local Central Office	LIF:	Line Interface Feature
LCP:	Link Control Procedure	LIH:	Line Interface Handler
LCP:	Link Control Protocol	LIM:	Line Interface Module
LCP:	Local Control Point	LIS:	Line Interface Subsystem
LCR:	Least Cost Routing	LIU:	Line Interface Unit
LCS:	Local Channel Support	LJS:	Loop Jack Switchboard
LCS:	Loop Control Statement	LLA:	Leased Line Adapter
LCS:	Loop Control System	LLA:	Long Line Adapter
LCT:	Line Control Table	LLA:	Low-Speed Line Adapter
LCT:	Logical Channel Termination	LLC:	Logical Link Control
LCT:	Logically Connected Terminal	LLE:	Long Line Equipment
LCU:	Line Control Unit	LLG:	Logical Line Group
LCV:	Loop Control Variable		
LCW:	Line Control Word		

LLM: Low Level Message	LSN: Line Stabilization Network
LLM: Low Level Multiplexer	LSP: Loop Splice Plate
LLN: Line Link Network	LSR: Local Shared Resources
LLN: Local Line Network	LSS: Loop Switching System
LLP: Logical Link Path	LST: Load Speaking Telephone
LME: Layer-Management Entity	LST: Low Speed Transmission
LMR: Land Mobile Radio	LSU: Line-Sharing Unit
LMS: Line Mode Switching	LSU: Link Set Up
LMT: Logical Mapping Table	LSU: Loan Signaling Unit
LMU: Line Monitor Unit	LTB: Last Trunk Busy
LMX: Local MultipleXer	LTC: Line Time Clock
LM/X:LAN Manager/X	LTD: Line Transfer Device
LNA: Line Number Access	LTE: Line Terminating Equipment
LNC: Local Area Network Controller	LTE: Load Telephone Exchange
LND: Local Number Dialing	LTE: Local Telephone Exchange
LNE: Local Network Emulator	LTF: Loop Transmission Frame
LNL: Line Noise Level	LTM: LAN Traffic Monitor
LNM: Logical Network Machine	LTP: Logical Terminal Pool
LNR: Low Noise Receiver	LTS: Line Transient Suppression
LOP: Line Oriented Protocol	LTS: Logical Terminal Subpool
LOR: Look Ahead On Request	LTU: Line Terminating Unit
LOS: Line Of Sight	LUE: Link Utilization Efficiency
LOS: Loss Of Signal	LUF: Lowest Usable Frequency
LPA: Link Pack Area	LUF: Lowest Useful High Frequency
LPC: Linear Predictive Coding	LUN: Logical Unit Name
LPC: LooP Control Relay	LVA: Line Voltage Analyzer
LPF: Low Pass Filter	LWC: Loop Wiring Concentrator
LPL: Local Processor Link	LWC: Loop Wiring Connector
LPT: Line PrinTer	LWE: Lower Window Edge
LRC: Longitudinal Redundancy Check	LWS: Local Work Station
LRI: Long-range Radar Input	LWS: Logical Work Station
LRL: Linking Relocating Loader	LWT: Listen While Talk
LRM: Line Response Mode	
LRR: Loop Regenerative Repeater	
LRT: Link Routing Table	
LRT: Local Routing Table	
LRX: Link Request to Transmit	
LSA: Line-Sharing Adapter	
LSA: Link State Algorithm	
LSA: Local Service Area	
LSB: Lower Side-Band	
LSB: Low-Speed Breaker	
LSC: Local Switching Center	
LSC: Loop Station Connector	
LSC: Low-Speed Concentrator	
LSC: Low-Speed Interface Control	
LSD: Line Signal Detector	
LSD: Low-Speed Data	
LSM: Line Select Module	
LSM: Line Switch Module	

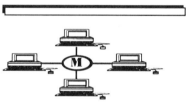

MAC: Medium Access Control
MAC: Message Authentication Code
MAF: Multiple Access Facility
MAG: Modem Approval Group
MAM:Memory Access Multiplexer
MAN: Metropolitan Area Network
MAO: Mini Access Office
MAP: Manufacturing Automation Protocol
MAP: Message Acceptable Pulse
MAP: Mobile Application Part

MAR: Malfunction Array Radar
MAS: Management Application Services
MAS: Multi-Access Signaling
MAT: Message Age Timer
MAT: Mobile Automatic Telephone System
MAU: Media Access Unit
MAU: Multiple Access Unit
MAU: Multi-Station Access Unit
MAX: Mobile Automatic EXchange
MBC: Medium-Bandwidth Channels
MBC: Multiple Basic Channel
MBF: Message Buffering Facility
MBN: Multidrop Bus Network
MCA: Malicious Call Alarm
MCA: Multi-Channel Analyzer
MCA: Multi-Processor Communication
    Adapter
MCB: Multi-Cast Bit
MCC: Miscellaneous Common Carrier
MCC: Multi-Core Cable
MCC: Multi-Point Channel Configuration
MCE: Multiple Carrier Environment
MCI: Microwave Communication Inc.
MCL: Mercury Communications Ltd (UK)
MCM: Multiplexed Circuit Modem
MCN: Micro-Cellular Network
MCP: Message Control Program
MCP: Multi-Channel Communications
    Program
MCS: Message Control Supervisor
MCS: Message Control System
MCS: Multi-Channel Communications
    Software
MCS: Multi-Channel Communications
    Support
MCT: Make-Up Codes Table
MCU: Multi-Processor
    Communications Unit
MCU: Multi-System Communications Unit
MCW: Modulated Continuous Wave
MDF: Main Distribution Frame
MDF: Multi-Datacenter Facility
MDL: Magnetic Delay Line
MDM: Multiplexer/DeMultiplexer
MDN: Multiple Domain Network
MDN: Managed Data Network
MDO: Message Delete Option
MDP: Main Data Path
MDP: Message-Driven Program
MDS: Message Data Set
MDS: Minimum Detectable Signal
MDS: Minimum Discernible Signal

MDS: Multi-Point Distribution Service
MDS: Multi-Point Distribution Systems
MDT: Merchant Deposit Transmittal
MDT: Multi-Drop Topology
MEC: Manual Error Control
MER: Message Error Record
MER: Multiple Explicit Routes
MET: Mobile Earth Terminal
MET: Multi-Button Electronic Telephone
MEX: Mobile Electronic EXchange
MFC: Multi-Frequency Code
MFG: Message Flow Graph
MFM: Modified Frequency Modulation
MFR: Multi-Frequency Receiver
MFS: Maximum Frame Size
MFS: Message Format Services
MGE: Modem Gateway Equipment
MHC: Modified Huffman Code
MHC: Modified Huffman Coding
MHD: Message HeaDer
MHP: Message Handling Processor
MHS: Message-Handling Service
MHS: Message-Handling System
MHS: Multiple Host Support
mhz: megahertz
MIA: Multiplex Interface Adapter
MIB: Management Information Base
MIC: Media Interface Connector
MIC: Microwave Integrated Circuit
MID: Message IDentifier
MID: Message Input Description
MIH: Multiplex Interface Handler
MIM: Modem Interface Module
MIP: Management Information Protocol
MIT: Message Intercept Table
MIU: Modem Interface Unit
MJF: Message Journaling Function
MLC: Main Loop Cabling
MLC: Multi-Link Control
MLM: Message Lock Mode
MLM: Multi-Leaving Line Manager
MLP: Multi-Link Procedure
MLT: Minimum Latency Time
MMC: Multi-Media Calls
MMF: Multi-Mode Fiber
MMI: Multi-Media Information
MMI: Multi-Message Interface
MMM: Multi-Media Mail
MMM: Multiple Message Mode
MMN: Man Made Noise
MMP: Multiplex Message Processor
MMR: Modified-Modified Read

MMS: Manufacturing Message Service
MMS: Manufacturing Message Specification
MMS: Manufacturing Message Standard
MNA: Main Network Address
MNA: Multi-Share Network Architecture
MNC: Master Node Control
MNF: Multi-system Network Facility
MNP: Micro-Com Networking Protocol
MOC: Manage Object Class
MOD: Message Output Description
mod: modulate
MOF: Monomode Optical Fiber
MOJ: Metering Over Junction
MOP: Meteosat Operational Program
MOS: Marine Observation Satellite
MPB: Multi-Port Bridges
MPL: Message Processing Language
MPL: Multi-Point Link
MPL: Multi-Schedule Private Line
MPN: Multi-Point Network
MPT: Ministry of Posts &
     Telecommunications (Japan)
mpt: multi-point channel configuration

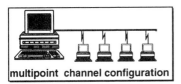

multipoint channel configuration

mpx: multiplex
MPX: MultiPleXer
MQE: Message Queue Element
MRE: Memory Register Exponent
MRF: Message ReFused Signal
MRK: Message Reference Key
MRP: Main Ring Path
MRP: Message Recovery Point
MRP: Multiple-Related Protocols
MRR: Multiple Response Resolver
MSC: Main Switching Center
MSC: Message Switching Center
MSC: Message Switching Concentration
MSC: Mile of Standard Cable
MSC: Mobile Switching Center
MSD: Modem Sharing Device
msg: message
MSG: Modulation Signal Generation
MSK: Minimal Shift Keying
MSM: Message Stream Modification
MSP: Major Synchronization Point

MSP: Manual Switching Position
MSP: Minor Synchronization Point
MSP: Multiband Sensor Package
MSR: Magnetic Send/Receive
MSS: Memory Switching System
MSU: Main Switching Unit
MTA: Message Transfer Agent
MTA: Multiple Terminal Access
MTB: Maximum Theoretical Bandwidth
MTC: Message Transmission Controller
MTF: Message Transfer Facility
MTF: Modulation Transfer Function
MTL: Message Transfer Layer
MTM: Modification Transmittal
     Memorandum
MTP: Message Transfer Part
MTP: Message Transfer Protocol
MTR: Message TRailer
MTR: Multiple Token Ring
MTS: Message Telecommunication Service
MTS: Message Transfer Service
MTS: Message Transfer State
MTS: Message Transfer System
MTS: Mobile Telephone Service
MTS: Module Tracking System
MTU: Modem Transfer Unit
MTU: Multiplexer & Terminal Unit
MTX: Mobile Telephone EXchange
MUF: Maximum Usable Frequency
mul: multiplexer
MUM: Multiple Unit Message
MUM: Multi-Unit Message
MUX: MUltipleXer

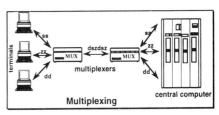

Multiplexing

MVS: Minimum Visible Signal
MWI: Message Waiting Indicator
MWR: Mercury-Wetted Relay
MWR: Minimum Weight Routing
MXA: Main EXchange Area
MXC: MultipleXer Channel
MXC: MultipleXer Circuit
MXE: Mobile Electronic EXchange

NAA: Noise Analysis Approach
NAB: National Association of Broadcasters (USA)
NAC: Network Access Controller
NAD: Node ADministration
NAD: Noise Amplitude Distribution
NAF: Network Access Facility
NAK: Negative AcKnowledge
NAK: Negative AcKnowledgement
NAM: Network Access Machine
NAM: Network Access Methods
NAM: Network Access Mirror
NAN: Network Application Node
NAP: Network Access Protocol
NAP: Noise Analysis Program
NAS: Network Application System
NAT: Neighbor Acquisition and Termination
NAU: Network Access Unit
NAU: Network Addressable Unit
NBH: Network Busy Hour
NBS: National Bureau of Standards (USA)
NCB: Network Control Block
NCB: Network Control Board
NCC: National Computer Center
NCC: Network Control Center
NCC: Network Coordination Center
NCD: Network Cryptographic Device
NCE: Network Connection Element
NCF: National Communication Forum
NCH: Network Connection Handler
NCI: National Computer Institute
NCI: National Computing Industries
NCI: Northeast Computer Institute (USA)
NCL: Network Control Language
NCM: Network Control Mode
NCM: Network Control Module
NCN: Network Control Node
NCP: Netware Core Protocol
NCP: Network Code of Practice
NCP: Network Control Phase
NCP: Network Control Point
NCP: Network Control Processor
NCP: Network Control Program (IBM)
NCP: Network Control Protocol
NCS: National Communication System

NCS: National Computer Systems
NCS: Netherland Computer Society
NCS: Network Control Station
NCS: Network Control System
NCS: Network Coordination System
NCT: Network Configuration Tables
NCU: Network Control Unit
NCU: Node Coupling Unit
NDB: Network DataBase
NDC: Network Diagnostic Control
NDD: Non-Delivery Diagnostic
NDF: No Defect Found
NDL: Network Database Language
NDL: Network Definition Language
NDS: Network Data Series
NDS: Network Data Services
NDS: Network Data Systems
NDT: Network Data Transfer
NDT: Network Description Table
NDU: Network Device Utility
NEA: National Electronics Association
NEF: Noise Equivalent Flux
NEM: Network Event Monitor
NEP: Noise Equivalent Power
NEQ: Non-EQuivalent Gate
net: network
NET: Network Entity Title
NET: Normes Europeennes de Telecommunications
NFD: Network Fault Diagnostic
NFE: Network Front End
NFF: No Fault Found
NFS: Network File Server
NFS: Network Filing System
NFT: Network File Transfer
NGP: Network Graphics Protocol
NHP: Network Host Protocol
nhz: nanohertz
NIB: Node Initialization Block
NIC: Network Information Center
NIC: Network Interface Card
NIC: Network Interface Control
NIC: New Image Communications
NIF: Network Information File
NIM: Network Interface Machine
NIM: Network Interface Monitor
NIS: Network Information Service
NIS: Network Information Source
NIS: Network Information System
NIS: Network Interface System
NIT: Network Interface Task
NIU: Network Interface Unit

NJE: Network Job Entry	NRM: Normal Response Mode
NJI: Network Job Interface	NRN: National Research Network
NLC: Network Language Center	NRP: Numbering and Routing Plan
NLM: Netware Loadable Module	NRT: Network Routing Table
NLR: Noise Load Ratio	NRU: Network Resource Unit
NMA: Network Management Application	NRV: Nodal Route Vector
NMA: Network Management Architecture	NRX: Network Request to Transmit
NMC: Network Management Center	NRZ: Non-Return-To-Zero Transmission
NMC: Network Manufacturing Center	NSA: National Standards Association
NMC: Network Master Controller	NSC: Network Switching Center
NMC: Null Modem Cable	NSC: Network Systems Corporation
NMI: Non-Maskable Interrupt	NSC: Nodal Switching Center
NMM: Network Measurement Machine	NSD: Network & Services Division
NMP: Network Management Profile	NSE: Network Service Element
NMS: Native Mail System	NSH: Network Services Header
NMS: Network Management Services	NSI: Non SNA Interconnection
NMS: Network Management Station	NSL: Non-Switched Line
NMS: Network Management Systems	NSM: Network Security Module
NMT: Network ManagemenT	NSM: Network Service Manager
NMT: Nordic Mobile Telephone	NSM: Network Status Monitor
NMU: Network Management Unit	NSO: National Standards
NNA: New Network Architecture	Organization (USA)
NNC: National Network Congestion Signal	NSP: Network Service Part
NND: National Number Dialing	NSP: Network Services Protocol
NNG: National Number Group	NSP: Network Support Plan
NOA: Network-Oriented Analysis	NSP: Network Support Processor
NOC: Network Operations Center	NSP: Non-Segmenting Protocol
NOC: Network Operating Center	NSR: Normal Service Request
NOC: Network Operator Console	NSS: Network Supervisor System
NOL: Network Operator Logon	NSS: Network Synchronization
NOS: Network Operating Services	Subsystem
NOS: Network Operating System	NST: Network Support Team
NPA: Network Point Of Attachment	NSU: Network Service Unit
NPA: Numbering Plan Area	NTA: National Telecommunications
NPA: Number Plan of America	Agency (USA)
NPD: Network Protector Device	NTA: Next Transfer Address
NPE: Network Processing Element	NTA: Norwegian Telecommunications
NPL: Negative Polling Limit	Agency
NPM: Network Performance Monitor (IBM)	NTC: Network Telecommunications
NPP: Network Protocol Processors	Conference (IEEE)
NPR: Noise Power Ratio	NTE: Network Terminating Equipment
NPS: Network Processing Supervisor	NTF: No Trouble Found
NPS: Network Product Support	NTI: National Telecommunications
NPT: Network Planning Technique	Industry
NPT: Network Planning Tool	NTI: Noise Transmission Impairment
NPT: Non-Packet Mode Terminal	NTM: Normal Transfer Mode
NPU: Network Planning Unit	NTN: Network Terminal Number
NPU: Network Processing Unit	NTO: Network Terminal Operator
NPV: Net Present Value	NTO: Network Terminal Option
NRC: Networking Routing Center	NTP: Network Terminal Protocol
NRD: Network Resource Directory	NTP: Network Terminating Point
NRL: Network Restructuring Language	NTP: Network Termination Processor

NTP: Network Time Protocol
NTP: Network Transfer Part
NTS: Network Television Station
NTT: Nippon Telephone and
Telegraph (Japan)
NTU: Network Terminating Unit
NTU: Network Transmission Unit
NUA: Network User Address
NUF: Network Utilities Field
NUI: Network User Identifier
NUI: Network User Identity
NUN: Network User Name
NVT: Network Virtual Terminal
NWD: Network Wide Directory
NWN: NetWork Node

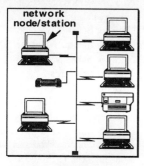

NWS: NetWork Station
NXA: Nodal EXchange Area

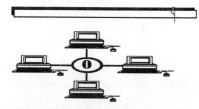

OAC: Operator's Access Code
OAS: Output Amplitude Stability
OAU: Operation Assistance Unit
OBH: Office Busy Hour
OBR: Optical Bypass Relay
OBS: OnLine Business Service
OCA: Optical Cable Attenuation
OCB: Out-going Calls Barred
OCC: Office Communication Cabinet
OCC: Other Common Carrier
OCD: OnLine Communication Driver
OCF: Open Channel Flow
OCL: Optical Connector Loss
OCL: Overall Connection Loss

OCN: Operation Code Number
OCR: Outgoing Call Restriction
OCS: Open /Cabling Strategy
OCS: Operation Control Station
OCS: Optical Communication System
OCS: Order Communications System
OC-1: Optical Carrier Level 1
OC-3: Optical Carrier Level 3
ODA: Office Document Architecture
ODA: Open Document Architecture
ODD: Operator Distance Dialing
ODD: Outward Data Dissemination
ODF: Office Distribution Frame
ODI: Open Data Interface
ODI: Open Datalink Interface
ODP: Open Data Path
ODP: Open Distribution Processing
ODP: Optical Data Processing
OEC: Open Enterprising Computing
OFC: Optical Fiber Cable
OFR: Over Frequency Relay
OIS: Operational Inter-
Communication System
OIW: OSI Implementors Workshop
OLG: Open Loop Gain
OLP: Operator Logical Paging
OLR: Open Loop Receiver
OLR: Open Loop Response
OMS: Optical Modulation System
ONA: Open Network Architecture
ONF: Optional Network Facilities
ONN: Open Network Node
ONP: Open Network Provision
OOB: Out-Of-Band
OPC: Originating Point Code
OPT: OPTion
ORF: Operator Response Field
ORS: Obtain Reply Service
ORT: Overland Radar Technology
OSD: OSI Service Driver
OSD: OSI Session Driver
OSE: Open Systems Environment
OSF: Open Systems Foundation

OSI: Open Systems Interconnection

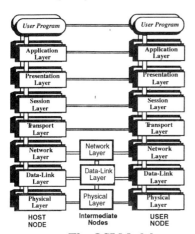

The OSI Model

OST: Operator Station Task
OSW: Operational SWitching Unit
OTC: Originating Toll Center
OTF: Optimum Traffic Frequency
OTM: Office of Telecommunications
      Management
OTP: Office of Telecommunications
      Policy (USA)
OTS: Operational Time Synchronization
OTS: Optical Technology Satellite
OTS: Optical Transport System
OTS: Orbital Test Satellite
out: outgoing
OWF: Optimum Working Frequency

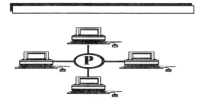

PAC: Polled Access Circuit
PAD: Packet Assembler-Disassembler
PAI: Protocol Addressing Information
PAL: Phase Alternating Line
PAL: Physical Access Level
PAM: Pass-Along Message
PAM: Pool Amplitude Modulation
PAM: Pulse Address Modem
PAM: Pulse Amplitude Modulation

PAN: Polled Access Network
PAO: Priority Access Opportunity
PAP: Phase Advanced Pulse
PAR: Perimeter Acquisition Radar
PAR: Positive Acknowledge and
      Retransmission
PAR: Precision Approach Radar
P/AR: Peak to Average Ratio
PAS: Process Array Signal
PAT: Program for Advanced
      Technology (EEC)
PAX: Parallel Architecture EXchange
PAX: Physical Address EXtension
PAX: Private Automatic EXchange
PBA: Piggy-Back Acknowledgement
PBM: Parity Bit Method
PBS: Physical Bad Signal
PBS: Public Broadcasting Service
PBT: PushButton Telephone
PBW: Proportional BandWidth
PBX: Private Branch EXchange
PCA: Percentage of Calls Answered
PCA: Programmable Communications
      Adapter
PCB: Program Communication Block
PCC: Personal Code Calling
PCD: Personal Computer Director
PCE: Packet Communications Experiment
PCI: Programmable Communications
      Interface
PCI: Protocol Control Information
PCL: Physical Control Level
PCM: Pulse Code Modulation
PCM: Pulse Count Modulation
PCN: Path Control Network
PCN: Personal Communications Network
PCN: Personal Computer Network
PCN: Problem Code Number
PCP: Private Cross-Connection Point
PCS: Plug-Compatible System
PCS: Presentation Context Set
PCS: Programmable Communications
      Subsystem
PDA: Personal Digital Assistants
PDC: Parallel Data Communicator
PDC: Permanent Data Call
PDD: Post Dialing Delay
PDM: Pulse Delta Modulation
PDM: Pulse Duration Modulation
PDN: Private Data Network
PDN: Private Digital Network
PDN: Public Data Network

PDN: Public Data Network
PDP: Pushbutton Dialing Pad
PDT: Parallel Data Transducer
PDU: Protocol Data Unit
PDX: Private Digital EXchange
PEP: Peak Envelope Power
PER: Primary Extended Route
PFM: Pulse Frequency Modulation
PFN: Prime Fan-Out Node
PFN: Pulse Forming Network
PGC: Programmed Gain Control
PGI: Parameter Group Identifier
PHE: Primary Element
PHM: PHase Modulation
PHY: PHYsical Layer
PIN: Program Identification Number
PIP: Path Independent Protocol
PLA: Programmable Line Adapter
PLC: Programmable Logic Controllers
PLD: Phase-Lock MoDulation
PLI: Packet Level Interface
PLI: Private Line Interface
PLP: Packet Level Protocol
PLP: Presentation Level Protocol
PLS: PhysicaL Signaling
PLS: Primary Link Station
PLS: Private-Line Service
PLT: Private Line Teletypewriter
PLU: Primary Logical Unit
PMA: Physical Medium Attachment
PMC: Personal Mobile Communications
PMD: Physical Media Device
PMD: Physical Medium Dependent Layer
PMG: Phase Modulation Generator
PMM: Pulse Mode Multiplex
PMN: Program Management Network
PMO: Packet Mode Operation
PMP: Peer Multi-Point
PMR: Phase Modulation Recording
PMR: Private Mobile Radio
PMS: Personal Message System
PMS: Picturephone Meeting Service
PMS: Public Message Service
PMT: Packet Mode Terminal
PMT: Page Mode Terminal
PMX: Packet MultipleXer
PMX: Protected Message EXchange
PNA: Packet Network Adapter
PNA: Project Network Analysis
PNA: Proprietary Network Analysis
PNI: Private Network Interface
PNM: Path Number Matrix

PNM: Pulse Number Modulation
PNN: Police National Network (UK)
PNS: Positional Numbering System
PON: Passive Optical Network
POS: Point Of Sale
PPM: Presentation Protocol Machine
PPM: Pulse Position Modulation
PPP: Ping-Pong Protocol
PPP: Point-to-Point Protocol
PPS: Public Packet Service
pps: pulse per Second
PPX: Packet Protocol EXtension
PPX: Private Packet EXchange
PRA: Primary Rate Access
PRF: Pulse Repetition Frequency
pri: rímary
PRI: Primary Rate Interface
PRI: Pulse Repetition Interval
PRK: Phase Reversed Keying
PRN: Packet Radio Network
PRP: Pulse Repetition Period
PRR: Pulse Repetition Rate
PRS: Partial Response Signaling
PRT: Pulse Repetition Time
PRU: Packet Radio Unit
PSD: Packet Switched Data
PSD: Phase-Sensitive Demodulator
PSD: Post Sending Delay
PSD: Protocol Specification Document
PSD: Pulse Spacing Distribution
PSE: Packet Switching Exchange
PSF: Packet Store-and-Forward
PSI: Packet System Interface
PSI: Programmable Serial Interface
PSK: Phase-Shift Keying
PSM: Packet Switched Signaling Message
PSM: Poll-Select Mode
PSN: Packet Switching Network
PSN: Packet Switching Node
PSN: Program Summary Network
PSN: Public Switched Network
PSO: Private Service Operator
PSP: Packet Switching Processor
PSP: Pre-Sending Pause
PSP: Programmable Signal Processor
PSR: Page Send-Receive
PSR: Partial Source Routing
PSS: Packet Switched System
PSS: Packet Switching Services
PSS: Packet Switching Stream
PSS: Packet Switch Stream

(British Telecom)
PSU: Packet Switching Unit
PTC: Pacific Telecommunications Councils
PTC: Phantom Telegraphy Circuit
PTC: Programmed Transmission Control
PTC: ProTocol Converter
PTM: Parallel Transfer Mode
PTM: Programmable Terminal Multiplexer
PTM: Pulse Time Modulation
PTM: Pulse Time Multiplex
PTN: Private Telecommunications Network
PTN: Public Telephone Network
PTO: Public Telecommunications Operator
PTO: Public Telephone Operator
PTP: Pass-Through Parameter
PTP: Point-To-Point Configuration

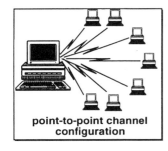

point-to-point channel
configuration

PTS: Parallel-To-Serial Conversion
PTS: Private Telephone Service
PTS: Proceed-To-Send
PTS: Public Telephone Service
PTT: Packet Transmit Timing
PTT: Postal Telegraph and Telephone
PVC: Permanent Virtual Circuit
PVR: Photo Voltaic Relay
PVS: Private Videotex System
PWD: Pulse Width Discriminator
PWM:Pulse-Width Modulation
PWM:Pulse-Width Multiplier
PWR: PoWeR

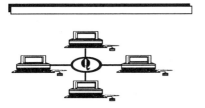

QAM: Quadratic Amplitude Modulation
QAM: Quadrature Amplitude Modulation
QBE: Query-By-Example

QBT: Quad Bus Transceiver
qdu: quantization distortion unit
QFM: Quantized Frequency Modulation
QOS: Quality Of Service
QPR: Quadrature Partial Response
QRC: Quick Reaction Communications
QRL: Quick Relocate and Link
QSA: Quad Synchronous Adapter

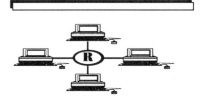

RAA: Remote Access Audio Device
RAC: Radio Adaptive Communications
RAD: Ring Attaching Device
RAE: Radio Astronomy Explorer Satellite
RAK: Read Access Key Station
RAM: Raw Accounting Merger
RAM: Remote Access Monitor
RAM: Remote Area Monitoring
RAP: Remote Access Point
RAT: Row Adaptive Transmission
RAV: Remove Attribute Value
RAX: Rural Automatic EXchange
RBA: Recovery Beacon Antenna
RBI: Ripple Blanking Input
RBL: Rubber-Band Line
RBO: Ripple Blanking Output
RCA: Radio Corporation of America
RCA: Reverse Charging Acceptance
RCB: Redundancy Check Bit
RCC: Radio Common Carrier
RCC: Redundancy Check Character
RCC: Remote Communications Central
RCC: Remote Communications Complex
RCC: Remote Communications
       Concentrator
RCE: Relay Communications Electronics
RCF: Remote Call Forwarding
RCF: Routing Control Field
RCI: Radar Coverage Indicator
RCO: Remote Control Office
RCO: Remote Control Oscillator
RCP: Remote Control Panel
RCP: Roll Call Polling
RCS: Radar Cross Section
RCS: Radio Command System

RCS: Reaction Control System
RCS: Remote Control Station
RCS: Remote Control System
RCS: Ring Control Scheme
RCT: Region Control Task
RCU: Remote Concentrator Unit
RCV: ReCeiVe
RDA: Receive Data & Acknowledge
RDA: Remote Database Access
RDC: Remote Data Collection
RDC: Remote Data Concentrator
RDE: Receive Data Enable
RDE: Remote Data Entry
RDF: Remote Distribution Frame
RDL: Reassembly DeadLock
RDM: Remote Digital Multiplexer
RDN: Relative Distinguished Name
RDP: Radar Data Processing
RDR: Request Data & Respond
RDS: Remote Data Station
RDT: Remote Data Transmitter
RDT: Rotational Delay Time
RDY: ReaDY Control Signal
rec: receipt
rec: receive
REJ: REJect
req: request
REQ: REQuire
RES: Remote Entry Service
RES: Remote Job Entry System (IBM)
REX: Route EXtension
RER: Rollback Error Recovery
RFC: Radio-Frequency Choke
RFC: Request For Comments
RFC: Request For Connection
RFI: Radio Frequency Interference
RFL: Routing Field Length
RFR: Request For Respond
RFS: Radio Frequency Shift
RFS: Ready For Sending
RFS: Remote File Sharing (AT &T)
RFS: Remote File Store (AT &T)
RFT: Request Functional Transmission
RGS: Radio Guidance System
RGS: Release Guard Signal
RHT: Register Holding Time
RIA: Ring Interface Adapter
RIC: Radar Interface Control
RIC: Radio Identity Code
RIF: Radio Influence Field
RIM: Radar Input Mapper

RIM: Read-In Mode
RIM: Request Initialization Mode
RIM: Resource Interface Module
RIP: Routing Information Protocol
RIS: Remote Information System
RIT: Radio Information Test
RIU: Ring Interface Unit
RIV: Radio Influence Voltage
RKM: Radar Keyboard Multiplexer
RKO: Range Keeper Operator
RKT: Routing Key Table
RLE: Run Length Encoding
RLG: ReLease Guard Signal
RLM: Remote LAN Module
RLN: Ring Local Network
RLU: Reassembly LockUp
RML: Radar Microwave Link
RML: Remote Maintenance Line
RMS: Remote Manipulator System
RMT: ReMoTe
RMU: Remote Multiplexer Unit
RMX: Remote Data MultipleXer
RNM: Ready for Next Message
RNP: Remote Network Processor
RNR: Receive Not Ready
RNT: Ring Network Topology

Ring Network Topology

ROS: Relay Open System
ROS: Remote Operations Service
RPC: Remote Procedure Call
RPD: Radar Planning Device
RPE: Receive Parity Error
RPE: Remote Peripheral Equipment
RPL: Radar Processing Language
RPL: Remote Program Load
RPN: Regular Processor Network
RPS: Remote Processing System
RPU: Radio Phone Unit
RPU: Radio Propagation Unit
RRE: Receiving Reference Equivalent
RRE: Royal Radar Establishment
RRN: Remote Request Number
RRS: Radio Research Station

RRT: Remote Routing Table
RSA: Remote Session Access
RSE: Real System Environment
RSF: Remote Support Facility
RSG: Reference Signal Generator
RSL: Received Signal Level
RSM: Remote Station Manager
RSM: Remote Switching Module
RSN: Radiation Surveillance Network
RSN: Rearrangeable Switching Network
RSS: Real-Time Switching System
RSS: Remotely Started Session
RSS: Route Switching Subsystem
RSS: Routing and Switching System
RSU: Relay Storage Unit
RSU: Remote Service Unit
RTA: Remote Trunk Arrangement
RTB: Remote Throughput Bias
RTD: Round Trip Delay
RTH: Regional Telecommunication Hub
RTL: Real-Time Link
RTM: Reliable Transfer Mode
RTN: Remote Terminal Network
RTP: Real-Time Protocol
RTS: Radar Tracking Station
RTS: Remote Testing System
RTS: Request Time Slots
RTS: Request To Send
RTT: Radio TeleTypewriter
RTT: Regie des Telegraphes et des
       Telephones (Belgian)
RUA: Remote User Agent
RVA: Recorded Voice Announcement
RVN: Requirements Verification Network
RWC: Ring Wiring Concentrator
RWM: Rectangular Wave Modulation
RWS: Remote WorkStation

SAA: Satellite Attitude Acquisition
SAA: Slot Array Antenna
SAA: Step Adjustable Antenna
SAB: Screen Attribute Byte
SAC: Special Area Code
SAD: Single Administration Document
SAL: System Assisted Linkage
SAM: Single Address Message
SAM: Stand-Alone Modem
SAM: Subsequent Address Message
SAM: Synchronous Address Module
SA-M: Stand-Alone Modem

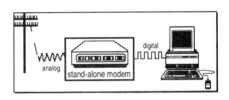

SAN: Small Area Network
SAP: Service Access Point
SAP: Shared Access Path
SAR: Session Activation Request
SAR: Synthetic Aperture Radar
SAS: Serial Associative Storage
SAS: Session Address Space
SAS: Single Attachment Station
SAS: Small Astronomy Satellite
SAS: Switched Access System
SAT: SATellite

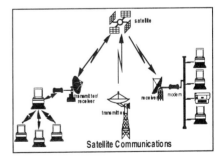

Satellite Communications

SAT: Societe Anonyme de
       Telecommunication
SAT: Synchronous Allocation Time
SAT: System Access Technique

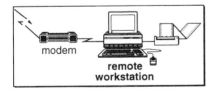

remote workstation

SAU:	Smallest Addressable Unit	SCT:	Suppressed Carrier Transmission
SAU:	System Availability Unit	SCX:	Selector Channel EXecutive
SAV:	Set Attribute Value	SDC:	Signal Data Converter
SBC:	Serialized Block Code	SDC:	Synchronous to Digital Converter
SBF:	Single-Route Broadcast Frame	SDD:	Service Definition Document
SBI:	Single Byte Interleaved	SDE:	Submission & Delivery Entity
SBM:	Semantic Binary Model	SDF:	Satellite Distribution Frame
SBS:	Satellite Business Systems (USA)	SDF:	Supergroup Distribution Frame
SCA:	Secondary Communications Authorization	SDH:	Synchronous Digital Hierarchy
		SDL:	Signaling Data Link
SCA:	Subsidiary Communications Authorization	SDM:	Sequency-Division Multiplexing
		SDM:	Space Division Multiplexing
SCA:	Synchronous Communications Adapter	SDM:	Statistical Delta Modulation
		SDM:	Synchronous Digital Machine
SCB:	Single-Channel Broadband	SDN:	Send-Data-With-No-Acknowledge
SCB:	Subscriber Control Block	SDN:	Single Domain Network
SCC:	Satellite Communication Concentrator	SDN:	Software-Defined Network
		SDN:	Synchronous Data Network
SCC:	Satellite Communications Configuration	SDN:	Synchronous Digital Transmission Network
SCC:	Satellite Communication Controller	SDR:	Signal to Distortion Ratio
SCC:	Satellite Control Center	SDS:	Space-Division Switching
SCC:	Serial Communication Controller	SDS:	Speaker-Dependent System
SCC:	Specialized Common Carrier	SDU:	Sequence Data Unit
SCC:	Sub-Carrier Channels	SDU:	Signal Distribution Unit
SCC:	Synchronous Communications Controller	SDU:	Subscriber Data and Message Unit
		SDX:	Satellite Data EXchange
SCD:	Short Code Dialing	SEN:	Single Enterprise Network
SCE:	Signal Conversion Equivalent	SER:	Satellite Equipment Room
SCF:	Satellite Control Facility	SFC:	Sectored File Channel
SCF:	Synchronous Communications Feature	SFC:	Selector File Channel
		SFM:	Switching Mode Frequency Multipliers
SCK:	Session Cryptographic Key		
SCL:	System Communication Location	SFM:	Synchronous Data Frame Synchronizing Module
SCM:	Single Channel Monitoring		
SCN:	Sensitive Command Network	SFS:	Shared File System
SCN:	Shortest Connected Network	SFS:	Single Frequency Signaling
SCN:	Switched Communication Network	SGA:	System Global Area
SCL:	System Communication Location	SGC:	Subvoice Grade Channel
SCP:	Secondary Control Point	SHF:	Super High Frequency
SCP:	Secondary Cross-connection Point	SHL:	Studio to Head-End Link
SCP:	Service Control Point	SHL:	System Handshake Logic
SCP:	System Communication Pamphlet	SHR:	Synchronous Hubbing Regeneration
SCR:	Session Control Record	SIA:	Sub-Miniature Integrated Antenna
SCR:	Single Character Recognition	SIC:	Standard Industrial Classification
SCS:	Secondary Clear to Send	SID:	Signal IDentification
SCS:	Separate Channel Signaling	SID:	Sudden Ionospheric Disturbance
SCS:	Sequence Coding System	SIF:	Signaling Information Field
SCS:	Single Cable System	sig:	signal
SCS:	System Conformance Statement	SIM:	Step Index Multi-Mode
SCT:	Self-CrossTalk	SIM:	Synchronous Interface Module
		SIO:	Service Information Octet

SIR: Session Initiation Request
SIR: Signal to Interference Ratio
SIS: Satellite Interceptor System
SIS: Signaling Inter-Working Subsystem
SIS: Swedish Information Technology Standard Institute
SIT: Societa Italiana per l'Esercizio delle Telecomunicazioni (Italy)
SIT: Special Information Tone
SLA: Shared Line Adapter
SLC: SeLector Channel
SLC: Single Line Control
SLC: Subscriber Line Charge
SLC: Synchronous Line Control
SLD: Synchronous Line Driver
SLF: Session Level Field
SLF: Signaling Link Function
SLI: Synchronous Line Interface
SLM: Space Light Modulator
SLM: Synchronous Data Line Connection Module
SLP: Session Level Pacing
SLR: Service Level Reporter
SLR: Side-Looking Radar
SLS: Secondary Link Station
SLS: Signaling Link Selection
SMB: Server Message Block
SMC: Service Modem Cable
SMF: Single Mode Fiber
SMF: System Management Function
SMM: Single Message Mode
SMP: Simple Mail Protocol
SMS: Satellite Multi-Services
SMS: Service Management System
SMS: Service Mode Switch
SMS: Synchronous-Altitude Meteorological Satellite
SMT: Screen Mode Terminal
SMT: Scroll Mode Terminal
SMT: Societe de Micro-Informatique et de Telecommunications (France)
SMT: Station ManagemenT
SMU: Secondary Multiplexing Unit
SMX: Subscriber MultipleXer
SNA: Source Network Addresses
SNA: System Network Architecture
SNB: Switched Network Backup
SNF: Signaling Network Function
SNG: Satellite News Gathering
SNI: Signal to Noise Improvement
SNI: Systems Network Interconnect
SNN: Single Node Network

SNP: Statistical Network Processor
SNP: Synchronized Network Processor
SNR: Signal-to-Noise Ratio
SNS: Secondary Network Server
SNS: Session Network Services
SNS: Simulated Network Simulations
SNT: Star Network Topology

Star Network Topology

SOA: Start Of Address
SOE: Single Office Exchange
SOF: Start Of Frame Delimiter
SOH: Start Of Heading
SOM: Start Of Messages Character
SOM: Synchronous Data Outgoing Buffer Module
SON: Synchronous Optical Network
SOR: Start Of Record
SOS: System Operator Station
SOT: Service Order Table
SPC: Semi-Permanent Connections
SPC: Switching and Processing Center
SPF: Segmentation Permitted Flag
SPF: Shortest Path First
S+DX: Speech Plus Derived TeleX
SPG: Synchronization Pulse Generator
SPL: Signal Processing Language
SPM: Session Protocol Machine
SPM: Synchronous Data Processor Interface Module
SPN: Service Protection Network
SPP: Signal Processing Peripheral
SPS: Solar Power Satellite
SPS: Solar Power System
SPS: Stored Program Signaling
SPX: Sequenced Packet EXchange
SQD: Signal Quality Detector
SRB: Single-Route Broadcast
SRC: Synchronous Remote Control
SRE: Sending Reference Equivalent
SRE: Stored Reference Equivalent
SRL: Square Root Limiter
SRM: Short Range Modem

SRN: Single Root Network
SRN: Slotted-Ring Network
SRS: Secondary Request to Send
SRS: Simulated Remote Sites
SSA: Single Line Synchronous Adapter
SSB: Single-SideBand Modulation
SSC: Sector Switching Center
SSC: Signaling And Supervisory Control
SSC: Special Services Centers
SSC: Station Selection Code
SSD: Secondary Send Data
SSF: Symmetrical Switching Function
SSI: Session Sequence Identifier
SSI: Synchronous Systems Interface
SSL: SubScriber Loop
SSM: Single-Sideband Signal Multiplier
SSM: Switching Statistical Multiplexer
SSN: Session Sequence Number
SSN: Switched Service Network
SSP: Service Seeking Pause
SSP: Service Switching Point
SSP: Signaling and Switching Processor
SSP: Sub-Satellite Point
SSR: Save System Right
SSR: Secondary Surveillance Radar
SSR: Solid State Relay
SSR: Sub-Synchronous Resonance
SSR: Synchronous Stable Relay
SSS: Strategic Satellite System
SST: Start-Stop Transmission
SST: Subscriber Signal Transferred
SST: Synchronous System Trap
SSU: Subscriber's Switching Unit
SSU: Subsequent Signal Unit
SSX: Supplementary Service EXchange
SSW: Satellite-SWitched
STA: STAtus
STA: Spanning Tree Algorithm
STC: Satellite Test Center
STC: Society for Technical Communications (USA)
STC: Standard Transmission Code
STD: State Transition Diagram
STD: Subscriber Trunk Dialing
STE: Signaling Terminal Equipment
STE: Signaling Terminal Exchange
STF: Supervisory Time Frame
STH: Satellite To Host
STL: Standard Telegraph Level

STL: Studio Transmitters Link
STM: SimplexTransmission Mode

Simplex Transmission Mode

STM: Synchronous Transport Module
STN: Satellite Tracking Network
STN: Switched Telecommunication Network
STP: Serial-To-Parallel Conversion
STP: Service Transaction Program
STP: Shielded Twisted Pair
STP: Signal Transfer Point
STP: Single-Token Protocol
STP: Spanning Tree Protocol
STR: Segment Table Register
STR: Side-Tone Reduction
STR: Synchronous Transmit Receive
STR: Synchronous Transmitter Receiver
STS: Satellite Tracking Station
STS: Shared Task Set
STT: Single Transmission Time
STU: Subscriber Terminal Unit
STU: System Transmission Unit
STV: Subscriber TeleVision
sub: subscriber
SUM: Synchronous Data Signaling Unit Module
SUN: Shared User Network
SUP: Service Update Process
SUP: SUPervisor
SVC: SuperVisor Calls
SVC: Switched Virtual Call
SVC: Switched Virtual Circuit
SVD: Simultaneous Voice Data
SVI: SerVice Interception
SWN: System-Wide Name
SWP: Sliding-Window Protocol
SWT: Sliding-Window Technique
SWU: SWitching Unit
SYN: SYNchronous
SYN: SYNchronous Idle Character
SYU: SYnchronization Signal Unit

TAC:	Telex Data Acquisition and Control
TAC:	Token Access Control
TAM:	Telecommunications Access Method
TAM:	Telephone Answering Machine
TAN:	Trunk Access Node
TAP:	Terminal Access Point
TAR:	Temporary Alternative Re-Routing
TAR:	Temporary Alternative Routing
TAR:	Terminal Address Register
TAS:	Telephone Answering Service
TAT:	TransAtlantic Telephone Cable
TAU:	Trunk Access Unit
TBB:	Transnational Broadband Backbone
TBC:	TimeBase Corrector Signal
TBC:	Token Bus Controller
TBM:	Tone Burst Modulation
TBN:	Token Bus Network
TBR:	Time BReak
TBR:	Transaction-Based Routing
TBS:	Tokyo Broadcasting System
TCA:	TeleCommunications Association
TCA:	Terminal Control Area
TCB:	Task Control Block
TCB:	Transfer Control Block
TCC:	Telecommunication Common Carriers
TCC:	Telecommunications Coordinating Committee
TCC:	Toll Center Code
TCC:	Transfer Channel Control
TCC:	Transmission Control Characters
TCD:	Telemetry and Command Data
TCL:	Transmission Control Layer
TCM:	TeleCommunications Manager
TCM:	TeleCommunications Monitor
TCM:	Terminal to Computer Multiplexer
TCM:	Time Compression Multiplexing
TCP:	Topology Change Procedure
TCP:	Transmission Control Program
TCP:	Transmission Control Protocol
TCP:	Transmitter Clock Pulse
TCP:	Transmitter Control Pulse
TCP:	Two-Phase Commit Protocol
TCS:	Telecommunication Control System
TCS:	Telephone Conference Summary
TCS:	Telex Computer Service

TCS:	Telex Computer System
TCS:	Test Call Sender
TCS:	Traffic Control Station
TCS:	Transmission-Controlled Speed
TCS:	Transportation and Communications Service
TCS:	Two-Channel Switch
T-CS:	Telecommunication Carrier System
TCT:	Termination-Codes Table
TCU:	Telecommunication Control Unit
TCU:	Transmission Control Unit
TCU:	Trunk Coupling Unit
TDC:	Time Derived Channel
TDE:	Tagged Data Elements
TDI:	Telecommunications Data Interface
TDM:	Time-Division Multiplexer
TDM:	Time-Division Multiplexing
TDM:	Time-Driven Monitor
TDR:	Time Delay Relay
TDR:	Tone Dial Receiver
TDR:	Transmit Data Register
TDS:	Time-Division Switching
TDX:	Time Division EXchange
TED:	Trunk Encryption Device
TEI:	Terminal Endpoint Identifier
TEL:	Termination Event List
TES:	Teleprinter Exchange Service
tex:	telex
TFC:	Transmit Flow Control
TGM:	Trunk Group Multiplexer
THD:	Total Harmonic Distortion
THF:	Tremendously High Frequency
THR:	Transmitter Holding Register
THT:	Token Holding Time
THZ:	TeraHertZ
TIA:	Telecommunications Information Administration
TIF:	Text Interchange Format
TIH:	Trunk Interface Handler
TJF:	Test Jack Frame
TLA:	Transmission Line Adapter
TLN:	Tiered Local Network

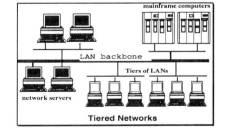

Tiered Networks

119

TLN:	Trunk Line Network	TRE:	Telecommunications Research Establishment
TLP:	Telephone Line Patch		
TLP:	Transmission Level Point	TRE:	Transmit Reference Equipment
TLX:	TeLeX	TRF:	Tuned Radio Frequency
TMA:	Telecommunications Managers Association	TRM:	Test Request Message
		TRN:	Token Ring Network
TML:	Terrestrial Microwave Links	TRS:	Telephone Repeater Station
TMN:	Telecommunications Management Network	TRS:	Terminal Receive Slide
		TRT:	Token Rotation Timer
TMP:	Test Management Protocol	TSA:	Time Slot Access
TMP:	Transmission Maintenance Point	TSC:	Transmitter Start Code
TMS:	Telephone Management System	TSC:	Transit Switching Center
TMS:	Time Multiplexed Switching	TSD:	Time Sequence Diagram
TMU:	Transmission Message Unit	TSD:	Time Sharing Driver
TMX:	Transaction Management EXecutive	TSE:	Terminal Switched Exchange
TNC:	Terminal Node Controller	TSE:	Terminal Switching Exchange
TNC:	Transport Network Controller	TSI:	Threshold Signal-to-Interference Ratio
TNS:	Transaction Network Service		
TNT:	Tree Network Topology	TSI:	Time Slot Interchange
		TSI:	Transmitting Subscriber's Identification

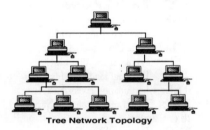

Tree Network Topology

		TSL:	Transaction Services Layer
		TSM:	Terminal Server Manager
		TSO:	Telephone Service Observation
TOL:	Two-Wire Open Line	TSP:	Time Sharing Priority
TOP:	Technical and Office Protocol	TSP:	Transmission Services Profile
TPB:	Token Passing Bus	TSR:	Time Stamp Request
TPC:	Three Party Call	TSS:	Time Share System
TPC:	Twisted-Pair Cable	TSS:	Time Sharing Service
TPD:	Transmission Path Delay	TSS:	Toll Switching System
TPD:	Transmission Propagation Delay	TST:	Time-Space-Time
TPE:	Twisted Pair Ethernet	TST:	Time-Space-Time Network
TPG:	Telecommunication Program Generator	TST:	Toll Switching Trunk
		TSU:	Transmission System Utilization
TPI:	Text Processing & Interchange	TSU:	Trunk Switching Unit
TPL:	Twisted Pair Line	TSW:	TeleSoftWare
TP-n:	Transport Protocol Class n	TTC:	Telecommunications Technology Committee (Japan)
TPP:	Token Passing Procedure		
TPR:	Token Passing Ring	TT & C:	Telemetry, Telecommand & Control
TPS:	Three Party Service		
TPU:	Telecommunications Processing Unit	TTK:	Tie TrunK
TPW:	Twisted-Pair Wire	TTK:	Two-Tone Keying
TRC:	Telegram Retransmission Center	TTL:	Transistor Transistor Logic
TRC:	Token Ring Cards	TTR:	Transmission Test Rack
TRC:	Transmit Receive Control Unit	TTR:	Trunk Test Rack
TRC:	Transverse Redundancy Check	TTS:	TeleTypeSetting
TRD:	Test Requirement Document	TTS:	Transaction Tracking System
		TTS:	Transmission Test Set
		TTT:	Touch-Tone Telephone
		ttw:	teletypeWriter
		TTX:	TeleTeX

tty: teletypewriter
TUA: Telecommunications Users Association (UK)
TUF: Transmitter Under-Flow
T&UG: Telephone & Utilities Group
TUP: Telephone User Part
TUR: Traffic Usage Recorder
TVC: TeleVision Camera
TWH: Three-Way Handshake
TWP: Twisted Wire Pair
TWS: Two Way Simultaneous
TWT: Travelling Wave Tube
TWX: TeletypeWriter EXchange
TXA: Terminal EXchange Area
TXC: Telephone EXchange - Crossbar
TXD: Telephone EXchange - Digital
TXD: Transmit Data
TXE: Telephone EXchange - Electronic
TXK: Crossbar EXchange
TXS: Telephone EXchange - Stowger

UIC: User Interface Circuit
UIP: User Interface Part
UIT: Union Internationale des Telecommunications
ULA: Upper Layer Architecture
ULM: Universal Line Multiplexer
ULP: Upper Layer Protocol
UMP: Usage Monitoring Plan
UNI: User Network Interface
UPU: Universal Postal Unit
URT: Universal Receiver-Transmitter
USB: Upper Side-Band
UTC: Coordinated Universal Time
UTC: Utilities Telecommunications Council
UTP: Unshielded Twisted Pair Cable
UWE: Upper Window Edge

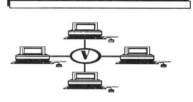

VAA: Voice Access Arrangement
VAB: Voice Answer Back
VAC: Value Added Carrier
VAD: Value-Added Data
VAN: Value-Added Network
VAP: Video Access Point
VAT: Voice Activation Technology
VBC: Voice Band Channels
VBD: Voice Band Data
VCA: Voice Connecting Arrangement
VCC: Virtual Call Clearing
VCE: Virtual Call Establishment
VCF: Virtual Console Function
VCI: Virtual Channel Identifier
VCI: Virtual Circuit Identifier
VCS: Video Communications System
VCS: Virtual Call Service
VCS: Virtual Circuit Service
VDA: Verbal Delay Announcement
VDE: Voice Data Entry
VDR: Voice Digitizer Rate
VDS: Voice Data Switch
VFO: Variable Frequency Oscillator
VFT: Voice Frequency Telegraphy
VGC: Voice Grade Channel
VG-T: Voice Grade Transmission

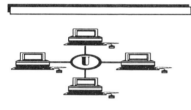

UAC: Uninterrupted Automatic Control
UAE: User Agent Entity
UAL: User Agent Layer
UAN: User-Application Network
UAX: Unit Automatic EXchange
UBA: UnBlocking Acknowledgement
UBC: Universal Block Channel
UBL: UnBLocking Signal
UCM: Universal Communications Monitor
UCS: Unacknowledged Connectionless Service
UCS: Uniform Communications Systems
UCS: Universal Call Sequence
UDH: Unthinkable Domestic Hexadecimal
UDL: Unbalanced Data Link
UDP: User Datagram Protocol
UDS: Urgent Data Signaling
UFI: Upstream Failure Indication
UFI: Usage Frequency Indicator
UFM: Universal Field Multiplexer
UHF: Ultra-High Frequency
UHS: Ultra-High Speed
UIC: User Interface Card

VHF: Very High Frequency
VIM: Vendor Independent Messaging
VLF: Very Low Frequency
VLS: Virtual Linkage Subsystem
VLS: Virtual Linkage System
VMS: Voice Message System
VNL: Via Net Loss
VNN: Vacant National Number Signal
VOS: Voice Operated Switch
VOX: Voice Operated Keying
VOX: Voice Operated Transmission
VPN: Virtual Private Network
VRC: Vertical Redundancy Check
VRM: Voice Recognition Modules
VRS: Voice Recognition System
VRS: Voice Recording System
VRS: Voice Response System
VSB: Vestigial SideBand Modulation
VSF: Voice Store-and-Forward
VSP: Virtual Switching Point
VSS: Voice Signaling System
VTC: Videotex Terminal Concentrator
VTE: Virtual Terminal Environment
VTF: Videotex Terminal Facility
VTP: Video Terminal Paging
VTP: Virtual Terminal Protocol
VTX: VideoTeX

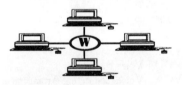

WAI: WAit for Interrupt
WAN: Wide Area Network
WAT: Wide Area Telecommunication
WBA: Wire Bundle Assembly
WBC: WideBand Circuit
WBC: WideBand Coupler
WBD: WideBand Data
WBL: Wide Band Limiting
WBS: Wide Band System
WCB: Will Call Back
WCC: Wire Common Carrier
WCI Waiting Calls Indicator
WCM: Word Combine and Multiplexer
WDB: WiDe Band
WDC: Wideband Directional Coupler
WDL: Wireless Data Link

WDM: Wavelength Division Multiplexi
WFP: Wideband Flexibility Point
WIB: When Interrupt Block
WLM: Wire Line MODEMS
WNP: Well-Non Ports
WPM: Word Parallel Mode
WRU: Who ARe YoU
WSC: Work Station Controller
WSE: Work Station Entry
WTD: World Telecommunications
         Directory
WTS: Word Terminal, Synchronous

XXX

XCT: X-Band Communications
         Transponder
XCU: Crosspoint Control Unit
XFC: TransFerred-Charge
xge: eXchange
XIC: Transmission Interface Converter
XID: EXchange IDentification
xmt: transMitter
XNG: TransmittiNG
XNS: Xerox Network System
XO-N: Transmitter-ON
XOR: EXclusive-OR
XPC: X.25 Protocol Control
XPD: Cross Polarization Discrimination
XPI: Cross Polarization Interference
XPS: Cross Point Switch
XPT: Cross-PoinT
XTA: X-Band Tracking Antenna
XTC: EXternal Transmit Clock
XTI: X/Open Transport Interface Defini
XTP: Xpress Transfer Protocol

YYY

YMU: YNET Management Unit
YTC: Yield To Call

ZZZ

ZBI: Zero Bit Insertion
ZCS: Zero Code Suppression
ZPM: Zero Power Modem